BOOK TWO
Second Edition

# Catechists in Formation

## Introduction to Theological Studies

Written by
**Peter Ries**

Consultant
**David Riley**

**Benziger Publishing Company**

*Mission Hills, California*

**Photo Credits**
Arnold & Brown 2-9, 2-10, 3-3, 5-13, 5-15, 7-14, 8-4, 8-12, 9-2, 10-7, 10-12, 11-2, 11-13;
Coleman Company 5-7; Myrleen Ferguson 12-16; Stephen McBrady 1-2, 1-12, 1-14, 2-14,
3-8, 3-14, 4-4, 6-2, 6-5, 6-10, 7-4, 7-11, 7-12, 8-8, 8-18, 9-12, 10-2, 11-3, 11-4, 12-12; Bob
Messina 9-4; Brent Phelps 3-4; Dana White Productions 1-8, 1-11, 4-2, 5-3, 11-14; Duane
R. Zehr 2-12.

*Nihil Obstat*
The Reverend Gregory A. Banazak, S.T.D.

*Imprimatur*
The Most Reverend Kenneth J. Povish, D.D.
Bishop of Lansing
May 13, 1994

The *Nihil Obstat* and *Imprimatur* are official declarations that a book or pamphlet is free of
doctrinal or moral error. No implication is contained therein that those who have granted the
*Nihil Obstat* and *Imprimatur* agree with the contents, opinions, or statements expressed.

Send all inquiries to:
BENZIGER PUBLISHING COMPANY
15319 Chatsworth Street
P.O. Box 9609
Mission Hills, California 91346-9609

Second Edition

ISBN 0-02-651188-6

Printed in the United States of America.

1 2 3 4 5 6 7 8 9   BAW   98 97 96 95 94

# Book Two  Table of Contents

# Book Two Introduction

Welcome to Benziger's *Catechists in Formation*, a complete introductory training program for catechists. Through the use of a four-part educational process, you will come to know the information, attitudes, and skills you need to be an effective catechist.

*Catechists in Formation* was designed to be used effectively in many types of religious education training programs. This Introduction will describe the program's philosophy and the content of its various books. You will be given several options for using this program and suggestions for implementing it under the model you choose.

## Audience

*Catechists in Formation* was written for the benefit of any man or woman engaged in the passing on of the Catholic faith, whether that person is a full-time, paid, professional teacher in a Catholic school setting or a first time, volunteer teacher in a Sunday morning parish religious education program. Because of its unique design, each level of teacher can take from *Catechists in Formation* what he or she needs in order to improve his or her catechetical skills and theological knowledge.

**Professional educators,** proficient in educational method, might use *Book One*, "Introduction to Catechetical Method," as a brief review or refresher course. Even the most experienced educator will find here valuable suggestions for teaching a particular age group. *Book Two*, "Introduction to Theological Studies," would then be used to update teachers in the beliefs of the Catholic faith, as well as demonstrate for them effective methods of communicating that faith to their students.

**Volunteer teachers** will want to pay special attention to *Book One*, using it as a workbook to develop the teaching skills they need in order to become more effective catechists. Once they become comfortable using effective teaching methods, volunteer teachers can turn their attention to *Book Two* and learn what the Church believes and practice teaching methods to effectively hand that faith on to the next generation of believers.

Throughout both books, "Introduction to Catechetical Methods" and "Introduction to Theological Studies," the term "catechist" is used to mean both the professional and the volunteer teacher. *Sharing the Life of Faith* names teachers and principals in Catholic schools, as well as parish catechists, parish coordinators, and Directors of Religious Education as catechists. Although their roles are different, both the professional and the volunteer teacher are vital to the students' growth into a mature, conscious, and active faith, and thus deserve the title of catechist.

## Philosophy of the Program

*Catechists in Formation* builds upon the National Catechetical Directory, *Sharing the Light of Faith* and the *Catechism of the Catholic Church*. There are eight basic assumptions integral to the philosophy of the program:

1. Religious education is more than the handing on of religious truths. Its goal is growth in faith, which implies both formation and transformation, leading one to live out the Gospel as a member of a believing community.

2. Religious education is a lifelong process. Everyone, including the catechist, is always a learner and is always growing in faith.

3. The role of catechist is central to the life of the Church. Systematic growth in faith is fostered through this ministry.

4. Adequate preparation and formation are indispensable for every catechist.

    *The response to this call [to be a catechist] includes willingness to give time and talent, not only to catechizing others, but to one's own continued growth in faith and understanding.* (Sharing the Light of Faith, #206)

    Volunteers as well as professionals need catechist formation.

5. Each local parish must determine its own approach to catechist formation by assessing and providing for its catechists' needs.

6. It is appropriate to promote and expect formation for all catechists because (a) the role of catechist requires specific skills and attitudes, (b) catechists

are central to the life of the Church, and (c) catechists themselves expect assistance.

7. Among the many possible approaches to promoting growth in faith, **experiential religious education** is of considerable value.

   *Catechists . . . should seek to teach the whole person, using both cognitive (intellectual) and affective (emotional) techniques.* (Sharing the Light of Faith, #176)

   *Catechists in Formation* reflects this experiential approach to religious education.

8. Sound religious education stresses the need to adapt the teaching and learning processes to the needs of the times and to the age levels of the people involved.

## The Components of the Program

There are three components to the program, *Catechists in Formation:*

- **Book One: "An Introduction to Catechetical Methods"**
- **Book Two: "An Introduction to Theological Studies"**
- The **Program Manual**

In addition, each chapter of *Book One* and *Book Two* may be ordered individually, separate from the books. This allows each parish to easily pick and choose the topics it wishes to teach and gives it an option on how the materials are presented to the teachers.

*Book One* and *Book Two* are designed to be used by the catechist as a workbook and journal. The catechist will use the books as their personal trainer in which they write notes, develop program ideas, and practice techniques to which they will frequently return. This introduction will describe Book One and Book Two in detail and will sketch out the contents of the Program Manual.

### Elements in Book One and Book Two

Book One, "Introduction to Catechetical Method," contains nine topics, all aimed at helping the catechist understand and apply the practical aspects of teaching religion, classroom management, and faith development.

Book Two, "Introduction to Theological Studies," contains twelve chapters focusing on the basic theological content required by most diocesan religious education guidelines.

Each chapter of *Catechists in Formation* is divided into four parts—**Experience, Message, Discovery,** and **Response**—that make up the catechetical process used in most modern religious education textbook series. Too often, catechists are taught using methods appropriate for the college classroom, but inappropriate for their students. In modeling the process by which catechists are to teach, *Catechists in Formation* better prepares the teacher to meet the needs of the students.

Each chapter begins with an introductory quote and a series of *learning outcomes.* From there, it moves quickly into the heart of the material.

- **Part I: Experience** The process of catechesis always involves sharing the stories of the Catholic faith following Jesus' example. Since the publication of *Christian Religious Education* by Dr. Thomas Groome, religious educators have recognized the importance, once again, of following Jesus' method.

  Part I contains realistic stories, directed toward the topic of discussion in the chapter, that are meant to capture the catechist's attention and touch upon their experience.

- **Part II: Message** It is here that the students are introduced directly to the topic in practical, clear, and readable prose. The basic points of content are introduced here.

- **Part III: Discovery** The content of the lesson is further developed here, with the catechist actually working with the material, exploring the faith dimension of the topic, and applying it to his or her situation.

- **Part IV: Response** The final part of the catechetical process is always a response to the message. Here, catechists use exercises and prayer to help them develop the skills presented in the lesson or determine how they will use what they've learned with their students.

Spread throughout *Catechists in Formation* are features, activities, and exercises. Of particular note are:

- **Pause a Moment . . .** These are questions for writing and discussion that appear regularly in the text.

- **The New Commandment** This feature highlights quotations from the New Testament appropriate to the topic being discussed.

- **The Church Teaches** This feature introduces catechists to Church teaching as presented in Catholic Church documents.

Because *Catechists in Formation* is designed to be used as a personal workbook by the catechist, writing rules are provided frequently to facilitate note-taking.

- **Memo** This feature asks the catechist to consider a question and provides a convenient space for the catechist's answer.
- **Activities** Many of the features in *Catechists in Formation* are actual worksheets for the catechist to use. Writing rules are provided so that the activity can be easily completed.
- **Notes** In many of the side margins, a "notepad" is provided to encourage the catechists' personal response to the questions raised in the narrative. **Notes** appears most frequently alongside the feature, **Pause a Moment.**

## Elements of the Program Manual

A Program Manual is available for use with *Catechists in Formation*. Detailed approaches for teaching each lesson are presented in the "Lesson Guides." Lesson Guides for Book One and Book Two are combined in the one Program Manual.

The Lesson Guides can be used effectively in both non-directed and directed group studies. Diocesan formation programs will also find that these lesson guides are correlated to catechetical guidelines.

# Using the Program

There are three basic models for using *Catechists in Formation*: (1) self-study, (2) non-directed group study, and (3) directed group study.

## Self-Study

In places where there is no director of religious education or very little opportunity for a formal program, *Catechists in Formation* provides an option for structured self-study. Professional teachers or volunteer catechists can use this program for personal or professional enrichment. The following list offers a step-by-step plan for using this program for self-study.

1. **Plan your schedule.** Although the two books are ordered in a logical, developmental sequence, each chapter is self-contained, and may be used when you need it. You decide what and when you will study.

2. **Complete your work.** Choose a quiet place to read, reflect, and finish the activities. The best material in the world is useless unless you take the time to study it, make it your own, and then decide how you can use it.

3. **Share what you have learned.** Discuss what you've learned with other catechists and apply your knowledge to your teaching. In this way you can clarify what you've discovered and can collectively support each others' efforts.

## Nondirected Group-Study

When the full benefit of using *Catechists in Formation* in a group setting is desired, but someone to direct the program is lacking, a nondirected group study approach can be used.

1. **Conduct a needs and interest survey** to determine which of the twenty-one topics in the two books are most relevant for your use. (Remember, you can order copies of just those chapters that you plan to study.) If there are many new volunteer catechists in the group, it is recommended that you begin with the topics in *Book One,* "Introduction to Catechetical Methods."

2. **Plan your calendar.** Consider how long the program will run (have definite beginning and ending dates), and which days you will meet. Determine how many topics you want to cover in the duration of the program.

3. **Determine length of meeting.** The length of your meetings affects the way you organize the session. With group discussion and the sharing of answers, there is enough material in each topic to last a full two and one-half hours. For shorter meetings, adjustments will have to be made.

---

- **One and one-half hour meetings:** Have the catechists read the material and complete the exercises at home during the week prior to the meeting. Use your time together to share answers, discuss ideas, and practice techniques.

- **Two-hour meetings:** Have the participants read **Part I: Experience** and complete the exercise found there before coming to the meeting. During the meeting, the catechists can read and discuss the remaining material together. Choose only a few of the many activities to complete together, concentrating on those in **Part IV: Response.** Allow for a 15-minute break in addition to the two hours of study.

---

4. If needed to harmonize schedules and choices of topics, consider forming a second group with its own agenda and schedule.

5. Order the books (or individual chapters) six to eight weeks in advance to allow time for shipment. If you wish to begin in September, order your books in May or June.

   *Remember, unauthorized duplication of Book One or Book Two (or any of the individual chapters) is a violation of copyright law.*

6. Decide where to hold the session. Groups can meet on the parish premises, in faculty rooms, or in individuals' homes. If the groups are to meet on the parish premises, schedule the program on the parish calendar early in the year.

7. Appoint a facilitator (an individual, a couple, or a team of two) to chair each meeting. Group participants can take turns (see "The Facilitator's Responsibilities" at the right).

8. Appoint a group coordinator to oversee the organizational details, including handling registrations and ordering the books.

## The Group Coordinator's Role

The role of group coordinator involves organizing the behind-the-scenes details so that the group meetings run smoothly.

1. Arrange for the registration of all participants and collect any necessary fees.

2. Order the materials. (See #5 under "Nondirected Group Study.")

3. Prepare for the first meeting. The first meeting, whether in a home or in the parish, is important. Inform the participants that the first meeting will last 15 minutes longer than future meetings. This will allow time for organizational details.

4. Organize the small groups at the beginning of the first session and ask one person in each group to act as discussion leader. Recall these points as you form the groups.

   • Small groups should consist of no fewer than five and no more than ten.

   • A mixture of ages and a variety of backgrounds affords a more extensive learning experience.

   • Husbands and wives (and best friends) benefit from being in different groups.

5. Prepare the meeting place so that it is comfortable. Have plenty of moveable chairs. Each small group should be given an area large enough so as not to interfere with other small groups. Make sure the space matches the size of the group. A large hall is not appropriate for one or two small groups. Good ventilation and proper temperature are important. Discourage smoking during the meeting.

6. Have all supplies on hand for each meeting: name tags, pencils, extra copies of *Catechists in Formation*, newsprint or chalkboard, any audio-visual equipment needed, and refreshments.

7. Evaluate each session. Sample evaluation sheets are provided in the Program Manual. Monitor the progress of the group by examining the participants' remarks and adjust future sessions to reflect their needs. Conduct a final evaluation at the end of the program.

## The Facilitator's Responsibilities

The role of the facilitator is to see that the meeting runs smoothly. A facilitator is neither the leader nor the teacher. Any adult who is enthusiastic about the program and who is willing to prepare for the meeting can facilitate. The facilitator's responsibilities include:

1. Prepare for the meeting. Read the material, complete the activities, and be prepared for discussion.

2. Begin on time, and move the group along so that you can finish the session on time. Keep the group informed on the amount of time remaining in the session.

3. Participate in a small group or in the overall group as an equal member. Do not take the position of teacher. You may, however, act as discussion leader in a small group.

4. Refer to the Lesson Guides in the Program Manual for step-by-step instructions for facilitating each lesson. Follow the topic page by page in the order presented unless there is good reason for not doing so. The following suggestions can help move the group through the process smoothly:

   • Have the group read the material either (a) before the session, (b) during the session quietly, (c) aloud in a large group, or (d) aloud in small groups. Ask the group how they would like to cover the material.

   • If you decide to do any part of the material at home prior to the session, adjust the time schedule, allowing time for group discussion of that material.

- Allow participants to ask any questions as they read. Do not attempt to answer those questions yourself, but encourage the group to search for answers together. Keep a watch on time and don't allow these activities to drag on.

- Allow plenty of time for participants to share their responses to the activities. Encourage discussion of people's responses, but accept no criticism of someone's answers. Do not let anyone dominate the discussion.

- End the meeting on time. If you haven't finished a topic or a section, ask the group if they want to finish where they left off at the next meeting, or complete the rest at home privately. Leave room at the next meeting for comments on the work studied at home.

- Include prayer as part of each session. Although the "Prayer Response" comes at the end of every topic, it can be used at any time during the process. Encourage participants to add prayer as they choose.

- When a topic is finished, evaluate the session.

## Directed Group Study

The main difference between nondirected group study and directed group study is the Catechist Trainer. A Catechist Trainer is a professional religious educator—religious or lay—who assumes the responsibilities assigned to the group coordinator and the facilitator and who also assumes the role of teacher.

### Suggestions for the Catechist Trainer

The following will help the Catechist Trainer use *Catechists in Formation* most effectively.

1. Use the Program Manual as your guide throughout the planning and implementation of the program.

2. Assess the needs of the group before setting a schedule. (See the Program Manual for instrument.)

3. Clarify what the program is intended to accomplish.

4. Based upon the needs of the participants, determine the number and order of the topics to be covered.

5. Design publicity for the program to ensure a good registration.

6. Be prepared to supplement the material presented in **Part II: Message** and **Part III: Discovery.**

Use the teaching suggestions found in the Manual as a guide.

7. Use various teaching techniques to promote understanding of the content and to make your presentations more dynamic. Refer to the Manual for suggestions on appropriate techniques to use.

8. Decide how you will use the writing and discussion activities throughout each session. You might want to have participants work through the material on their own prior to the sessions.

9. Monitor group progress through regular evaluations.

## Scheduling the Program

One attractive feature about *Catechists in Formation* is its flexibility. If the individual chapters are purchased, you can arrange the topics in any order you choose. Of course, each book is self-contained and may be followed exactly in the order given, which is a logical presentation of the topics.

The following list offers optional ways of scheduling the program:

1. One topic a week for twenty-one weeks. Or do the same for shorter programs of three, four, or six weeks.

2. A one-day seminar covering two or three topics.

3. One topic at monthly catechist meetings or grade level planning sessions.

4. A week-long summer program.

5. An in-service program for the catechists of the Catholic school.

6. A mini-series of topics as part of a summer program.

7. Pair up experienced catechists with new catechists and have them work through the material together.

8. In cooperation with another parish or parishes. Share each others' resources, discussion leaders, and Catechist Trainers.

We are confident that *Catechists in Formation* is an excellent approach to helping individuals prepare for their role as catechists. We are interested in your comments and observations about this program. Send them to Benziger Publishing Company, 15319 Chatsworth St., P.O. Box 9609, Mission Hills, CA 91346-9609.

# Benziger

# Understanding the Theological Process

Theology is the fruit of a reflective process. Theological content is not a timeless [set of materials], a historical body of information couched in language that can be understood readily in any time or place. Theological reflection is a process of making meaning of selves and the world in light of God, carried on by persons with particular questions arising from particular experiences in particular cultural situations who are members of particular communities of faith. Each generation and community must translate its experience . . . if its theology is to be life-giving and faithful.

"Assisting Adults to Think Theologically,"
by Patricia O'Connell Killen, Ph.D. *PACE 22* February 1993.

Written by
**Peter Ries**

Consultant
**David Riley**

BOOK TWO

## In this chapter you will:

- Consider several definitions of theology and recognize the purpose and uses of each.

- Explore various categories and approaches to theology.

- Examine the relationship of religious education to theology and story.

- Study how different theological approaches can be used in catechesis.

Second Edition

▲ *The highlight of the festival was the pageant. People dressed in period clothing acted out the history of the community.*

## Everything You Ever Wanted to Know

Everyone knew the story of Greg Cecil. He was a hero, the greatest man to come out of Harlan County these past 200 years. The people of Balltown celebrated Greg's birthday every year with a parade and festival. People came from miles around to feast on pan-fried chicken, mashed potatoes, and country biscuits. The farmers and artists of the county displayed their handiwork during this festival; it was the most important weekend in the life of the community each year, both financially and spiritually.

The highlight of the festival is the play. Members of the community retell the highlights of Greg's life in dramatic fashion. People who have seen the show say that it was "beautiful" and "very moving." At least that's what the brochure says. I'm not making this up. According to the brochure,

> *"This story has affected my life greatly. Here's a man who changed the life of his community through kindness and generosity. After watching this play, I understand why the people of Balltown hold him in such high esteem."*

You would thing that this Greg Cecil was the second coming of Jesus. Here was a story waiting for me to write it.

The magazine I write for is always looking for interesting people and celebrations to publicize. We are not interested in providing free publicity so much as we attempt to put people in touch with the wider American culture. Our articles are written for the more discriminating reader, people who will look at a situation critically before making a decision. They don't believe everything they read and neither do I. This looked like an opportunity to investigate what these country people hold sacred and hold it up for the world's critical judgment. Few, if any, legends escape our magazine untouched.

I was right about the story. People swore by Greg Cecil. He was Paul Bunyan, Abe Lincoln, and Tom Cruise all rolled into one. Greg single-handedly defeated the Germans in World War I. For a lark he would outdo George Washington by throwing rocks across the Salt Lick River at high flood—a toss of a quarter mile, at least. He was a great scholar and athlete at the old county high school; he must have held a dozen records. Too bad the school had burned 30 years ago, all documents destroyed.

People not only talked about Greg's amazing feats of strength, but they also hinted at his tremendous goodness. No one had ever been that generous. Why, during the Depression, Greg must have helped half the farmers in the county pay their mortgages, never asking for interest in return. What a man.

These stories about Greg were too good to be entirely true without embellishment. It was clear to me that people had taken actual events and retold them so many times that they no longer knew where the facts ended and the legend began. Still, I had to admit, Greg was important to the community. I actually heard a woman ask her daughter, "How do you think Greg Cecil would have handled this problem?"

After spending a week in town, talking to people, looking up county records, and enjoying the festival, it was time for the pageant. The little community theater was packed. The children, dressed up in clothes like those worn by their great-grandparents, acted out the history of the community. Then the storyteller—a white-haired woman simply dressed in a prim farm dress and apron—walked onto the stage. She carried herself strongly erect—shoulders back, head held high—as if the guardian of a sacred trust.

She stopped in the center of the stage and began to speak in a rich, vibrant voice that carried to the farthest corner of the building. As she spoke, people from the community acted out the life of Greg Cecil. But it was the storyteller who held our attention. The legend melted away from the man under her spell. Here was no American myth of greatness, but a simple farmer who went out of his way to make a difference in people's lives. Amazingly, the more the man was revealed, the more attractive he became. Here was an example of the reality being greater than the legend.

I went to Balltown a skeptic; no, make that an atheist. I didn't believe the legend and the festival were anything but excuses to make money. And there is certainly some of that taking place. But what I wrote in my article was:

> Here is an event that cannot be explained in mere words. To truly appreciate the power of this celebration you have to experience it for yourself. You may come to enjoy the fun and hospitality, you may come looking for gifts handmade by local artisans. You can spend a day here and leave untouched by the events celebrated here. But I guarantee that if you see the results and hear the story, you will leave a different person than when you arrived. I did.

*Memo*

How does this story express the challenge catechists face in using theology with students?

## YOUR STORY

The truth of a story resides in the human heart, not in books or records. Just reading about someone or something does not make it real. Only by experiencing the story can one vouch for its veracity. The same is true for theology. Knowing about religious teaching is not enough, one must also experience the truth of the story. From your reading, answer the following questions:

1. What is the importance of story in understanding truth? What can imaginative remembrances tell us about someone or something?

_____

2. How does theology help us understand a popularly held belief? Offer an example of when a theological explanation has clarified a belief for you.

_____

3. As a catechist, how important do you feel it is to study and understand theology?

_____

_____

4. From reading this story, what would you say is the relationship between faith and theology?

_____

_____

## What Is Theology?

The early Church, during the first 200 years after Jesus died, lacked many of the clear guides we take for granted.

- The last books of the New Testament were not finished until the second century A.D. and questions were raised about which books were to be accepted as Scripture for several hundred more years. (You may have heard of ancient books such as the *Gospel of Thomas* which were written during the first century but never were accepted into the scriptural canon.)

- There were no formal professions of beliefs or *creeds* until the late second century (the Roman Creed which later developed into the Apostle's Creed in the fourth century)—the Nicene Creed prayed at Mass was not formalized until the Council of Nicaea in 325.

- The rich tradition of the Church had not yet developed—the great Christian thinkers Origen and Tertullian (third century), Augustine (fourth century), Anselm (eleventh century), and Aquinas (thirteenth century) had not yet written systematically on the issues of faith that now provide us a comfortable starting place.

The early Christian communities struggled to understand how to live faithful to Jesus' Way, often through trial and error. Many of the letters written to these communities that we now accept as part of our Scriptures were written to try and correct theological efforts that had missed the mark.

One of the greatest dangers faced by these early communities came from the *Gnostics.* From the Greek word, "gnosis" (meaning "knowledge"), the Gnostics taught that salvation came from having special knowledge that was available only to a few. The Letters of John and the writings of Saint Irenaeus argued the contrary case: that salvation comes through Jesus and is offered to all through the guidance of the Holy Spirit and the faithful teaching of the bishops.

When many people today think of theology, they seem to fall into the trap of gnosticism: theology is a special knowledge offered only to a few. Such thinking does a disservice to the process of theology and to the teachings that come to us from over the centuries from people engaged in the process of theology.

Most people recognize the word "theology," but few have a clear understanding of its full meaning and scope. Although theology is the basis of the teaching ministry of the Church, it still remains a mystery to the average churchgoer, who places theology in the domain of scholars. The theories and skills of theologians seem to be beyond many people's reach.

When people say that they are studying theology, they often mean that they are studying the historical record, learning what the Church teaches about the faith and what great thinkers have written over the years. They are, in a sense, searching for knowledge. Theology, however, is more than a body of knowledge to be learned. It is also, more importantly, a process, a way of understanding the meaning of God. People engage in the theological

▲ *Theology is much like a blueprint to help us build a life with God. To work freely with theology, we must learn how to use the theological process.*

process when they reflect on the ways God enters human history and attempt to articulate the meaning of such experiences within the faith community.

As catechists we are participants in this process when we reflect on the ways we have experienced God and articulate this experience to others. In this way, as Thomas Groome points out in *Christian Religious Education,* "Theology and Christian religious education cooperate as mutual partners in promoting lived Christian faith in the world."

## Finding an Explanation

There are many ways that a person could explain the word "theology," with each attempt arising from a different perspective. However, since no one definition adequately spans the breadth of the theological process, a number of explanations are needed. Consider the following:

1. *Theology is both the act and the result of reflection on the meaning of the experience of revelation.* God has been and continues to be revealed to us in human history. The Jews experienced God as one who cared for them—saving them from slavery in Egypt and leading them to freedom in their own land. Through Jesus, God was revealed as a loving father, someone dedicated to our well-being, who called us to serve others in peace, justice, and joy.

   People experienced these revelations as lived events—something as real as escaping from Egypt or being healed of a hemorrhage by Jesus—not as cognitive knowledge. These revelations of God were deep, basic, human experiences that touched people to their core. Later, as they reflected on the meaning of these experiences, people sorted out the various implications of each event and considered aspects of the experience that were not clear to them. First as individuals and then as members of a faith community, people pondered God's role in their lives and tried to make sense of what they had experienced. The individual and communal shared reflections come to us as theology.

2. *Theology is faith seeking understanding.* As people experienced God's self-revelation, they accepted God into their lives, and a faith relationship began. After continued reflection, people came to recognize

a deeper significance in their experience of revelation. They allowed their faith to influence this reflection and their resulting growth.

3. *Theology is a process of reflecting on the meaning of God in life and articulating this meaning within the faith community.* As individuals, people reflect from time to time on the meaning of life and how God acts in their lives. As members of a faith community, people do this reflecting together, seeking meaning as they worship, live, learn, and serve with others. In the community, one individual's reflections influence the thinking of others. The community becomes a guide in the search for meaning, giving direction based on a tradition of belief and the presence of the Spirit.

4. *Theology is an activity in which the human mind seeks to comprehend the depths of revealed truth in rational terms.* Many of the realities present in God's revelation are mysteries waiting to be pondered. These mysteries, when probed, yield layer upon layer of meaning without ever being fully understood. Although believers perceive and accept God's revelation through the eyes of faith, it is also appropriate that they use their intellects to add to their understanding of the revelation they have received.

5. *Theology is the systematic study of God's self-revelation conducted by the human mind enlightened by faith.* God's revelation is found in the Bible and in the tradition of the Church. The human mind seeks to better understand this revelation, to derive conclusions from it, and to assemble all these insights and conclusions into a logical system. Such activity has a method and proceeds in an orderly fashion, guided by the Holy Spirit, the tradition of the Church, and the teaching of the bishops reflecting the faith of the community.

## What Theology Does

Theology is a tool which we can use to *interpret* both the experience of God's self-revelation and the Church's expression as to what that experience means. Theology helps us put into words, images, and phrases the meaning of these events.

Theology also gives us *insight.* Reflections, both verbal and written, either shared within the context of the faith community or those resulting from a personal, prayerful dialogue with God, can uncover realizations not previously understood.

Theology can help strengthen our *identity* as Catholics because it can lead us to a better understanding of the beliefs which identify us as Church and motivate our way of life.

Each of these functions intends a *practical* or *applicable* purpose—better understanding of God, or ourselves, the meaning and purpose of life, and how we ought to live out our relationship with God and with others in the complex arena of daily life.

No matter how it is defined, theology attempts to make statements about and to draw conclusions from the *experience* of revelation. For people who have never experienced the things that theology speaks about, theological explanations will not make sense. For example, Christian theology traditionally has placed a great deal of importance on virginity for the sake of the kingdom of God. When this theological message was taught in cultures where virginity was not considered a value, the message was often not understood. Or, consider the person who has never experienced the warmth, power, and energy of a loving Christian community. That individual may have a great deal of difficulty understanding the communal aspects of worship or of sin.

**People do not engage in theology to gain faith.** In fact, theology presupposes that people have faith from the beginning of the dialogue. People of faith participate in the study of theology and the theological process in order to understand their experience of faith.

Religious education textbooks are a result of theologizing. They are attempts to make the teachings of faith understandable for people today. As catechists, we engage in theology when we prepare and present a lesson. We need to be sensitive to student needs and continue to look for ways to help them reflect upon and articulate their own faith experience.

## Pause a Moment . . .

- Describe the value of theology to the Church. For yourself. For a catechist.

- Describe a topic that you hear the Church talking about but that does not mean much to you because you have not personally experienced that reality.

*Memo*

Jot down your reflections regarding the meaning of God in your life.

# Listening to Different Voices

There is no one correct way of doing theology, although there are theological statements that are absolute and true. There have been many voices over the years raised to explain God's role in the world.

## Theological Voices Within the Church

Since the earliest years of its history, the Church has possessed a variety of theological approaches, usually developed as an extension of a major thinker's work. One can thus speak of *Pauline theology* developed in the letters of Paul, *Johannine theology* in the writings of John, and *Thomistic theology* from the *Summa Theologica* of Thomas Aquinas. Theologies also developed around particular religious cultures (e.g., the theology of the Eastern Rite Catholic Church).

Some theological approaches today are a bit more open-ended and less precise than some of those used in the past. More recent approaches have included attempts to speak to our multi-cultural and multi-denominational society. Theology can never stop developing. It always attempts to understand the mystery of God in terms of the culture and circumstances of the era from which it comes. Every theology reflects a world view; they develop out of a particular culture and time, and were shaped by the reigning philosophy of the day. To truly understand what any theological statement means we first must understand its historical and cultural context.

Recent years have seen the development of *Liberation theology.* This theological approach stresses that people first must exercise their fundamental human rights before they can experience and understand the basic insights of faith. The love and providence of God, the dignity and value of people, and the place of peace and justice in the scheme of things are difficult to grasp when people experience repression and dehumanizing conditions. Liberation theology stresses the Christian's duty to work for change when faced with repression and the denial of human rights.

The 1960s saw the development of *Black theology* in the United States. This theological approach attempted to integrate developing social activism among African-Americans with prejudicial structures and attitudes present in the Church. It also focused on the Church's obligation to respond to racial inequality in our society.

Today, African-American voices within the Church try to relate Church traditions to the African-American experience of family, oppression, and the value of developing personal self-esteem. Contributions made to the Church by its Negro members are emphasized (black popes and saints), as well as the importance of Africa on the early development of Christianity. This theology attempts to show that becoming Catholic does not cause one to cease to be black; the African-American community has much to offer to the Church if only the Church is open to receive it.

The women's movement of the past 20 years has introduced yet another approach to Christian theology. *Feminist theology* addresses issues of equality and justice for women, especially in the Church's structures. Some of the topics explored include women's full participation in the ministry of the Church and the removal of sexist language from its theological and liturgical expressions.

## The Importance of Story

Another recent approach to theology looks at the use of story to express our experience of and relationship with God. Theology is not a collection of knowledge to be held but a collection of stories to be told in order to survive difficult times and to prolong good times. A leading proponent of this thought is Rev. John Shea.

> We all seem to be under the sentence of Scheherazade. We tell our stories to live. . . . God not only loves to hear our stories, [but also] he loves to tell his own. And, quite simply, we are the story God tells. Our very lives are the words that come from his mouth. This insight has always fired the religious imagination, refusing to be rationalized or dismissed. The conviction that we are God's story releases primordial impulses and out of a mixture of belligerence, gratitude, and imitation we return the compliment. We tell stories of God.

> Someone has outlined the perennial Christian strategy as: 1. Gather the folks. 2. Break the bread. 3. Tell the stories. . . . As Christians we have inherited ancient stories that carry the faith convictions of our people. Although these stories may start with "long ago," they end with "right now." There is an enduring world-creating ability to the stories of God. . . .

> Before telling the stories of God we must understand ourselves as storytellers. . . . since we are inescapably related to Mystery, we inescapably talk about its [meaning]. . . . To tell a story of God is to create a world, adopt an attitude, suggest a behavior. But stories are first, we are second. We are born into a community of stories and storytellers. In interpreting our traditional stories of God we find out who we are and what we must do. In telling the stories of

▲ *Nothing holds our attention like a good story. In many ways, theology is a process of telling stories about God.*

*God we ourselves are told.* (Stories of God: An Unauthorized Biography, pages 8–9)

Proponents of this method argue that no matter how well we use human reason to explain God's workings, it is still an imperfect attempt to capture the perfect. There is always the unexplainable lurking behind the rational response. Humanity has always expressed the unexplainable through story. The use of story doesn't replace theology, but enhances it. Story moves the human heart—unlike theology which tends to focus on rational explanations. Story carries the expression of faith to a deeper level.

## A Process in Tension

Theology is always a servant of faith. Theology starts from revelation and doctrine and attempts to explain it so that it is understandable to the hearer. It does not create Church teachings. Only the teaching office of the Church, the *Magisterium,* is capable of officially expressing doctrine, which it does through the pope or bishops meeting in a council, advised, in most cases, by professional theologians. However, theological explanations can both wander from the truth and clarify the truth for us. As we become more familiar with the theological process and learn to critically evaluate it, we will be better equipped to recognize when a theological statement explains what we believe and when it becomes unacceptable.

Understand here that many of the theological expressions we now use developed out of disagreements about the faith. For example, the statement of the Nicene Creed that Jesus is "God from God, Light from Light, True God from True God" was developed to contradict heresies that challenged Jesus' divinity. These false teachings were being widely accepted throughout the Church. Only by clearly expressing the truth of faith were the bishops in council able to rescue the Church from its error.

Even when theological expressions are faithful to what the Church teaches, various theological approaches can sometimes lead to disagreements. This makes sense when we recognize that:

- Traditional approaches are concerned with *understanding* Church teaching. They attempt to explain and defend what the Church believes, *preserving* foundational expressions of belief.

- Modern approaches to theology tend to be creative in the way they explain and apply Church teaching to current problems and questions. The focus of this approach is *interpretive;* "How are ancient teachings understandable in the modern world?"

Tension can develop between proponents of traditional expressions of theology and those who advocate more modern explanations. Both sides have valid points; this tension can actually be healthy for the Church.

## Pause a Moment . . .

- With which different theological voices are you familiar? Do they express different faiths or different expressions of faith? Explain your answer.

- How is the process of theology the act of telling stories of God?

- How can the tension that exists between the traditional and the modern voices of theology be both harmful to and helpful for the Church?

---

### Developing Doctrine

As Catholics we believe that all Divine Revelation was completed in Jesus. Since then, the People of God have attempted to express the meaning of this Revelation fully and clearly. The Church has, through the pronouncements of popes, bishops, and the meeting of bishops in councils, expressed what the Church believes as *doctrine.* Those truths that the Church requires the faithful to accept as being revealed by God (e.g., Jesus Christ is fully God and fully man) are known as *dogmas.* These teachings have been promulgated by the Church's highest authority. How a doctrine is understood naturally develops over time as it is reexplained according to changing historical circumstances and developing knowledge.

# $\mathcal{P}$art III $\mathcal{D}$iscovery

## The Theological Process and Catechesis

$\mathcal{N}$otes

_____
_____
_____
_____
_____
_____
_____
_____
_____
_____
_____
_____
_____
_____

Theology and religious education are intended to help each other. As the *National Catechetical Directory* states: "[Religious education] draws on theology, and theology draws in turn on the richness of the Church's [religious education] experience." *(#37)*. Theology and religious education are not identical, however. The *National Catechetical Directory* elaborates on this point.

> *Theology seeks fuller understanding of the gospel message through reflection on the life of Christians and the formal teachings of the Church. It employs systematic and critical methods. It uses philosophy, history, linguistics, the social sciences, and other disciplines in an attempt to understand and express Christian truth more clearly.*

> *[Religious education] also makes use of the sacred and human sciences. It does this not as theology does—for systematic study and analyses of the faith—but in order to better proclaim the faith and, in cooperation with the Holy Spirit, lead individual Christians and the community to maturity of faith, a richer living of the fullness of the gospel message. (#37)*

*Revelation* is the starting point—God's manifestation to people. The people *experience* God through key events and lasting impressions. If people accept God's self-revelation, *faith* results. Later, they *reflect* and *theologize* on the meaning of their experience. As time goes on, certain people (theologians) take up this activity in a systematic way (although all believers theologize from time to time). When the faith community shares with believers the results of this reflection we have catechesis. Catechesis (or in a broader sense, religious education) is the process whereby a person of faith shares God's Word with other believers in order that they, too, may grow in faith.

Catechists need a solid background in theological studies because they present more than their personal beliefs to their students. They need to know what the Church teaches, its history, and the reasons why Catholics believe what they do. The truly effective catechist will have a basic foundation in historical theology and an understanding of the theological process. However, the effective catechist also knows that:

- Simply giving people theological information does not form them as believers or lead them to conversion. (e.g., telling people that God is forgiving is not the same as helping them experience God's forgiveness.)

- Giving people only "second-hand knowledge"—the rational conclusions derived from a long process to make sense out of mystery— is deceptive, if not dishonest. (e.g., teachers should themselves have experienced God's forgiveness before they can honestly teach others about this forgiveness.)

- Using these rational conclusions in place of the experience of God's mystery suggests that God—the ineffable mystery—is really quite manageable and understandable, and thus reduces God to our size. (e.g., God is greater than anything we can say about God.)

- Such a misuse of theological knowledge confuses the symbol (language) with the reality (experience of God).

The catechists' experiences serve as proving grounds for theology, determining whether certain explanations are apt vehicles for articulating God's revelation to believers today. Catechists serve as links between theologians and the people by discovering the new, important questions that arise in everyday life. Together, both theology and religious education are at the service of the Church.

## Pause a Moment . . .

- How would you describe the relationship between theology and catechesis?
- How should theological knowledge be used in catechesis?

▲ *In sharing our experiences, we relive the original event to some degree.*

# Doing Theology

Along with a solid foundation of theological knowledge, effective catechists develop the ability and the skill to think theologically. Then, as part of their teaching, they pass on both to their students. If all the people of God are called to "think theologically," then developing a theological process must be an essential part of religious education. As Patricia O'Connell Killen says,

> There is no task more crucial for anyone working with adults in the Church today than helping them to think theologically. Without this skill, they will not have the conscious and critical access to the resources of their tradition which both the Church and the world desperately need.
>
> ("Assisting Adults, to think Theologically," PACE 22)

Killen offers the following suggestions for assisting adults to think theologically:

- Begin with the nonjudgmental narration of experience.
- Identify significant aspects.
- Connect the present experience and the Church's tradition.
- Name the new learnings and determine the new actions that are to be taken.

Let's look at each of these in more detail.

## Narrate Experience

Two brothers, ages nine and three, lie on the living room floor looking at the older brother's photo album. Pointing at a picture, the older brother says, "That's me at the Grand Canyon. When you get bigger maybe we can go together." Dad, sitting there quietly reading the paper is suddenly moved to tears remembering that trip. What a joy it was!

What are the experiences that people have? How have they been touched by family, nature, religious culture, and the modern world? By talking about these experiences, a person relives the original event. As Killen says, "It makes the incident present again as we re-experience the feelings and actions, see the scene, smell the smells, sense the impressions."

By returning to the event we regather at a place where God was experienced. By asking the basic questions "who," "what," "when," "where," and "how" we can begin to unpack this experience. The question "why" is not answered at this time. To answer a "why" question always involves interpretation. If we were ready to give a meaningful interpretation to the experience at this time, we would not need this process. Interpretation of the experience will occur at the end of the process.

This applies not only to personal experience. The same questions also need to be asked of Church traditions, Bible readings, or current events, especially familiar ones with ready-made answers. Learning to see these events with new eyes means that the event will be seen afresh without any preconceived answers.

## Identify Significant Aspects

What are the most significant aspects of the experience? Name several that strike you as most important. Then choose one to explore. This will keep the reflection focused. Any aspects not considered can be the source for later reflections.

While this process is important, it need not be serious or somber. Neither does it have to be limited to only the rational part of our brains. We can express our theological discoveries through any artistic media we choose: draw a picture, sing a song, or dance out your experience.

## Connect Present Experience and the Church's Tradition

The challenge here is to confront the experience with questions from Church teaching. These questions should find their origin in classic Christian themes. This brings Church teachings, which are often known out of context and without meaning, into an active dialogue with everyday life.

Killen suggests:

*Form a single question which you use to probe the material . . . Knowing what question to ask and how to shape it requires practice. Learning to listen for the theological themes about which people talk in their ordinary language is one step in developing such a skill.*

## Name New Learnings, Determine New Actions

For some people, studying theology is simply an academic exercise, something to learn. Theological reflection should always be more than merely another "something to do." Theological thinking needs to lead to a meaningful response. How will your life change because of this reflection? What can you do differently? What help will you need to begin living your new insights?

## Pause a Moment . . .

*   What benefit do you see in using a method to help you participate in theological thinking?

*   What are some aspects of this process that you can practice using? Where do you start to use this process?

▲ *For some people, theology is only an academic exercise. The study of theological writings is only one part of the entire theological process.*

# Part IV Response

## Using Theology with Students

How can you use what you have learned about theology with students? One way is to introduce them to the process of theological thinking you have just learned. Once they have become familiar with this process, introduce them slowly to the traditions of the Church.

Most religion textbooks operate on this very principle. They introduce the students to a way of thinking about God and then offer them an opportunity to consider what the Church teaches and what various people over the years have said about a particular issue. In this way students learn not only information, but also how to use it.

### Branches of Theology

The Church traditionally divides the study of theology into various categories. These categories of theology are clearly demonstrated in most major religious education textbook series. Quite often, individual lessons deal with several of these categories at once. There seems to be a growing attempt today to present the various categories of theology as an integrated whole, both in religious education textbooks as well as in seminary training. The following list contains many of these categories:

- **Dogmatic theology:** the study of the Church's beliefs using logical principles and comprehensive methods. Often dogmatic theology establishes the norms and sets the tone for other branches of theological study.

- **Moral theology:** the study of how one should live. What is the meaning of sin, conscience, the Commandments, the Beatitudes, virtues, and social justice?

- **Mystical theology:** the study of our spiritual life. How does a person grow in one's relationship with God? How is the Holy Spirit active in the life of each Christian? What is the role of prayer in the Christian life? What are various approaches we can take to prayer?

- **Mariology:** the study of Mary and doctrines relating to her. What is Mary's role as a model of the faithful disciple?

- **Ecclesiology:** the study of the Church. What was Jesus' idea of the Church? the early Christian community's experience of Church? How has the Church been understood over the centuries? What did the Second Vatican Council teach about the Church, authority, papal infallibility, or collegiality?

- **Biblical theology:** the study of doctrine as found in the Old and New Testaments. Additional research comes from the findings of history, archaeology, and anthropology that help explain various parts of the Bible and their meaning for the Christian community. How is God revealed through the teachings of Scripture?

- **Christology:** the study of who Jesus was and the doctrines relating to him. What does Jesus' life and death reveal about God and salvation?

- **Pastoral theology:** approaches belief and life from the standpoint of pastoral needs and practices. What are the practical considerations necessary for effective and meaningful parish and diocesan life? What are the personal and faith needs of people?

## Using These Categories

How can you use these theological categories to help your students become theological thinkers?

1. To begin with, recognize that the students do not need to know the names of the categories. Whether they can identify something as moral theology or pastoral theology is unimportant.

2. Listen to your students talk about their lives. Help them identify where God may be acting for them. Learn to ask good questions about their experience of mystery.

3. Help students come in touch with an experience of God. Tell the story of what God has done or have them find such stories in their textbooks. Let the mystery speak for itself. Don't try to explain what has happened.

4. With the students, identify an important aspect to be studied. Does the story raise questions about Jesus, how we forgive others, or being a friend? While there can be numerous aspects, choose one to explore. Come back to the other ones later.

5. Introduce the students to what the Church teaches, connecting, as Thomas Groome says, our little story to the BIG story. This is where theological categories are important for the catechist. If a student talks about the joy he or she felt when he or she was forgiven by a friend, use that time to talk about how Jesus forgave others. The student now has a sense of what it feels like to imitate Jesus.

6. Look for ways to use this process to affect your and the students' behavior. "From what I have discovered about God, how should I act toward a friend? a stranger? an enemy? a brother or sister? What is God calling me to do?"

## Some Approaches to Teaching

How can your student's text and teacher's manual help you to bring the theological process to your students? Here are some suggestions.

**Christology.** The human nature of Jesus is presented in the story of his birth, finding the child in the Temple at age 12, and in his passion and death. Take the finding of the child in the Temple.

- Read the story directly from the Bible, have the students act it out, or use a film or video.

- Have younger students discuss how Jesus belonged to a family taken care of by Mary and Joseph. Ask them to describe how Jesus felt being loved this way. Tell them that Jesus knows what it is like when they feel close to their families.

- Upper elementary and junior high students can discuss how Jesus might have become separated from his family when on pilgrimage to Jerusalem. How might Mary and Joseph have felt when they realized that Jesus was lost? Did Jesus know he was in trouble? Have them locate

▲ *Prayer is always a part of the theological process. Candles and music help establish a prayerful environment.*

Jesus' "But I" statement in the story. How does Jesus understand the misunderstandings that sometimes make family life difficult and how these misunderstandings can be worked out?

- How would you use this story with high school students?

**Mystical Theology.** Engage your students in a prayer experience. Incorporate quiet reflection, a concrete object (a rock, a lock and key, a mirror, a plant) and meditative music. Let the students handle the concrete object in some way.

- Lower elementary students can pray a short litany of thanksgiving for the presence and care Jesus offers them.

- Upper elementary students can name when the presence and concern of Jesus for them was special.

- Junior high students can write a short prayer about their life now and how Jesus knows about this situation and wants to help them.

- High school students will be able to name a time when prayer has helped them through a difficult situation.

*Memo*

In light of what I have learned about theology and religious education, I want to keep the following considerations in mind for the next time I meet with my students:

## YOUR STORY

From the following examples, how would you use them to stimulate the students to think theologically?

**1.** What it means to be Church (Ecclesiology):

_____

**2.** The Feast of the Immaculate Conception (Dogmatic theology):

_____

**3.** The parish food bank (Moral theology):

_____

**4.** Preparing for First Eucharist (Pastoral theology):

_____

**5.** A careful look at your teacher's manual and student textbook will help you locate examples of theology (theologizing). Notice two beliefs that are mentioned and how they are explained.

**First belief?** _____

Why is this belief being presented? _____

What teaching method is used to present this belief? _____

What application is made to your students' daily lives? _____

**Second belief?** _____

Why is this belief presented? _____

What teaching method is used to present this belief? _____

What application is made to your students' daily lives? _____

# The New Commandment

> The kingdom of God . . . is like mustard seed that, when it is sown in the ground, is the smallest of all the seeds, on the earth. But, once it is sown, it springs up and becomes the largest of plants and puts forth large branches, so that the birds of the sky can dwell in its shade.
>
> (Mark 4:31–32)

## Prayer Response

Consider your place in the process of God's self-revelation to your students and how you lead your students in a reflection on the meaning of that revelation in their lives.

Read the following Scripture passages, pausing to reflect for a few moments on each one. Consider the connection between each passage and your own ministry as a catechist.

> I charge you . . . proclaim the word; be persistent whether it is convenient or inconvenient; convince, reprimand, encourage through all patience and teaching . . . be self-possessed in all circumstances; put up with hardship, perform the work of an evangelist, fulfill your ministry. (2 Timothy 4:2–5)

> And some seed fell on rich soil and produced fruit. It came up and grew and yielded thirty, sixty, and a hundred-fold. (Mark 4:8)

## BIBLIOGRAPHY

Bokenkotter, Thomas. "The Creed: Faith Essentials for Catholics," *Catholic Update*. Cincinnati, OH: St. Anthony Messenger Press, July 1985.

Butcher, H. Maxwell. *Story as a Way to God*. Portland, OR: Resource Publications, 1991.

Diocese of Baker, Oregon. "Our Catholic Creed," *The Desales Program*. Video.

Foley, Leonard, O.F.M. "What Catholics Believe: A Popular Overview of Catholic Teaching," *Catholic Update*. Cincinnati, OH: St. Anthony Messenger Press, October 1986.

Groome, Thomas H. *Christian Religious Education: Sharing Our Story and Vision*. San Francisco: Harper & Row, 1980.

_____ *Sharing Faith: A Comprehensive Approach to Religious Education and Pastoral Ministry*. San Fracisco: Harper, 1991.

Helwig, Monika. *Understanding Catholicism*. New York: Paulist Press, 1981.

Hill, Brennan R. "Chapter 3, Theology: Interpretation of the Christian Experience," *Key Dimensions of Religious Education*. Winona, MN: St. Mary's Press, 1988.

Killen, Patricia O'Connell. "Assisting Adults to Think Theologically," *PACE 22*, February, 1993.

Manternach, Janaan and Pfeifer, Carl J. "Chapter 9, Ecclesial Signs: Creeds and Doctrines," *Creative Catechist*. Mystic, CT: Twenty-Third Publications, 1991.

Meagher, OP, S.T.M., Paul Kevin, O'Brien, Thomas, Aherne, SSJ, Consuelo Maria, editors. *Encyclopedic Dictionary of Religion*. Washington, D.C.: Corpus Publications, 1979.

National Conference of Catholic Bishops. "Chapter II, The Catechetical Ministry of the Church," and Chapter III, Revelation, Faith, and Catechesis." *Sharing the Light of Faith: National Catechetical Directory for Catholics of the United States*. Washington, DC: USCC Publications, 1979.

Pilarczyk, Archbishop Daniel E. *"We Believe:" Essentials of Faith*. Cincinnati, OH: St. Anthony Messenger Press, 1990.

Rohr, Richard, O.F.M. and Martos, Joseph. *Why Be Catholic? Understanding Our Experience and Tradition*. Cincinnati, OH: St. Anthony Messenger Press, 1989.

Shea, John. *Stories of God*. Chicago: Thomas More Press, 1978.

*Nihil Obstat*
The Reverend Gregory A. Banazak, S.T.D.

*Imprimatur*
The Most Reverend Kenneth J. Povish, D.D.
Bishop of Lansing
May 13, 1994

The *Nihil Obstat* and *Imprimatur* are official declarations that a book or pamphlet is free of doctrinal or moral error. No implication is contained therein that those who have granted the *Nihil Obstat* and *Imprimatur* agree with the contents, opinions, or statements expressed.

Send all inquiries to:

BENZIGER PUBLISHING COMPANY
15319 Chatsworth Street
P.O. Box 9609
Mission Hills, California 91346-9609

Second Edition

**ISBN 0-02-651223-8**

Printed in the United States of America.

1 2 3 4 5 6 7 8 9   BAW   98 97 96 95 94

Benziger

# Understanding the Bible

*In speaking of God's self-revelation and of our grace-inspired response of faith . . . [we have] referred to the profound dialogue between God and humankind. [Religious education] draws attention to this dialogue and seeks to shed light upon it.*

*National Catechetical Directory, #61*

BOOK TWO

## In this chapter you will:

- Develop an understanding of what the Bible is and how it was written.

- Examine three approaches to studying the Bible.

- Consider several ways of using the Bible with students.

*Written by*
**Peter Ries**

*Consultant*
**David Riley**

Second Edition

# $\mathcal{P}$art I $\mathcal{E}$xperience

## A Personal History

▲ *Betsy Keifer had lived a full life, much of it centered around Saint Luke's parish. Her memories told an important part of the church's history as well.*

Betsy Keifer had been a member of Saint Luke's for more than half of the parish's life. As the parish prepared to celebrate its 175th anniversary, the planning team thought that Betsy might like to share her stories about the parish. Never the shy type, Betsy readily agreed.

Betsy had seen and done it all at Saint Luke's. The church had been so important to her these past 90-something years:

- Baptized in January, 1900.
- First Communion and Confirmation in May, 1912.
- Graduated from Saint Luke's school, June, 1913.
- Wed her sweetheart, Don, just after he returned from the war in 1919.
- Four children, eight grandchildren, all baptized there.
- Funerals, all too many funerals: her parents, two children, and, most recently, Don's. For the last eight years, since Don's death, Betsy had helped the parish comfort other families with a loved one to mourn.

Yes, Betsy's life and the life of Saint Luke's had been intertwined for all of her life. And Betsy had given as much back as she had received. The membership lists of organizations, causes, and fundraisers would wallpaper the church building itself. Her service was not finished though; God had something more planned.

Betsy was asked to put together an album of memories. The organizing committee had all of the written records, but they lacked the day-to-day stories that Betsy had lived. Betsy was asked to bring to life all of the characters who had made Saint Luke's what it was. Betsy was the perfect person for the task.

"I remember Father Giancomo very well," Betsy said, speaking into the tape recorder.

> *"He was the young associate when I was a school girl. He taught us religion classes on Saturday. He stayed with us for eight years before he volunteered as a chaplain in World War I. He could have stayed safely behind here at the parish, but he felt that his duty was with the men at the front. He's one of the 18 men from this parish buried in France who never came home from that war."*

For two months, Betsy told story after story of the people—priest, religious, and lay—who had been a part of Saint Luke's last 100 years. Her stories were typed by a secretary. They were then read by other older members of the community who added their stories to Betsy's. Dates and spellings were checked against parish records. A month before the parish's celebration, the *Book of Memories* was finished.

Betsy never got to see the final book, however. Around the fourth of July, Betsy's daughter, Irma, noticed that her mother was not well. Irma took Betsy to the doctor on July 7 and he admitted her into the hospital that night. Betsy's condition steadily worsened. Soon she could not see and began to lose her ability to speak.

The pastor, Monsignor Parente, anointed Betsy on her third day at the hospital. "You have two months and two days to be on your feet, Elizabeth," he challenged.

Her health stabilized but did not improve. Betsy realized that she would not be able to take part in the parish's jubilee. That didn't bother her, though. She'd lived through too much that was truly important to worry about a party. But she did have something else to say to the church she loved. She painstakingly dictated her thoughts to Irma:

> *Dear Friends,*
>
> *Saint Luke's has been my home, and I give thanks to God for giving me such a beautiful one. The building has changed over the years, and I never did like the color they painted the sanctuary, but I'm not talking about the building. I'm talking about the people who brought the parish to life.*
>
> *Saint Luke's has always been a place of compassion. It welcomed the immigrant people at the turn of the century—our fathers and mothers—provided aid to struggling families during the Great Depression, and now reaches out to the homeless and abused of our city today.*
>
> *The people of this parish have never been afraid to show their love or to celebrate God's goodness. Think about how many people are touched by our hospitality each week. The joy we share surely is the mark of our Christian faith. "See how they love each other," people must say.*
>
> *We are, above all, a people of faith in Jesus Christ. May he continue to bless us into eternity.*
>
> *Elizabeth Keifer*

Irma Pisano, Betsy's second daughter, read the statement at the anniversary Mass on September 12. Betsy died on August 11. The *Book of Memories* and Betsy's final message are kept in the parish museum for all to see. New parishioners are given a copy when they register.

*Memo*

What stories would your parish's "Book of Memories" include?

## YOUR STORY

**1.** Why is the *Book of Memories* held in such high esteem by Saint Luke's parish?

_____

**2.** While Betsy was the main storyteller, the final book was also shaped by other members of the parish community. Whose name would you put on the album as the author? Explain your answer.

_____

_____

**3.** Betsy's oral history of the parish was supported by the parish's records. Since the parish had these records, why was Betsy's story even needed?

_____

_____

# $\mathcal{P}$art II $\mathcal{M}$essage

## What Is the Bible?

*"The Bible is undeniable, unchangeable truth."*

*"The Bible is the demanding Word of God."*

*"The Bible is the faith story of all people who believe in one God."*

*"The Bible is a guide for living."*

*"The Bible is never wrong."*

You may have heard all of these statements before, either in church, from a door-to-door missionary, or in a Bible-study group. The curious thing about all of these different statements is that they all are true (depending, of course, on how they are understood).

This chapter will examine how the Bible came to be written. Other aspects about the Bible will be covered in the chapters "Reading the Bible" and "Using the Bible."

The Bible can be an intimidating book at first glance. Even when printed on very thin paper, a Bible can be almost two inches thick. Depending on the size of type used, the Bible can run to almost 2,000 pages in length. Tolstoy's *War and Peace* is short in comparison.

Don't be alarmed by the size or length of the Bible. While it is substantial in size, it is not all one book. The Bible is actually a collection of books, each divided into chapters and verses. People who are familiar with the Bible know that it is actually a small library of many different types of writing.

## The Library

The word, "bible" comes from the Greek *biblia* meaning "books." This library contains a wide variety of writings—stories, speeches, poems, songs, and wise sayings.

There are 46 books in the Old Testament grouped into four categories: Pentateuch, Former Prophets, Wisdom, and Latter Prophets. The New Testament has 27 books: four gospel accounts, the Acts of the Apostles, 21 letters (or Epistles), and the Book of Revelation.

## Finding Your Way Around

Each book of the Bible is divided into chapter and verse, marked by numbers at various points. These numbers are not part of the original text. The Bible was divided and numbered into chapters during the thirteenth century A.D.—more than 1,000 years after the last book of the New Testament was written—and into verses in A.D. 1551.

Gradually, you will become familiar with the location of the books of the Old and New Testaments, and the Bible will become less of a mystery to you.

---

### Look It Up

Usually when you see a Bible verse quoted or cited in a book or magazine, you will see a reference given: e.g., **Matt. 8, 5–13** or **Matthew 8:5–13.** Although written differently, these citations reference the same passage: the Gospel of Matthew, Chapter 8, starting with verse 5 and reading through verse 13. Once you know the code, it's easy to find your way around the Bible. Do the following for practice:

1. Locate the Gospel according to Matthew in the table of contents of your Bible. Turn to that page. Remember that the gospel accounts are in the New Testament and so will be toward the back of the Bible.

2. Now, turn to the eighth chapter following the large, boldfaced numbers. The first line in the *New American Bible* (NAB) reads, "When Jesus came down from the mountain." Your Bible, if it's not a *NAB,* may have a slightly different wording. Ignore that for the moment.

3. Look for the superscript number 5 printed within the text. If you have the story of the healing of the centurion's servant, you've succeeded. Congratulations! The passage ends with the line, "And at that very hour [his] servant was healed."

*Pause a Moment...*

- What does it mean to say that the Bible is a library of books?
- Find the following passages in the Bible: Matthew 3:13–17, Ezekiel 37:1–14, Luke 8:4–15, Genesis 11:1–9, 1 Corinthians 12:12–31. Then, label each with one of the following titles: (a) The Tower of Babel, (b) The Parable of the Sower, (c) The Vision of the Dry Bones, (d) The Body of Christ, (e) The Baptism of Jesus.

# A Developing Story

You should now be able to find any passage in the Bible if given the reference. That's the first step toward biblical literacy. The next step is understanding what you will find in the Bible. Keep an open mind as you read this section; you might find that some of what is written here challenges your preconceived notions of what the Bible is.

## A Written Document

The Bible is, first and foremost, the collected stories of a people of faith. Written and edited over many centuries, they document the history of God's communication with the people of the Covenant.

The Bible is an ancient document.

- The earliest written part of the Old Testament dates to around 1050 B.C., although many of the Old Testament stories are as much as 800 years older than that.
- The last books of the Old Testament were written during the second century B.C.
- The earliest books of the New Testament are the letters written by Paul during the middle part of the first century A.D. (Not all of the letters that bear Paul's name were written by him.)
- The last books in the New Testament were written around A.D.100, possibly as late as the beginning of the second century.

Writing styles, political situations, and social customs evolved and changed many times during that 1,100-year period. In fact, biblical scholars are able to accurately date books using these criteria. Since the Bible is neither one continuous piece nor a planned anthology, knowing when a particular book was written will help you better understand what is written.

The Bible has many different authors. These authors wrote without the knowledge or intention of being included in one collected book. The authors wrote, not for money or prestige, but to convey God's message at a particular time and place to a particular group of people. That these writings still have meaning says much about the power of God's inspiration.

**The books of the Bible developed over many years.** Where a modern author might sit down and compose a book, the books of the Bible developed slowly, some over many centuries.

At various times there were many separate versions of the Bible. The Septuagint is a Greek translation of the Hebrew Bible made in the late third century B.C. When the Jewish Bible was finalized in the late second century A.D., some of the books in the Septuagint were left out. This explains why

B.C. and A.D. are the traditional designations given for dates, meaning "before Christ" and "in the year of the Lord (in Latin, *anno Domini*) respectively. This system was developed by a Christian monk, Dionysus Exiguus (Dennis the Short!) around the year 550. Because of the specifically Christian roots of these designations, members of other religious traditions are often uncomfortable using them. In scholarly works on the Bible, you will sometimes see **B.C.E.** and **C.E.** used, meaning "before the common era" and "common era." These terms were developed as more neutral terms for dating events. The dates remain the same whatever initials are used.

versions of the Old Testament are different between Catholic and other Christian or Jewish Bibles.

The Catholic Bible was finalized at the Council of Trent in the sixteenth century A.D. to include 46 books in the Old Testament and 27 in the New Testament. These books finally agreed to by the Church are called the scriptural canon—the Church's certification of their authenticity.

## From Spoken Word to Written Word

Betsy's story in Part I of this chapter is similar in many ways to how the Bible developed. It reflects the way by which much written communication develops:

1. A person has a significant experience: sickness, success, discovery, failure, or death.

2. The person will reflect upon the experience and talk with others about it. Through this reflection and conversation, further meaning is gained.

3. The person may write down some thoughts about the experience, including his or her subsequent understanding of its meaning. This process might involve any number of rewrites and stages of development.

If it was a group experience, a number of people might write their recollections, each perhaps focusing on a different part of the event. Later, an editor would collect the material, inserting transitions between the separate parts, add an introduction and conclusion, and thus form a completed work. Thus, what were separate efforts becomes one book.

The pattern repeats itself when people read the book: they learn of the writer's original experience, reflect on what they have read, discuss it with others, then reach new insights of their own. This cycle of development of written communication is seen in God's relationship with humanity.

The Bible grew out of the faith experience of people, which was usually orally transmitted to the community. Eventually, those reflections that the community found most valuable or used in worship were written down. Over hundreds of years these writings took a final form, with additional sections being added, old sections being revised, and the entire collection being edited. Eventually, these efforts resulted in the books of the Bible as we know them today.

The Bible retells God's actions among us and shares the significance that people found in those events. Readers today reflect on those events and their meaning. We use these writings in our worship. We discuss what we read and hear with others, and discover how God acts in our lives.

Each of these three elements—the event, oral tradition, and written documentation—shaped the Bible as we know it. "The Bible is the result, the end product, of the living faith of our ancestors" (Fr. Isidore J. Mikulski).

## Pause a Moment . . .

- Review the three stages of Bible development: oral, written, and edited. At what stage(s) in the process would God be involved?

- When you read a Bible passage, what process do you use to understand what you have read? What process do you use to interpret a passage for your students? How do these processes further apply the message of the Bible to modern situations?

# The Inspired and Living Word of God

The Bible is often defined as the "inspired and living Word of God." *Inspiration* means that God influenced the human writers of the Bible in such a way that God can be said to be its author. In some way, God influenced human writers to produce what God wished written. Inspiration is God's active participation through the writers of sacred Scripture.

Because the Bible is a result of God's self-revelation, God is the author of the Bible. This cannot be understood simplistically, however, to mean that God literally dictated the Bible word-for-word. Human handprints can be seen all over the biblical formation process. As discussed above, God's revelation was first experienced by God's people. They thought about its significance and developed various ways of speaking to one another about it. Eventually, these stories, reflections, and interpretations were written down, faithful to the community's understanding of God's revelation. The writers creatively wrote and organized their effort. For all these reasons, we can say the Bible was written by human authors.

Unlike God, human beings are limited in their ability to understand divine concepts. For this reason, God chose to be revealed in ways appropriate to the knowledge and culture of the biblical authors. The writers, through that inspiration, expressed God's revelation in terms their contemporaries could understand. For this reason, we can say both God and the human writer are the authors of the Bible.

What all this means is that it is a mistake to take each word of the Bible as coming straight from the mouth of God. That's not how the process of inspiration works. God's revelation touches people in their hearts and souls, at a level deeper than speech. When the biblical authors put that revelation into words, they chose terms and concepts which were meaningful for their time. In doing so, they captured the truths about God which remain essential for our salvation. Nevertheless, their words contain all the limitations and partial understandings of human communication. One of your roles as a "teacher" of Scripture will be to help "translate" the experience of God which underlies the Bible in terms and concepts appropriate for your students.

In addition to its being the inspired Word of God, the Bible is also the living Word of God. Today, we usually regard a word as a written or spoken tool used to convey a message. But for the people of the Old and New Testament periods, words had much richer and more dynamic meanings.

Words were thought to possess the life and presence of the one who originally uttered them. For instance, the Jews regarded the messenger who conveyed the king's statement as the king himself speaking. Killing a king's messenger was a symbolic way of killing the king (see *Matthew 21:33–45*).

To the Jews, anytime a word was spoken, a past event was relived. In the retelling of the Exodus from Egypt, the Jews experienced once again God's saving action.

The Bible presents a living God who acts in history. When it is read today, God is again present. This living Word invites our free response. We are called to meet God in the present moment of our lives in a personal and communal way. God continues to act as Savior, leading us from slavery to new levels of freedom. The Bible leads beyond information. It calls us to an ongoing conversion and continuing transformation.

## The Church Teaches

"Those divinely revealed realities which are contained and presented in sacred Scripture have been committed to writing under the inspiration of the Holy Spirit . . . having been written under the inspiration of the Holy Spirit they have God as their author . . . In composing the books, God chose [men and women] and . . . they made use of their powers and abilities. . . . they, as true authors, consigned to writing everything and only those things which he wanted.

Therefore, since everything asserted by the inspired authors . . . must be held to be asserted by the Holy Spirit, it follows that the books of Scripture must be acknowledged as teaching firmly, faithfully, and without error that truth which God wanted put into the sacred writings for the sake of our salvation. *Dei Verbum*, *#11* ("Dogmatic Constitution on Divine Revelation"). See also the *Catechism of the Catholic Church, #105–109.*

## The Communal Context

In her diary, Anne Frank told the story of her family's life in hiding. She wrote for her own understanding, but also as a record for future generations. Her diary was intended to be read by whomever found it. Anne had no particular audience in mind when she wrote.

The Bible was neither written as a private journal nor intended for simply anyone who happened to read it. The stories in the Bible were each written for a particular audience, and they attempt to express something particular about God to that audience. The books that have survived as the Bible did so because they were accepted by their faith community. The community recognized God's spirit in what was written and made it their own. Just as Betsy's story was cherished and preserved by Saint Luke's parish, so too were the books of the Bible cherished by the Jewish and early Christian communities. The books that we have come to us because an earlier faith community believed these writings to be God's Word to them!

## Intended Outcomes

The Bible is not a naive or innocent collection of stories. These writings were carefully crafted to accomplish a specific end. The authors addressed the faith-needs of their community. Consider the differences in the Gospel accounts of Matthew and Mark.

> *Mark was written between A.D. 60 and 70 for Christian communities that were not Jews and so lacked an understanding of Israel and its history. The author translates and explains Jewish sayings and practices for this audience.*

> *Matthew, however, was obviously written for an audience of Christians with a knowledge of Jewish beliefs and practices. The author of Matthew does not need to explain references to Jewish life or translate Hebrew words as Mark did. Matthew's audience understands.* (See Matthew 5:22; 10:25; 27:6.)

When you read the Bible, you need to be aware of the author's intended audience and any particular problem or question that audience was experiencing (along with when the book was written, which was discussed earlier) in order to understand it correctly.

### Pause a Moment . . .

• What does it mean to say that the Bible is the "living Word of God"?

• How would knowing the audience and context of a particular book affect how you would understand that book?

## Approaches to Studying the Bible

Knowing how the Bible came to be written is not the same as knowing how to interpret what is in the Bible. There are basically three ways or approaches for studying the Bible: *the literal, the rational,* and *the exegetical.* Each of these approaches includes certain presuppositions. How one understands what the Bible means is shaped by these presuppositions.

## The Literal Approach

People who follow the literal approach presuppose the Bible to be accurate in every detail—literally, scientifically, and historically. They take each word at face value; words cannot have symbolic meaning or reflect poetic license. For example, Judges 15 says that Samson killed 1,000 Philistines; literalists would insist that exactly 1,000 people died. In their opinion, a body count would not have revealed 999 or 1,001 dead.

Literalists not only take a word-by-word approach to interpreting the Bible, but they also insist that the Bible be read as a history and science book. For example, the theory of evolution is impossible because the Book of Genesis describes how the world was created by God in seven 24-hour days. They use a modern understanding of science to interpret ancient books.

This difference in perspective is important, going to the heart of what the biblical authors were trying to accomplish. Today, we expect statements about nature to be scientific in character unless otherwise indicated. For example, if someone says that water consists of hydrogen and oxygen, we assume that this statement is intended to be taken as a literal description of events, not as a symbolic description. In the ancient world, this was not so. Most people regarded nature in religious categories, so that their descriptions of natural events were infused with their religious beliefs. This was natural and accepted. For us to assume that Genesis 1–2, containing the creation stories, was intended to be read as scientifically accurate is therefore a serious mistake which fails to respect the cultural differences separating us from the original audience.

In addition, the literalist approach imposes a modern understanding of history on biblical history. Literalists forget that the Hebrew notion of history often placed more emphasis on the meaning of an event than on accurately related details. Biblical authors felt that they were being loyal to the original event by using exaggerations or decorative additions to clearly project the event's significance to their readers. For example, great leaders of Israel all had unique childhoods—Moses was rescued from death, Samuel was born to an aged, barren mother, David slew Goliath with a slingshot. The Bible authors used these stories to show that God had been with these leaders all of their lives, chosen by God to rescue Israel.

A literalist approach to the Bible can cause serious difficulties for the believer. When the Bible is read carefully, discrepancies and contradictions are found. For instance, the first two chapters in Genesis reveals not one creation story, but two. In Genesis 1, man and woman are created last. In Genesis 2, man and woman are created first.

As Walter M. Abbott points out:

> The Bible is a book of religion and is not authoritative in any other realm. It is not a textbook in mathematics [or useful in] . . . analyzing the meteorological factors that lead to a flood. Mark 4:31 says that a mustard seed "is the smallest of all seeds on earth." Botanists would not agree with that but this does not invalidate Jesus' word about the power of a little faith. (The Bible Reader, pp. xi-xii)

## The Rationalist Approach

The rationalist approach presupposes that only those things that can be proved are true. This outlook colors the way that a rationalist reads any

▲ *Young children are literal minded. Whatever is read to them is understood to be truth. They are not capable yet of distinguishing between fact and fiction.*

biblical passage. By trying to explain miraculous events with natural explanations, a rationalist tends not to experience the presence of God or the message of faith contained in the event.

Take, for example, the Exodus story: God leads the people with a pillar of cloud by day and a pillar of fire by night (see *Exodus 13:21*). People who follow the rationalist approach are most interested in the physical causes of this phenomenon, such as an active volcano in the Sinai Peninsula whose eruptions produced a cloud in the daytime and a fiery glow at night. This explanation does not consider the saving action of God in the fire and the cloud. For Jews, the fire and the cloud were symbols that conveyed the intensity and mystery of their experience: God had intervened in the natural course of events to protect the Jewish people and deliver them from Egypt. They used these symbols to dramatically express an experience that was far more intense than the sight of clouds or fire could ever be. But without the use of symbols, it would be impossible to describe. The rationalist approach does not leave room for symbolic interpretation, believing instead that the Jews' escape from Egypt was a combination of "the political situation and good luck."

Because they cannot accept the miraculous, however, rationalists dismiss the Bible's explanations of events as fanciful and inaccurate. When interpreting the story of the Exodus, for example, rationalists will attempt to find scientifically sound alternative explanations for the parting of the Red Sea and the pillar of fire which led the Israelites. Like the literalist approach, rationalism ignores the religious significance of the symbolism in such stories. Following this approach, the individual can become boxed into another corner, this one devoid of faith.

## The Exegetical Approach

The exegetical approach offers a solution to the problems raised by the other approaches. An exegete is a scholar who explains and critically interprets a text. A biblical exegete attempts to discover what biblical authors intended to say about God's revelation. The exegete does not take the Bible at its face value but asks:

- What central truth is communicated?
- How is this truth conveyed?
- Who was the audience?
- What was the author's purpose in writing?
- What kind of writing do we have here?

The exegetical approach understands that the Scriptures are not biographies or histories, but testimonials to faith. For instance, the Scriptures do not describe the life of Jesus in the sense of reporting what went on. Rather, they show how the early Christian community proclaimed his life for its meaning as Savior of the world. The New Testament writers sought to establish, deepen, and widen people's faith in Jesus. The Catholic Church encourages us to read the Bible from this approach.

Exegetes look at the religious or faith meaning of the text. Consider the miracle of the loaves and fishes *(Mark 6:34–44)*. Where the literalist will praise God for the miracle and the rationalist will wonder how everyone could be fed, the exegete will ask what this story says about God's saving action. The fact that Jesus may have physically fed 5,000 people with five

▲ *Rationalists read the Bible to find provable fact. Anything that cannot be proven by reason or scientific explanation is considered untrue, and thus worthless.*

loaves and a fish is not important. The issue is not to understand how Jesus worked a miracle, or to explain the miracle through natural causes, but to understand that God's kingdom is a place where all will be fed.

The exegetical approach also attempts to determine literary style. The Bible with its different sections is much like a newspaper. When we read a newspaper, we understand that its front page is different than the editorials or the comic section.

If, 2,000 years from now, our descendants found the sports section in a time capsule and did not understand its type of writing, they could easily be confused. A headline such as **"San Diego Padres Clobber Atlanta Braves"** might cause them to ask why priests were fighting Native Americans in the 1990s. A headline like **"Giants Lose Four Straight to Orioles"** might have our descendants wondering if there really were giants and how small birds could defeat them!

The exegete realizes that the Bible contains many different kinds of writing, many different *literary forms.* There are stories that are not literally true but teach truths *(see Genesis 1–11).* There are different types of history, such as the books of Kings, Maccabees, and the Acts of the Apostles. There is poetry, as in Psalms. There is prophecy, as in Isaiah. There is the symbolic, or *apocalyptic,* type of writing as in parts of Daniel and Revelation. Knowing what kind of writing is contained in a certain scripture passage helps one to interpret its meaning more accurately.

The exegetical approach understands that various factors influenced the formation of the Bible.

- Reflecting the culture in which it developed, the Bible has a very concrete and down-to-earth view of life.

- The Bible resonates with the Jewish language, mentality, and culture with its emphasis on story.

- All of the surrounding peoples believed in many gods. It was difficult at times for the Jews to hold on to their belief in one God. Frequently, they were heavily influenced by their pagan neighbors' social and legal customs.

The daily life of the people influenced the developing collections of teachings and sayings in the Bible. In the Old Testament, these were the numerous rules and laws for the life of the Jewish nation. In the New Testament, the early Christians would try to remember what Jesus had said or meant as they attempted to apply his message to some situation in their lives or answer some questions that had arisen.

Scholars who study the Bible are aware of these various influences. They try to answer "What is the central truth(s) being communicated? What are the descriptive additions or details used as vehicles to convey this truth(s)? What is the message intended for the original audience?" The answers to any and all of these questions affect the way we should interpret the particular passages today.

## Pause a Moment . . .

- How do the literal, rational, and exegetical approaches to reading Scripture differ?

- What's the problem with interpreting Scripture using only the scientific method?

## Helping Students Understand the Bible

This section will help you deepen your understanding of the information you have just read and prepare you to use what you've learned in your role as a catechist.

Complete the following exercises.

1.  Describe in your own words the three approaches to studying the Bible and one or two consequences of using each approach.

Literal _____

_____

Rational _____

_____

Exegetical _____

_____

▲ *When you look through a photo album you relive the past events of your life. The same is true for the Bible; when you read it, you relive the life of our ancestors in faith.*

2.  Read Matthew 8:23–27 about Jesus and the storm at sea. How would each of the three approaches to studying the Bible attempt to explain this passage?

a.  The Literalist's Approach _____

_____

b.  The Rationalist's Approach _____

_____

c.  The Exegetical's Approach _____

_____

Four general comments can be made about helping students understand the Bible:

1.  **Be careful about how you present to students the ideas discussed in this chapter.** For example, God's role in the formation of Scripture could be described in such a way that students might conclude that God had no role at all. One could say, "God did not write the Bible, the human author did." Though the catechist might understand all the subtleties of that statement, and though the statement itself is partially true, it could easily mislead the students and leave them with the wrong impression. Young students (below the sixth grade) usually have not reached the stage of development where they can make the abstract distinctions necessary for understanding this process.

2. **Choose an appropriate way to explain an idea.** One need not conclude that ideas are too dangerous, too confusing, or too deep for the students. The key is choosing the appropriate approach. There are some adults who have difficulty seeing how the Bible could really be the Word of God unless God dictated it word-for-word to the human writer. They have grown so accustomed to this explanation that anything else seems misleading, incomplete, and wrong. Students studying the Bible for the first time, however, usually do not have this same difficulty. They hear, discuss, and work with the explanations and simply conclude that God is the author and the human writer is the author, and without God there would be no Bible. (Note that the New Testament is usually easier for younger students to understand than is the Old Testament.)

3. **Methods and exercises for teaching the Bible to adults may not work with children or teens.** Portions of the Bible that are of interest to adults may not be compelling for younger people. Catechists always need to be sensitive in selecting appropriate methods of presenting the material from this topic to their students.

4. **Finally, it is crucial that in our teaching we allow the Bible to be itself.** The Bible does not need to be squeezed into particular boxes of meaning or forced into certain usage to help students grow in faith. Like all great literature, the Bible has universal appeal and a wide-ranging validity that is readily apparent to the students. With a prepared catechist's gentle prodding and commentary, the Bible's positive effectiveness with students will be enhanced.

You can never go wrong by teaching students of any age the basic skills for locating books in the Bible, recognizing references, or finding particular chapters and verses. With practice, they will develop a familiarity with the Bible that will serve them well. The more comfortable a person is in using the Bible, the more likely it is that the person will read the Bible on a regular basis.

One additional rule of thumb: **Never teach what must later be untaught.** That is, don't teach as history what may be legend or myth. Children read all kinds of stories and enjoy them as stories. Don't lean heavily on *analysis* or draw out the *"moral."* Let them enjoy the story simply as story. In the Noah story, for example, emphasize that God saved Noah, not how many animals can fit on a boat as described in the Bible. If students want to know how it happened, invite them to share what they think. In this way you invite them to develop their reasoning skills and avoid the temptation toward literalism.

## Pause a Moment . . .

- Why is it important to teach younger learners about the Bible differently than you would teach adults?

- What are some examples of appropriate and inappropriate ways of teaching the Bible to first grade students? sixth grade students? tenth grade students?

## The New Commandment

He got into the boat and his disciples followed him. Without warning a violent storm came up on the lake, and the boat began to be swamped by the waves. Jesus was sleeping soundly, so they made their way toward him and woke him: "Lord, save us! We are lost!" He said to them: "Where is your courage? How little faith you have!" Then he stood up and took the winds and the sea to task. Complete calm ensued; the men were dumbfounded. "What sort of man is this," they said, "that even the winds and the sea obey him?"

(Matthew 8:23–27)

# Part IV Response

▲ *Incorporate the Bible into your students' prayer. One way of doing this is to set up a prayer corner where the Bible is honored.*

## Some Ideas for Catechists

How you teach the Bible to your students should be determined by their age and ability. Here are a few age-appropriate suggestions for you to consider. For each age level, confer with your teacher's manual for ideas and approaches for using the Bible with your students.

### Early Childhood

Begin using the Bible gradually with these young children. Pick a special place in your classroom to enthrone the Scriptures. Gather around the Bible when you pray. Avoid full-fledged Bible stories at this time. The children will begin exploring the stories in more detail in the first grade. If you wish to use the Bible directly, read or paraphrase from it in short passages.

### Primary

Bible stories are very effective when used with primary students.

- Use short, colorful stories from the Old or New Testament. Arch Books has developed a large selection of appropriate titles. Gather the students around you in the story corner and read or tell the story to your students. Choose stories with care. The stories should not be too frightening, confusing, or lengthy. Be familiar with the story and how you will tell it ahead of time. If you are using a book with illustrations, show the students the pictures as you read the story. Show the students where that same story is found in the Bible.

- Young children enjoy acting out stories. Have a number of old pieces of clothing available to make various costumes. Be imaginative in describing what the characters are wearing. Assign one simple line to each character while you serve as the narrator. Or have students make simple puppets of the characters in the story by drawing the face of a character on a paper plate and using that plate-face as the character when they say their line(s).

- Have students make a creative project to express the main idea of a Scripture story (e.g., David's slingshot, the tower of Babel). Exhibit their work in your prayer corner near where your Bible is enthroned. If your parish has the Liturgy of the Word for children during weekend Masses, consult the materials used for additional approaches.

### Intermediate Students

- Intermediate students often enjoy working in groups of three or four. Have a **"Scripture Scavenger Hunt."** List objects on the board and give the groups five minutes to find two or three of those objects somewhere in your classroom. Tape the title of a particular book of the Bible to each object. After the teams find the objects, they need to find the books in their Bibles. If your students have learned how to find particular Bible verses, have them find a Bible chapter and verse in each book that relates to a Scripture story or quote you have used in a previous lesson.

- Scripture can become more relevant for intermediate age students if it is related to other subjects they study. Use a map of the Middle East to show where the major Scripture events took place. Locate and use Scripture/history timelines which give an idea of major historical events in relation to major biblical events and the writing of the Bible. Include as part of your story material on living in an ancient culture. For example, "What was ancient warfare like?" or "How do nomads live?"

## Junior High

- Junior high students are drawn to heroes and heroines. Make a list of biblical heroes and heroines. Have groups of three or four students research a person they select and prepare a brief report for the class. They can help their classmates find the section(s) of the Bible where their hero or heroine is described and answer questions about their subject.

- Occasionally use games such as "Bible Pictionary," "HolyWord Squares," or "Bible Trivia" as review or learning tools. Catechists can make up their own sets of questions. Divide the class into two teams competing in mock baseball or football games, each successful question being worth a certain number of bases or yards, each unsuccessful question being an out or a down lost.

## High School

- All of the above activities, appropriately modified for level of difficulty, can be used effectively with high school students as well.

- High school students frequently relate positively to reflective prayer services. Dim the lighting in the room. If allowed, place a lighted candle in the middle of the group. Then pass around a hat filled with short passages from the Book of Wisdom and from the sayings of Jesus in the Gospel. Each student will select a quotation and read it to the group. Invite the entire group to comment on its meaning and how it might apply to their lives today. The person who picks the sayings starts the sharing.

- Use the Bible as part of a guided image prayer. Pick a Bible story, like "The Woman at the Well" *(John 4:4–30)*. As someone reads the story aloud, they are to see in their imagination what is taking place. The reader is to read the verses very slowly, pausing after each one. When the prayer time is finished, ask the student to write or discuss what they saw and how they felt.

## Adult

Many of the exercises intended for high school students can be used with adults as well. Adults are usually capable of much greater abstract thought and can struggle with the questions raised by serious scholarship. That does not mean that adult learning should be strictly academic. Do not be afraid to have adults draw their images of scripture, engage in guided imagery prayer, or act out a Bible story. The more they enjoy Bible study, the more they will participate, and the more they will learn.

Notes

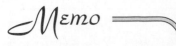

## Memo

In light of what I have learned about the Bible, I want to keep the following considerations in mind for the next time I meet with my students:

## Prayer Response

Relax and quietly reflect on your relationship with God. Use the following Scripture passage to consider the Bible's importance in your life. Reflect on how God's Word penetrates and gives clarity for you and helps you appreciate the basic meaning of life. Ask God for the interest, energy, and stamina to continue to grow in your understanding of the Bible so that God's Word enriches you as a catechist.

*Indeed, God's word is living and effective, sharper than any two-edged sword. It penetrates and divides soul and spirit, joints and marrow; it judges the reflections and thoughts of the heart. Nothing is concealed from him; all lies bare and exposed to the eyes of him to whom we must render an account.* (Hebrews 4:12–13)

## BIBLIOGRAPHY

Abbott, Walter M., S.J., et al. *The Bible Reader.* Milwaukee, WI: Bruce, 1969.

*About the Bible.* South Deerfield, MA: Channing L. Bete Co., 1971.

*Basic Tools for Bible Study.* The DeSales Program, Franciscan Communications, video.

*The Bible and You.* Scriptographic Booklet. South Deerfield, MA: Channing L. Bete Co., 1971.

Boadt, Lawrence. *Reading the Old Testament.* Mahwah, NJ: Paulist Press, 1984.

Brown, Raymond. *Responses to 101 Questions on the Bible.* Mahwah, NJ: Paulist Press, 1990.

Foley, Leonard, OFM. "How the Gospels Were Written." *Catholic Update.* Cincinnati, OH: St. Anthony Messenger Press, May, 1983.

Fujita, Neil S. *Introducing the Bible.* Mahwah, NJ: Paulist Press, 1981.

Glavich, Sr. Mary Kathleen, S.N.D. *Leading Students into Scripture.* West Mystic, CT: Twenty-Third Publications, 1987.

National Conference of Catholic Bishops. "Chapter III, Revelation, Faith, and Catechesis," *Sharing the Light of Faith: National Catechetical Directory for Catholics of the United States.* Washington, D.C.: USCC Publications, 1979.

Ralph, Margaret. *And God Said What?* Mahwah, NJ: Paulist Press, 1987.

Scott, Macrina, O.S.F. "A Popular Guide to Reading the Bible," *Catholic Update.* Cincinnati: St. Anthony Messenger Press, 1984.

*Scripture from Scratch.* St. Anthony Messenger Press, video series.

Smith, Virginia. "Whole Bible at a Glance: Its 'Golden Thread' of Meaning," *Catholic Update.* Cincinnati, OH: St. Anthony Messenger Press, April, 1989.

*What Catholics Believe About the Bible.* St. Louis, MO: Liguori Publications, video.

*Nihil Obstat*
The Reverend Gregory A. Banazak, S.T.D.

*Imprimatur*
The Most Reverend Kenneth J. Povish, D.D.
Bishop of Lansing
May 13, 1994

The *Nihil Obstat* and *Imprimatur* are official declarations that a book or pamphlet is free of doctrinal or moral error. No implication is contained therein that those who have granted the *Nihil Obstat* and *Imprimatur* agree with the contents, opinions, or statements expressed.

Send all inquiries to:

BENZIGER PUBLISHING COMPANY
15319 Chatsworth Street
P.O. Box 9609
Mission Hills, California 91346-9609

Second Edition

**ISBN 0-02-651211-4**

Printed in the United States of America.

1 2 3 4 5 6 7 8 9   BAW   98 97 96 95 94

# Benziger

# Reading the Bible

*The Bible . . . offers us a way of understanding the world in a fresh perspective, a perspective that leads to life, joy, and wholeness. It offers us a model, a pattern, through which we make, think about, perceive, and live life differently.*

Walter Brueggemann

*Written by*
**Peter Ries**

*Consultant*
**David Riley**

## In this chapter you will:

- Identify some of the types of literature in the Bible.
- Practice a technique for reading Scripture.
- Develop a realistic Bible-reading plan.

Second Edition

## *It's Hard to Tell*

"It's got to be around here somewhere," said Joy, as she peeled off Sunset Boulevard and meandered into the Hollywood Hills. Like Caroline, a friend from out of town, Joy was a big fan of Raymond Chandler's detective novels. That evening they were searching for a gangster's retreat featured in *The Long Goodbye.* Unfortunately, they didn't have much luck. "Wasn't there something in the first chapter about a gargoyle fountain?" asked Joy. Caroline grabbed a dog-eared paperback from a pile of marked books at her feet. "I don't think so," she said. They swung back around and tried the next street.

Caroline and Joy read most of Chandler's novels while in college. They liked how narrator Philip Marlowe's dark, descriptive tone captured the grimy elements of Los Angeles during the 1930s. In the stories, the pragmatic and honest private investigator attempts to make sense of a deceptive and corrupt society. Although the character had many faults, in many ways Marlowe was like a modern knight. Caroline and Joy hoped to retrace routes from his adventures.

Joy backed the car up a cobblestone driveway. "Can this be it?" she wondered, as they stepped out of the car and walked around the perimeter of the yard. The doorway conformed to a passage from the book and the windows faced the right direction. Even the trees were in place. Caroline reached through the open car window to get her camera. "You can put that back," sighed Joy. "This isn't it. The garage is on the wrong side." She pointed out the structure as she walked back to the car.

"How about the house in Silverlake?" suggested Caroline. Joy steered the car out of the hills and headed east. Fifteen minutes later, they were in the proper area. "I think it's close to the reservoir," she said. "Tell me if you recognize any landmarks." The road was narrow and there weren't many streetlights, but Caroline glimpsed a driveway that matched a scene from *Farewell, My Lovely.* Behind a wrought-iron fence, a paved road turned behind overgrown shrubs. "What do you think?" she asked. Joy responded, "It's hard to tell, but it could be. Make a note of it, and let's try another block."

Stopping at a nearby coffee shop, Joy and Caroline compared passages from Chandler's books with their road atlas. Now everything began to make more sense. Many of the streets Marlowe investigated were fabricated. Avenues that did exist often went in different directions, weren't to scale, or didn't connect. The houses probably weren't real, either. Although Chandler effectively conveyed the atmosphere and geography of certain parts of Los Angeles, he certainly didn't adhere to road maps. No wonder they couldn't find anything.

"Why don't we drive out on the San Bernadino freeway?" asked Joy, alluding to a trip made in *The Big Sleep.* "Sure," said Caroline. "At least we know that exists. Chandler's a great writer, but he's no cartographer."

1. Why do you think Caroline and Joy wanted to find the sites mentioned in Chandler's novels?

_____

_____

2. Did their discovery that much of Chandler's geography was fabricated make his novels any less "true" or enjoyable? Why or why not?

_____

_____

3. What do you think Caroline and Joy valued more about Chandler's books: the accuracy of their details, or the overall "feel" for the city and the characters the novels provide?

_____

_____

4. What do you think this story has to do with reading the Bible?

_____

_____

*M*emo

Do you have a favorite author? What appeals to you about him or her?

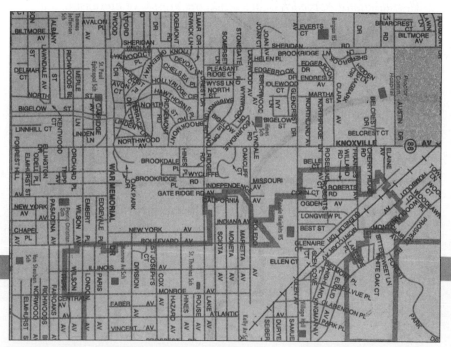

▲ *Caroline and Joy tried to use Raymond Chandler's novels as if they were a travelogue. Just as Chandler did not intend for his books to be used as road maps, the writers of the Bible did not intend to write a simple history book.*

## What Is the Bible?

Before describing a technique for reading the Bible, it is important to review four main ideas that help form a proper understanding of what the Bible is. These issues are covered in more detail in the chapter "Understanding the Bible."

**The Book**

- The Bible explains who and what God is, and presents a living God active in the lives of people. In the Bible, we see God calling, challenging, and leading people to holiness.

- In the Bible, we see specific faith communities responding to their experience of God. The Bible is not a static, once-and-for-all historical record, but a living invitation to meet God today.

- The Bible is a library of 46 Old Testament and 27 New Testament books representing diverse writing styles, themes, and points of view.

**Approaches to Studying the Bible.** People wise in the ways of the world know that what you expect from something has a lot to do with what you get out of it. This insight applies to the Bible as well. Before you begin reading the Bible, it's a good idea to talk about what you should expect to find there.

- *The Literalistic Approach* expects the Bible to be historically and literally accurate in every detail.

- *The Rationalist Approach* is, in a sense, the flipside of literalism. Rationalists also read the Bible on a literal level, insisting that only what can be proved is true.

- *The Exegetical Approach,* the one adopted here, realizes that the Bible was written for various communities of faith. This approach emphasizes that the authors of the Bible belonged to a different culture, with different ideas about the world and human behavior.

**Various Kinds of Writing.** It is crucial to know that different kinds of writing (literary forms) make up the Bible (e.g., poetry, wise sayings, prophecy). Each kind of writing has a somewhat different purpose reflecting the author's intent for the reader.

**Influences on the Formation of the Bible.** Usually any one book of the Bible developed over a period of many years. After experiencing God's saving presence among them in some memorable way, the people would reflect upon the significance of that event. An oral tradition would develop as each succeeding generation heard the message. Eventually, parts of this tradition would be written down.

▲ *The Bible is like a library with 46 different books in the Old Testament and 27 different books in the New Testament. To better understand the Bible, you will need to know the type of literature you are reading.*

## Pause a Moment . . .

- How could you identify a person who approaches the Bible from a literalistic perspective?

- The biblical authors adjusted and reshaped their religious traditions to meet the needs of their faith communities. In what ways is the role of the catechist similar?

## Types of Literature in the Bible

Since the Bible is a library, it will help for you to know something about the genres (types of literature) you will encounter. Each genre has its own purpose and structure, and a familiarity with them puts you in a much better position to understand what you're reading.

**Myth.** In everyday speech, the word "myth" has come to mean a story that lacks truth. Initially, most of your students will probably understand the term this way. As catechists, however, we must stress that a myth is not an "untrue" story, but a story whose truth is religious and symbolic rather than historical. Its truth is so deep, profound, and complex that it can only be expressed in story.

A myth is an imaginative story, usually concerned with the beginnings of the universe or of humanity, which uses story to communicate abstract ideas about God, nature, society, and human behavior. Students of myth often talk about these abstract ideas as the four "functions" of mythology:

- **The Theological Function:** Myths tells us about the nature of God and God's attitude towards the world and towards human beings.

- **The Cosmological Function:** Myths orient us towards our environment and tell us what we can expect from the natural world.

- **The Social Function:** Myths give us a picture of human society, both how it actually operates and what it should be like.

- **The Ethical Function:** Myths depict models of human behavior, both positive and negative, as guides in ethical decision-making.

Let's take an example. Genesis 3 relates the story of the fall of humanity. At the theological level, we find that God demands obedience from humanity, but also has the capacity to forgive when people fail. We also find that God created the natural world to be a source of pleasure for humanity, but that the potential exists for us to abuse that intention. Socially, the story in Genesis 3 suggests that men and women were intended to function as partners. Finally, the actions of Adam and Eve in Genesis 3 serve as negative moral examples, suggesting the importance both of obedience and of accepting responsibility for one's actions.

Taken as a whole, myth has the power to capture the feelings of people—of whole societies—and move them to action. The story of the fall of humanity draws forth from us a resounding "yes." We recognize the truth of sin and its power over us. The power of this truth leads us to pray for God's great mercy and forgiveness.

**Legend.** Legends are stories concerning famous figures from the past which serve to express a community's values and identity. Unlike myths, the central characters in legends are generally historical figures.

Notes

The history of Israel captured in the Bible is a record of God's ongoing involvement in the fate of the Hebrew people. Here are the significant periods and events:

- **B.C. 1800–1600** Prehistory. The time of the Patriarchs.

- **B.C. 1280–1260** Moses forms a covenant with God and leads the Hebrew slaves out of Israel into freedom. Known as the Exodus.

- **B.C. 1260–1040** The Hebrews take control of the land promised to them by God. The conquest is not immediate nor permanent. It is the time of the Judges.

- **B.C. 1040–922** Under the leadership of Saul, David, and Solomon Israel becomes a united kingdom.

- **B.C. 922–721** The nation of Israel divides into the kingdom of Israel (ten northern tribes) and Judah (two southern tribes). The kingdom of Israel was destroyed by the Assyrians in 721. This is the time of the prophets.

Continued on next page

Chapters 12 to 40 in Genesis contain legends about the famous founders of Israelite culture, such as Abraham, Sarah, Hagar, Isaac, Jacob, Rachel, and Joseph. The legends in Genesis concern events that date to as early as 1800 B.C., even though they were not collected and written down until at least 1,000 years later.

All cultures have legends about their important founding figures. In America, we tell stories about George Washington telling the truth and throwing a silver dollar across the Potomac River. These stories emphasize American values such as honesty and physical strength. Although these events are obviously exaggerated, the stories communicate important truths about the American culture.

The legends in Genesis are similar to the ones about George Washington. The stories about Abraham's obedience to Yahweh in his near-sacrifice of Isaac, Jacob's cunning in stealing his brother's birthright, and Joseph's compassion in forgiving his brothers, all stress qualities highly prized by the ancient Israelites. Read in this light, the legends of Genesis open an important window on the cultural world of the Bible.

Their importance doesn't end there, however. They continue to show us the values we need to live fully human lives. The legends found in the Bible continue to empower the reader even after thousands of years.

**Ancient History.** Neither myths nor legends are intended to relate historical events. There are several biblical texts, however, that record historical events. In the Old Testament, the "former prophets," a set of texts including Joshua, Judges, 1 and 2 Samuel, and 1 and 2 Kings are called historical books. In the New Testament, the four gospel accounts are quasi-historical works, as is the Acts of the Apostles. The characters and events recorded in these books are historically genuine.

We must realize, however, that ancient people regarded history-writing much differently than we do. In the modern world, history writers are trained to separate their opinions and judgments of events from "how things actually were," meaning the dates, names, places, and other details of the past. Ancient historians, however, were trained to include their analysis *in* this record. In other words, the task of an ancient historian was not necessarily to "get the facts right," but to present the meaning of the past to the reader.

To take an example of how this works, the author of Joshua presents the Israelite settlement of the promised land as the result of swift military conquest. In fact, the actual process probably took much longer, was more complex, and despite the occasional battles, was largely the product of peaceful assimilation. The author of Joshua wished to stress, however, that the Israelites enjoyed the support and protection of Yahweh in their acquisition of this land. The presence of such "distortions" in the Bible's historical books does not make them poor historical sources, but neither can one simply assume that each and every historical claim in the Bible happened exactly as described. Each story must be read in light of the author's overall theme, as well as the evidence of other biblical texts, to get a more complete picture.

**Prophecy.** The prophets spoke for Yahweh in ancient Israel. Some of the prophets, such as Elijah, Elisha, and Huldah, left no written record. In the case of Isaiah, Jeremiah, Ezekiel, and the 12 "minor prophets," the Bible contains collections of their teaching. These works are collectively known as "prophecies."

People often think of a "prophet" as someone who predicts the future. This is a very small part of what the Israelite prophets did. Mostly they addressed specific situations in Israelite society, criticizing, condemning, and encouraging the people in light of Yahweh's word. Their task was to apply the religious values of Israel to the current political, economic, and social challenges facing the people.

There are many types of literature within the general category of "prophecy." Prophets spoke oracles, sang hymns, told stories, and engaged in symbolic actions. *In each case they strove to recall for Israel its commitment to Yahweh and the Covenant.* More importantly, they sought to apply that commitment to specific circumstances. They spoke for justice on behalf of the poor and the oppressed. Their words were intended for a specific people, time, and place. They spoke honestly and forthrightly without fear.

**Wisdom Literature.** The part of the Bible known as the "wisdom literature" actually contains a wide variety of literary genres, including poetry (the Psalms), religious fiction (Jonah), theological essays (Ecclesiastes) and moral instructions (Proverbs). The Book of Jonah, for example, is a satire on faithless prophets, in the spirit of satirical works by authors such as Jonathan Swift. It would be a mistake to read this as a literal story about someone being swallowed by a large sea-creature, who somehow survived the experience. Instead, the story pokes fun at Jonah's inability to outrun God's persistent request, and his unwillingness to speak the word God has chosen him to deliver.

Quite different in tone is the Book of Ecclesiastes. There, the author means to be taken literally when he says "all is vanity and a chasing after wind." The author's pessimism should not be avoided by trying to interpret the text on a non-literal level. Instead, Ecclesiastes should be read as a moving testament to the difficulties faced by human beings as they attempt to cope with life's pain. In this case, however, the literal approach is the appropriate one, since this type of literature (theological essay) is meant to be read that way.

As you read through the wisdom literature, bear in mind that each book may call for a different kind of interpretation depending on the kind of literature it contains. This flexibility in approach flows from a healthy recognition of the Bible's diversity.

**Epistles.** In the New Testament, the most widely employed literary genre is the epistle, or "letter." The New Testament contains 14 epistles traditionally attributed to the apostle Paul, along with seven "Catholic" letters whose authorship is unknown. In addition, the Book of Revelation opens with seven letters to Christian churches in Asia. Of the 27 New Testament books, therefore, epistles figure in all or part of 22 of them.

Epistles are letters written by leaders of early Christianity to Christian communities in various locations. In the case of Paul's letters, you can usually tell the location from the title; the Letter to the Romans, for example, is addressed to the fledgling Christian community in Rome. With the Catholic epistles, it is sometimes more difficult to identify the exact audience intended by the author. In any case, these letters are generally not intended to be universal formulations of Christian faith, but answers to the specific problems and questions faced by that community.

The epistles are witnesses to the growth of Christianity in the first few decades after the death and resurrection of Jesus. Read properly, they

- **B.C. 720–587** Judah survives as a separate kingdom until it, too, is destroyed by Babylon in 587. This is also the time of the prophets.

- **B.C. 587–538** The people of Judah live in Exile in Babylon. Synagogue worship and the Law develop as signs of Judaism.

- **B.C. 538–333** Jews rebuild Jerusalem and the Temple and develop religious reforms.

- **B.C. 333–167** Greek culture influenced and shaped Jewish beliefs and practices.

- **B.C. 167–63** Maccabean uprising against Greek rule. See 1 and 2 Maccabees.

- **B.C. 63–135 A.D.** Roman Rule. Jerusalem and the Temple were destroyed in A.D 70. By 135 the nation of Judah no longer existed.

communicate the values and convictions which fueled the expansion of Christianity and which still animate the Church today.

**Apocalyptic Literature.** In the Old Testament, there are several examples of apocalyptic writing: the Book of Daniel, parts of Ezekiel, and parts of Isaiah. In the New Testament, the Book of Revelation is also an apocalyptic work. The word "apocalypse" is Greek for "uncovering," suggesting that apocalyptic books reveal previously hidden truths. In general, these hidden truths concern God's future plans for humanity and the world.

When reading an apocalyptic book, it is important not to become too concerned with establishing the precise meaning of each symbol and reference. This sort of writing is intended to be mysterious. Instead, let the symbols affect you emotionally, as they were intended to do with their original audiences. Experience fear at the images of God's wrath and destructive power, and then joy in the description of the restored life Yahweh has planned for us.

The most important idea contained in apocalyptic literature is that history is not open-ended; instead, it is building to a climax, in which God will act to deliver the faithful. Our present difficulties and pain, therefore, are endurable, because we have God's promise of a happy ending. Read this way, apocalyptic literature can be a profound source of comfort and optimism.

## Pause a Moment . . .

- How would you respond if, after telling a student that the creation stories in Genesis are myths, she asks, "Does that mean they're not true?"

- How will knowing about these different kinds of writing influence the way you read the Bible?

▲ *Letters have their own style: they begin with an introduction, discuss important matters, and then close with a fond remembrance. Paul's letters to the churches he founded follow a similar pattern. They always begin with a greeting and end with a note of praise and blessing.*

## REFLECTION

The following exercise will give you an opportunity to see if you can use the ideas you have just read. Answer the following questions in a way that might be understood by your neighbor.

1. In a very few words, describe what the Bible is.

_____

_____

_____

_____

2. In general terms, describe the factors that are important to keep in mind when reading the Bible.

_____

_____

_____

_____

# Part III Discovery

## A Technique for Reading the Bible

To understand what we read, we must first know the type of material that is being read. Is it poetry, the newspaper, scientific or technical studies, a joke book, novels? Each type is approached uniquely as its purpose dictates. Similarly, we must be concerned with certain basic considerations when developing a technique for reading the Bible. The most basic ones are "What did the text mean to the writers and their contemporaries? Why did the authors write? What was happening at that point in time in their communities? What were the authors trying to say?"

Once the original meaning of a passage is clear, the reader is ready to apply that insight to his or her own life. Ask, "What does the text say to me in my situation?" The mystery here is that the Bible speaks not only through the dust-filled roads of Palestine, but also through the sweat and struggle of our lives today. The reader is challenged to remain faithful to the original message of the text, while also being open to the Holy Spirit's invitation to personal discovery and growth in faith.

In learning about the writers' world, it is crucial that one honestly recognize and accept the Bible's limitations. The Bible is not a history book or science manual. It is not an answer book for all of life's problems—although it does contain insights, directions, and much meaning.

### An Effective Technique

Peter (10) and Sarah (12) were going to surprise their parents with a special breakfast for their anniversary. They had helped their parents cook many times and felt very comfortable making pancakes and orange juice. They worked hard together, not arguing even once, and placed before their folks a beautiful anniversary gift.

Although their mom and dad complimented them on the wonderful breakfast, the kids knew that something was amiss. Finally, Sarah broke into tears, "Mom, I'm sorry that the pancakes taste so yucky and the OJ is watery. We mixed everything together according to the recipe and instructions. I don't know what went wrong."

Mom asked a few simple questions: "Did you stir in the baking soda and salt before you added the milk? When did you stir up the juice?" From these questions they discovered why the breakfast did not taste as it should: good results come from using the proper ingredients in the proper way.

The same is true with reading the Bible. There are many ways to do it, some better than others. Even when you have the "basic ingredients" you need, it helps to have a time-tested "recipe" to help you produce the best results. Here is a five-step method that you can use to improve your results as you read the Bible.

**Step 1: What Does the Passage Say?** What did the writer intend to say in a particular passage? What kind of writing is it: poetry, prophecy, a parable, perhaps? How does the literary genre of this passage affect its meaning?

Quite often the Bible you are using includes an introduction to each book and footnotes for some of the verses. These can begin to answer some of the questions just raised. Your parish center or local library may have introductions to the Bible or biblical commentaries that also indicate what the writer was trying to say. A biblical concordance and dictionary are also invaluable aids.

**Step 2: What Does the Passage Mean?** What is the real message being offered here? What meaning did the writer intend? This questioning goes beyond Step 1, moving from what was said to what was meant. From a simple reading, you may know what the author said, but not necessarily know what the passage means. The same resources listed above will help with this step as well.

**Step 3: What Does the Passage Mean in My Life?** What is the significance of this passage for your own faith-life? With this step, a person begins making connections between God's Word and his or her own life. You know what the author meant in the context of his time, but do you know what this passage means for you today?

**Step 4: Be Judged by the Text.** Ask, "What can I do to truly let this passage affect my life and cause a conversion in my own relationship with God and others?" This step begins to deal with the mystery, spontaneity, and complexity of relationships. The reader needs to be open to the action of the Holy Spirit. This openness is not always easy as it calls for a selflessness that is painful. This step leads to decision.

**Step 5: Apply What You've Learned.** How does this biblical passage relate to the content you are now covering with your students? How can you apply its meaning to their lives? What are some ways you can help the students to consider how they could live out this meaning in their lives? In this step, the catechist strives to remain faithful to the message of the passage, while sharing the meaning he or she has uncovered as well as encouraging the students to explore the meanings they may perceive.

## Applying the Technique

Let's use the technique just described. Read the following biblical passage and see how the technique helps you to understand its meaning. As you start please realize that there are many layers of meaning to explore, not just one.

> *You are the salt of the earth. But if salt loses its taste, with what can it be seasoned? It is no longer good for anything but to be thrown out and trampled underfoot. You are the light of the world. A city set on a mountain cannot be hidden. Nor do they light a lamp and then put it under a bushel basket; it is set on a lampstand, where it gives light to all in the house. Just so, your light must shine before others, that they may see your good deeds and glorify your heavenly Father.* (Matthew 5:13–16)

**Step 1: What Does the Passage Say?** As a wisdom saying, this selection is using common imagery to express a spiritual insight. In the ancient world, salt was highly prized both as a spice, which added flavor to meals, and as a preservative, which kept meat from going bad. By calling his disciples "salt," Jesus means that they, too, are highly prized; they are people who add meaning to life and who preserve his word. The saying about the lamp presumes the one-room house of ancient Palestine, in which a single lamp was used in common by all. Jesus calls upon his followers to share their gifts with others. (A good commentary will offer this type of insight on a Bible passage.)

**Step 2: What Does the Passage Mean?** The implication here is that just as salt without flavor is thrown out and a covered light is useless, the Christian life that does not show forth the goodness of God is a contradiction. Such a life does not fulfill the purpose for which it was intended.

**Step 3: What Does the Passage Mean in My Life?** Sandra, a catechist and mother, reflecting on this passage said,

> *I must allow my light to shine before the people I am with every day if I am to fulfill the purpose of my Christian calling. I must season my surroundings with the salt of Christian conduct. If my spouse, my children, my neighbors, or my coworkers see no "goodness" in my actions or are not reminded about the meaning of their lives and the place of God in their lives, then somehow, as a Christian, I have become as worthless as a lamp under a bushel basket.*

**Step 4: Be Judged by the Text.** Sandra continued her reflection,

> *What can I do to truly let this biblical teaching affect my life and deepen my relationship with God and others? If I am really convinced of the value of God's revelation, then I will demonstrate it by living according to Christian values even in difficult situations. I will be appropriately straightforward without being pushy or preachy. For example, I will not hesitate to set a good example for and to offer sound guidance to my children or students. As a follower of Jesus, what value would I have if the light of his revelation were hidden in my life? Would I continue to experience a sense of meaning and purpose if the flavor of God's Word grew flat within my spirit?*

**Step 5: Apply What You've Learned.** Finally, Sandra reached the stage of action:

> *How can I apply what I have gained to my teaching situation? How can all this apply to my students' lives? Perhaps I can point out to my students their real value and importance, that they can have a refreshing influence on the world, particularly their peers, when they live Christian values in a simple, direct way. I could affirm the quality of my students' witness and remind them about how they experience the positive influence of their friends. I can challenge them to live the Christian message. I could point to the example of some saints or current heroic Christians to reinforce this message.*

## Pause a Moment . . .

- What do you suppose it means to let a Biblical passage "judge" you? How might this work in practice?

- What are other applications for this passage? What other ideas or responses does it evoke from you?

- What other ways can you use to affirm to your students the value of their role as witnesses to the Gospel?

---

### Reflection

Apply Steps 1–4 of the technique given in this essay to the following Scripture passages. Answer each of the steps as completely as you can and include your reflections.

Matthew 6:19–21

**1.** _____

_____

**2.** _____

_____

**3.** _____

_____

**4.** _____

_____

Jeremiah 1:4–10

**1.** _____

_____

**2.** _____

_____

**3.** _____

_____

**4.** _____

_____

1 Corinthians 12:12–31

**1.** _____

_____

**2.** _____

_____

**3.** _____

_____

**4.** _____

_____

# A Bible-Reading Plan

To develop a realistic and permanent Bible-reading plan, it is necessary to be specific in regard to three factors: time, location, and amount of reading.

## Time

How much time do you honestly have to read the Bible? Some people read the Bible one hour a day, every day. Others read the Bible for short periods, perhaps ten to fifteen minutes each time, and not necessarily every day. A great deal of value can be obtained from even short periods of concentrated Bible reading.

In developing your own Bible-reading plan, select the length of time that you can realistically spend and stick with it. Most people find it easier to begin with as few as ten minutes and work up to a longer sitting. Be realistic and build upon small successes!

You will also need to specify when you will spend this time. Some people read the Bible very early in the morning before beginning their day's activities. Others read at the end of the day to focus on the deeper significance of the day's events. Some people open and close their day with Bible reading as a form of prayer.

Decide for yourself when you will read the Bible during the day and whether you will read every day or less frequently. Once you decide, stick with your choice until you discover that a change better suits your needs. If for some reason you can't keep your chosen time, select an alternate time and be determined to read the Bible then.

## Location

Where will you do your reading? Location is an important factor that can contribute to the quality of your reading time. Is the place you have selected quiet? Are there visual distractions? Does the place remind you of all the activities on your schedule or the matters and people for which you are responsible? Is the place really conducive to concentration?

Wherever you decide to read, remove as many distractions as possible before you begin. Put on the answering machine, turn off the TV, close the door behind you, and become quiet. Elijah learned, as we must too, that God can often be heard best in the "still, small voice" audible when we are quiet.

## Amount of Reading

How much reading do you want to do? This decision will be influenced by your reason for reading: are you reading to gain information or spiritual insight, or are you reading for pleasure?

- If you intend to read for broad information, you may decide to read as much as several chapters or an entire book at any one time.

- If you are reading for spiritual enlightenment, you may want to read slowly and meditatively, pausing whenever you feel inclined to reflect on the significance of what you've read. You may want to repeat certain phrases or words over and over, allowing them to move you as they will. In this case, you may cover only a few verses at a time, which is fine.

- Many people find it helpful to keep a journal. There they can record their reading experience, what they have read, and what they have gained from the experience.

## Factors for Success

**Realism** must guide your decisions in this plan. You have a much better chance at succeeding if you plan to read too little than to read too much. Becoming discouraged by not meeting your goal could cause you to drop the effort entirely before you develop a reading habit.

**Consistency** is another important factor in carrying out a practical Bible-reading plan. Whatever you decide in regard to time, place, and amount of reading, follow your plan consistently for at least three to four weeks. Adjust your plan as needed, just don't postpone or skip parts of it.

## Final Considerations

Use the following suggestions to gain a better perspective of and satisfaction from your Bible-reading plan.

1. Read with an open mind. Try to discover what is there.

2. Read with a sense of context. Consider how each passage fits in with the preceding and subsequent passages.

3. Read with a purpose. Keep in mind what you want to achieve.

4. Read with care. Try to learn the writer's meaning for each passage you read.

5. Read with sensitivity. Fill your reading time with prayerful openness to God. God's Word lives and speaks to you today.

6. Read for application and connection with your life. What does this passage mean for you in this day and age? How can you apply the insights you are gaining here to your own faith-life? Does this passage help you in your marriage and family? How does this passage apply to your parish? Are strength and guidance there for times of crisis in your life? What connection does this passage have with current social justice needs?

A Bible-reading plan is often most successful as part of a group discussion or study experience. This type of group reading can bring about a special feeling of community in Christ Jesus. The interchange among participants enriches one's own understanding of what has been read.

Choosing what you will read may be the most important step in your reading plan. While some people start at Genesis with the intent of reading the Bible all of the way through, many people are discouraged by the sheer weight of this attempt.

Many people find success reading the Scriptures that will be read the following Sunday. They report how this has enhanced their worship. Other people focus on a particular epistle or gospel account. They reread that book until they gain a mastery of it. Whatever you choose is up to you.

## Pause a Moment . . .

- What has been your personal experience with reading the Bible? Was it successful for you? Why or why not?

- What would you expect to gain from regular Bible reading? What would be your reason(s) for doing it consistently?

## Reflection

Work out your own realistic Bible-reading plan. Be sure to include details for each of the sections that follow.

1. My purpose in reading the Bible at this point of my life is:_____

_____

_____

_____

_____

_____

_____

_____

2. Time of day:_____

_____

_____

3. Frequency:_____

_____

_____

4. Length of time: _____

_____

_____

5. Place: _____

_____

_____

6. Amount of material to cover each time: _____

_____

_____

7. I will begin with: _____

_____

_____

# $\mathcal{P}$art IV $\mathcal{R}$esponse

## Some Ideas for Catechists

In this chapter, we have focused on how knowing the kind of literature you are reading should influence the expectations you have of the text. The importance of a personal Bible-reading plan has been stressed. The benefits of such a plan accumulate quietly and gradually over a period of time. You can gather various insights, explanations, and methods to use with your students. In this section, some ideas for translating these points into classroom practice wil be developed.

### Younger Students

Children at the elementary level will generally not be able to distinguish literary genres, and there is no reason you should expect them to. Children are drawn to stories. Narrative material from the Bible should be presented to them in story form. Generally, they will not be concerned with "interpretation" and neither should you. Instead, they will absorb the values and insights of the stories naturally; although, of course, you as the catechist will help the students to clarify and express what those values are.

**Dramatic Reading.** When using Bible stories, assign characters and parts of the narration to different students. They enjoy making the stories come to life.

**Role-Playing.** A variation of this method is role-playing. Students can take various parts, both spoken and silent, and act out a Bible passage. The catechist usually reads or tells the Bible story for the students to role-play. This becomes a concrete point of reference when the catechist initiates a discussion about the meaning of the story.

After hearing or seeing a Bible story, ask the students to draw a picture or make some creative project that expresses one aspect of the story's significance. For example, you might ask them to go through magazines to find pictures that illustrate what certain characters were thinking or feeling at important moments in the narrative.

### Middle-Grade Levels

At this stage of development, students will begin to become alert to the historical and scientific plausibility of many Bible stories. It may be useful to introduce some very basic distinctions between myth, legend, and history. Be clear, though, to distinguish this from the question of a particular passage's "truth:" something can be true without being historically factual.

Further, students will be looking for ways to apply Bible material to their own life situations. They also enjoy working as members of a group. Develop your assignments to reflect this need. For example, you might encourage students to "update" their performances of Bible scenes, bringing the characters and situations into the modern world but retaining the point of the original story. This encourages students to begin moving from the story itself to how it might apply to their own lives.

▲ *Children love to role-play. Tell them a story and let them act it out. Have several sets of "play" clothes available for the children to use. Don't tell them what to do; let them figure out their parts with only the minimal amount of help from you.*

You may also want to introduce the idea of the spiritual journal at this time. Students at this age level are just beginning to distinguish their own ideas and feelings from those of their parents and peers, and a journal gives them an excellent outlet for this. Again, the goal here should be to focus students on seeing the relevance of Bible passages for their own faith situation.

## Older Students

High school students are developing the intellectual capability needed to understand the more complex distinctions between literary genres previously discussed. They are also learning to make the more sophisticated connections needed for true biblical scholarship. This is also a time in many students' lives when they need to see the relevance of the scriptures for themselves. They may express a mistrust of religion, but they have a spiritual hunger that the Bible can help satisfy. Before you introduce these concepts, prepare the students.

When you are using particular Bible passages with older students, ask them to answer the following questions:

1. How is God's message expressed in this passage?

2. What does this passage mean in my life?

3. What are some ways I could live out the deeper significance of this passage in my daily life?

Adolescents are particularly introspective and concerned with their own thoughts and feelings. Therefore, life application should become a most important emphasis in Bible study. As a creative writing assignment, you may want to ask them to rewrite a particular story, interjecting themselves into the narrative. How would they react? With whom would they identify? These questions will encourage students to see connections between the reading and the choices they make.

No matter what methods you use, you will achieve better results if you personally work through the particular Bible passage using the five-step technique outlined in this topic first. The technique will bring the implications of the Bible passage to the forefront of your consciousness and highlight many of the possible connections that you could use with your students.

## Pause a Moment . . .

• What has been your experience of presenting Bible stories to students? What issues or problems did you encounter?

• How could you persuade a student that reading the Bible could be of benefit to him or her? How would your approach differ with the age level involved?

### IMPLICATIONS

Complete the following exercises; refer to any of the previous sections as needed.

1. Review the exercise you completed at the end of "Part III Discovery." Read what you wrote for Steps 1–4. Now, apply what you've learned. How can these passages apply to your students' lives?

---

### The New Commandment

*Love never fails. If there are prophecies, they will be brought to nothing; if tongues, they will cease; if knowledge, it will be brought to nothing. For we know partially and we prophesy partially, but when the perfect comes, the partial will pass away. When I was a child, I used to talk as a child, think as a child, reason as a child; when I became a man, I put aside childish things. At present we see indistinctly, as in a mirror, but then face to face. At present I know partially; then I shall know fully as I am fully known.*

(1 Corinthians 13:8–12)

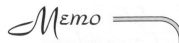

**Memo**

In light of what I have learned about reading the Bible, I want to keep the following considerations in mind for the next time I meet my students:

**2.** Consider one of the lessons you have taught. How would you teach your students to read the Bible within the context of that particular lesson?

## Prayer Response

Use the following activity to help you to better pray and listen to the Word of God.

Read and reflect on the following scripture passage. Compare the message of the reading with some aspect of your life. How does the message affect you today? How can you apply the message? Ask for help to truly hear what God is saying to you.

*Therefore, putting away falsehood, speak the truth, each one to his neighbor, for we are members of one another. Be angry, but do not sin; do not let the sun set on your anger, and do not leave room for the devil. . . . No foul language should come out of your mouths, but only such as is good for needed edification, that it may impart grace to those who hear. . . . All bitterness, fury, anger, shouting, and reviling must be removed from you, along with malice. [And] be kind to one another, compassionate, forgiving one another as God has forgiven you in Christ.* (Ephesians 4:25–27, 29, 31–32)

## BIBLIOGRAPHY

Auer, Jim, and Delaney, Robert. *The Bible: A Simple Introduction.* Los Angeles: Franciscan Communications, 1991.

"Basic Tools for Bible Study," *The DeSales Program.* Los Angeles: Franciscan Communications, video.

Brueggemann, Walter. "Why Read the Bible," *PACE 6.* Collegeville, MN: St. Mary's Press, 1975.

*How to Study the Bible.* South Deerfield, MA: Channing L. Bete Co., 1978.

Montague, George T. *How to Interpret the Bible.* Collegeville, MN: The Liturgical Press, 1983.

National Conference of Catholic Bishops. Chapter III, "Revelation, Faith, and Catechesis" in *Sharing the Light of Faith, National Catechetical Directory for Catholics of the United States.* Washington, DC: USCC Publications, 1979.

Scott, Macrina, O.S.F. "A Popular Guide to Reading the Bible," *Catholic Update,* Cincinnati, OH: St. Anthony Messenger Press, December, 1984.

_____. *Picking the "Right" Bible Study Program.* Chicago: ACTA Publications, 1994.

Smith, Virginia. "Whole Bible at a Glance: It's 'Golden Thread' of Meaning," *Catholic Update,* Cincinnati, OH: St. Anthony Messenger Press, April, 1989.

*Nihil Obstat*
The Reverend Gregory A. Banazak, S.T.D.

*Imprimatur*
The Most Reverend Kenneth J. Povish, D.D.
Bishop of Lansing
May 13, 1994

The *Nihil Obstat* and *Imprimatur* are official declarations that a book or pamphlet is free of doctrinal or moral error. No implication is contained therein that those who have granted the *Nihil Obstat* and *Imprimatur* agree with the contents, opinions, or statements expressed.

Send all inquiries to:

BENZIGER PUBLISHING COMPANY
15319 Chatsworth Street
P.O. Box 9609
Mission Hills, California 91346-9609

Second Edition

**ISBN 0-02-651212-2**

Printed in the United States of America.

1 2 3 4 5 6 7 8 9   BAW   98 97 96 95 94

# Using the Bible

*Everything written before our time was written for our instruction, that we might derive hope from the lessons of patience and the words of encouragement in the Scriptures.*

Romans 15:4

*Written by*
**Peter Ries**

*Consultant*
**David Riley**

## In this chapter you will:

- Explore the interplay between audience and message in the Bible.
- Use principles for applying the Bible to life situations.
- Practice ways of using the Bible with different age groups in catechetical situations.

Second Edition

▲ *Mr. O'Neill was very committed to the Church, and had strong opinions about how things should be done. He had not, however, had much experience with using the Bible.*

## Definitely from the Old School

As on every other class day, Arthur stayed apart from the rest of the boys and girls until Mrs. Cavaletti called the students to line up. Only then did Arthur's grandfather, Patrick O'Neill, release the boy from his grasp to go with Mrs. Cavaletti and the rest of the second grade religion class at Our Mother of Sorrows.

Mrs. Cavaletti had been warned about Patrick O'Neill when she agreed to teach the First Communion class. "He's definitely from the old school," Jim Andrews, the DRE, told her. "Patrick O'Neill thinks only priests should distribute communion. He wrote a letter to the bishop when the parish stopped using the communion rails. He and his wife take Arthur to the hospital for Sunday Mass. The chaplain there, Monsignor O'Flaherty, says the Mass in Latin. Patrick and he see "eye to eye."

Arthur was the only son of Patrick's daughter, Connie. Connie was never married to Arthur's father. When Arthur was four, Connie was killed by a drunk driver. The O'Neills adopted Arthur shortly thereafter. Although Connie had graduated from Our Mother of Sorrows and Arthur was baptized there, Patrick found the parish too "progressive" for his taste. The only reason he allowed Arthur to attend religious education there at all was so the boy could make his First Communion. Monsignor O'Flaherty required Arthur to have formal religious training before receiving the sacrament.

Arthur joined the other second graders as they went to church to practice for Sunday's children's liturgy. Mrs. Cavaletti gathered the boys and girls in the front pews. "We have a special opportunity to participate this Sunday at Mass. Some of you will bring up the gifts of bread and wine. Others will help greet the people as they arrive for Mass. And, I need two of you to read the Scripture," Mrs. Cavaletti told them.

She tried very hard, but it was impossible to ignore Arthur's arm waving madly after she asked for volunteers. Arthur was the only one who wanted to read.

"This will never work," Mrs. Cavaletti thought as Arthur trudged from his place to the ambo. "Patrick O'Neill will never let his son come to Mass here, much less do something that he thinks only clergy have a right to do."

Still, Arthur went on with the practice. Mrs. Cavaletti didn't have many other options. "A reading from the first letter to the Cor-in-thi-ans," Arthur began.

It was just then that Mrs. Cavaletti saw Patrick O'Neill take a seat in the back of the church. He was an immovable figure as his grandson read on: "But now Christ has been raised from the dead, the first fruits of those who have fallen asleep. For since death came from a human being, the resurrection of the dead came also through a human being."

Mr. O'Neill seemed to leap from the pew at these words and to walk to the sanctuary. Mrs. Cavaletti moved towards him to avoid what could become an embarrassing scene for everyone. "For just as in Adam all die, so too in Christ shall all be brought to life." The words rang on.

"Mr. O'Neill? Hi, I'm Arthur's teacher. Isn't he doing a marvelous job?" Mrs. Cavaletti began.

Patrick O'Neill looked past her to his grandson, seeming not even to see her. "The last enemy to be destroyed is death." The old man's eyes were filled with tears.

"Mrs. Cavaletti, do I say 'This is the Word of the Lord' or 'The Word of the Lord'? Somebody crossed out the 'this' in your book," Arthur asked.

"I will explain in a second, Arthur. I'm speaking with your grandfather just now," she said. "Mr. O'Neill, can he read those words from Scripture on Sunday at our family Mass?"

Patrick spoke softly. "Madam, I don't know much about the Bible and such, but what that boy just read meant quite a bit to me. I remember when his mother made her First Communion right here. What a blessed day. She was taken away from us all too soon. The words that Arthur just read were spoken at his mother's funeral. I never realized just what they meant, until now. I wonder if I might have a copy of it that I could take home to show his grandmother."

Patrick O'Neill let Arthur play on the school yard with the other kids for the first time at the end of class. While he waited, he sat on the bench and thumbed through the Bible Mrs. Cavaletti had given him.

"The word of the Lord." Patrick repeated the phrase he heard his grandson speak in church. Patrick would bring Arthur to church here on Sunday to hear him read God's word once again.

Memo

As a catechist, how can you deal sensitively with parents who are uncomfortable with either your teaching methods or the content of what you present?

## YOUR STORY

1. Why do you think Patrick O'Neill was so protective of Arthur?

_____

_____

2. Why did the passage from 1 Corinthians mean so much to Patrick? Would it have meant as much if he had encountered it under different circumstances?

_____

_____

3. Can you recall a time when a passage from Scripture suddenly took on new meaning for you?

_____

_____

4. What conclusions do you draw from this story about the relationship between life experience and the appreciation of Scripture?

_____

_____

# Part II  Message

## It Begins with Experience

As catechists, our goal for students is not merely that they gain a knowledge of Scripture, not simply that they know important names, dates, and terms. More importantly, we hope to awaken in students a living appreciation of the Bible as a source of guidance, comfort, and challenge. While people can acquire information (even religious information) at almost anytime, under what circumstances do they develop an appreciation for something? Generally, this appreciation grows when the subject speaks to their life situation. Scripture comes alive for students when they see that it can help them make sense of their own experience.

This was the discovery Patrick O'Neill made in the opening story in this chapter—the reading from Scripture offered words of comfort which helped him come to terms with the loss of his daughter. This is where effective use of the Bible begins, with a consideration of the experiences and needs people bring to the learning situation.

The process of shaping the message of Scripture so that it speaks to the experience of a particular audience is modeled in Scripture itself. The books of the Bible were all written with specific audiences in mind, and the content of each book was carefully crafted to be meaningful for the people to whom it was directed. The authors took their inherited religious traditions, and put them together in new combinations to help their faith communities interpret its life in the light of revelation. In this way, the biblical authors modeled the approach to religious education that good catechists employ. In this section, we'll see how the authors of the Bible wrote with the needs of their audience in mind.

## The Deuteronomic Historian

One of the most traumatic events experienced by the ancient Israelites was their exile to Babylon following the capture of Judah in 587 B.C. by the Babylonian emperor Nebuchadnezzar. Israelites lost their homes, their property, and their political independence. Many were forced to relocate to Babylon, where they lived under the domination of a foreign power.

For the Israelites, this was a crushing blow. They believed that Yahweh had made a covenant with David, that one of David's descendants would sit on the throne of David "forever." Further, the Israelites believed that God had promised the land of Israel to Abraham and his children. Where were those promises now? The symbol of that promise and the abiding presence of Yahweh—Jerusalem and the Temple—lay in ruins. Was Marduk, the Babylonian god, simply more powerful than Yahweh? Or had Yahweh abandoned them?

With this experience in mind, a group of people Bible scholars call the "Deuteronomic historians" crafted a message which spoke to the needs of these people. The books of Joshua, Judges, 1 and 2 Samuel, and 1 and 2 Kings—the historical books of the Old Testament—were written by this group. They wrote about much earlier times in light of their present

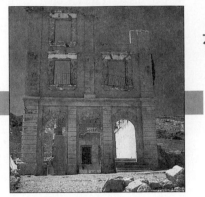

▲ *How would you feel if your home was destroyed and you were forced to flee for your life? Following the destruction of Jerusalem, the Deuteronomic historians explained to the people of Judah God's promise of hope.*

understanding and experience. They are called the "Deuteronomic" historians because their analysis of history is based on the Book of Deuteronomy in the Pentateuch.

Looking back over the history of Israel, the Deuteronomic historians found an explanation for the tragedy of the Exile. God's Covenant promises, they said, had always been conditional, dependent on the obedience of the people. Although they found occasional moments of fidelity in Israel, such as in the reign of King Josiah, the Deuteronomic historians thought that the people had often failed to honor their promises to God. Israel's disobedience showed in two primary ways:

- **Social Injustice.** The people failed to care adequately for the poor, widows, aliens, and orphans.

- **False Worship.** Failing to honor their vow to worship Yahweh alone, the people were often attracted to the religious practices of their neighbors, most notably the Canaanites.

Although God's prophets had warned about the consequences of disobedience throughout their history, Israel failed to listen. Based on these offenses, the Deuteronomic historians explained, Yahweh had no choice but to allow the Babylonians to destroy Judah.

This explanation addressed the needs of the people in two ways. First, it made sense of their tragedy; the Exile was not merely senseless, random suffering. Through the eyes of the Deuteronomic historians, their pain could now be seen as purposeful and consistent with their beliefs about God. Second, this explanation offered people hope. If their suffering had been the result of disobedience, then they could hope for redemption through renewed obedience. This idea became the basis for a vigorous renewal of Jewish religious life in the Exile.

In the Deuteronomic history, we see a classic example of how religious tradition can be molded to take on new meaning in the light of changing experience. The people of Israel had experienced a tragedy which caused them to doubt some very fundamental beliefs about God and themselves. Knowing this, the Deuteronomic historians delivered a message which both reassured and challenged their audience. This is the heart of the catechetical process at work.

## The Gospels

Many people assume that the four gospel accounts are eyewitness reports of the words and deeds of Jesus. In fact, it is doubtful that any of the gospel accounts were written by an eyewitness. The earliest of the gospel accounts was not put on paper until some 40 years after Jesus' death and resurrection. The gospel accounts do record some of what Jesus said and did, but they also reflect this teaching through the filter of at least 40 years of teaching by the early church. Because of this fact, the gospel accounts bear the mark of having been shaped with particular faith communities in mind.

To understand this idea, it's necessary first to focus on the term "gospel." In the very beginning of the Church, gospel (a word meaning "good news") referred not to a written work, but to the message about Jesus' death and resurrection as proclaimed by Christian missionaries. This is the sense in which St. Paul uses the term in his epistles.

While there are four gospel accounts, there is only one Gospel of Jesus. For many years, his words and deeds, the "Good News" of his teaching, were

*Notes*

# The New Commandment

*Now there was a man in Jerusalem whose name was Simeon. This man was righteous and devout, awaiting the consolation of Israel, and the holy Spirit was upon him. It has been revealed to him by the holy Spirit that he should not see death before he had seen the Messiah of the Lord. He came in the Spirit into the temple; and when the parents brought in the child Jesus to perform the custom of the law in regard to him, he took him into his arms and blessed God, saying: "Now, Master, you may let your servant go in peace, according to your word, for my eyes have seen your salvation, which you prepared in sight of all the peoples, a light for revelation to the Gentiles, and glory for your people Israel."*

(Luke 2:25–32)

kept alive in the Church through an oral tradition. They were used in preaching, in the liturgy, and in the prayer of early Christians.

After a period of time, perhaps as the original generation of apostles began to disappear, individual communities began to feel the need for more permanent collections of Jesus' sayings and actions. In response, the written Gospel emerged. Therefore, the gospel accounts originated out of a desire to adapt the traditions about Jesus to the needs of specific faith communities.

When the authors of the gospel accounts sat down to put their works together, they had the Hebrew Scriptures and about 40 years of Christian tradition to draw upon. There were oral and written collections of Jesus' sayings, stories about his miracles, and remembrances of his other deeds. In addition, there were ideas and concepts which originated in the teaching of the early Church as it attempted to answer questions Jesus himself had not resolved in the course of his life. From such an abundance of tradition, the Gospel writers were forced to make selections. Their choices were not random; they selected material they believed would speak to the experiences and needs of their audiences.

We can see this principle of selection (or "redaction" as it is called by scholars) at work in the gospel account of Matthew. Matthew wrote for a community of Jewish-Christians, who were struggling to maintain their Jewish heritage in light of their faith that Jesus was the Messiah (the anointed one of God). In response to this belief, Matthew developed a literary device called the "formula citation," quoting from an Old Testament prophecy in support of the claim that Jesus fulfilled the messianic hopes of ancient Judaism. His famous quotation of Isaiah 7:14, "The virgin shall be with child and give birth to a son, and they shall call him Emmanuel," is an example of this formula.

Matthew also emphasizes Jesus' reverences for the Law of Israel: "Do not think that I have come to abolish the law or the prophets. I have come not to abolish but to fulfill" *(Matthew 5:17)*. In fact, throughout his account, Matthew presents Jesus as a teacher of the Law, similar to Moses but greater in stature. Both the formula citation and this view of Jesus as lawgiver are unique to Matthew's gospel account, and represent his effort to make Jesus' message relevant to the situation faced by his Jewish-Christian audience.

The same process is evident in the gospel account of Luke. Unlike Matthew, Luke is writing for an audience of Gentile Christians. Luke wishes to assure his readers that despite Christianity's Jewish origins, all people are included in the saving message of the Gospel. Luke's emphasis that the saving actions of Jesus extend to Gentiles as well as Jews echoes from the very beginning of his account. In Luke 2:32, the elderly pious man named Simeon calls the child Jesus a "revealing light for the Gentiles."

Luke alone contains the parable of the Good Samaritan, a saying of Jesus. In this saying, Jesus tells of an injured man whose needs were ignored by Jews, but who was then rescued by a Samaritan, a bitter enemy of the Jews. The point, as Jesus says, is that anyone who does God's will is a member of the community.

In both Matthew and Luke, then, we see the Jesus traditions taking shape in light of the audiences being addressed. Once more, the catechetical process is on display: good teaching begins by knowing the audience.

## Paul

Unlike the other biblical authors we've looked at, Paul is explicit about his method of adapting his message to the experiences of his audience. Speaking about his role as an apostle in 1 Corinthians, Paul says:

> *To the Jews I became like a Jew to win over Jews; to those under the law I became like one under the law—though I myself am not under the law—to win over those under the law. To those outside the law I became like one outside the law—though I am not outside God's law but within the law of Christ—to win over those outside the law. To the weak I became weak, to win over the weak. I have become all things to all, to save at least some.* (1 Corinthians 9:20–22)

When speaking to a Jewish audience, Paul's technique was to emphasize his Jewish roots: he was a member of the tribe of Benjamin, a well-educated Jew zealous for the traditions of his ancestors. He would quote from the Old Testament and debate points of the law in order to win Jewish converts.

When facing a Gentile audience, Paul was equally comfortable. He spoke fluent Greek, the language of the Eastern Roman empire. He was familiar with the great Gentile poets, and even quoted them from time to time. He was also familiar with the religious traditions of the Greeks and Romans, and could adjust his proclamation of the Gospel in light of their background and expectations.

This flexibility in Paul is clear from his statements in 1 Corinthians 10:23–30 concerning the question of whether Christians could eat meat that had been sacrificed to pagan gods in Greek temples. Jewish law forbade eating such meat. Paul begins by making clear that Christians can eat meat from the temples, since Jesus has taken the place of the Jewish law. Paul goes on to say, however, that it may not always be wise to exercise this freedom. If your neighbor will see such behavior as an endorsement of idol worship, Paul says, then do not eat the sacrificial meat. Such restraint comes not from any law, but from a careful consideration of how your audience will interpret your behavior.

In Paul, therefore, as with the other biblical authors, we see the insistence that catechists (in other words, people who teach the Gospel) form their messages in light of the experience of their community.

## Pause a Moment . . .

* How can the explanation of the Deuteronomic historian offer a sense of purpose and hope to someone who is suffering?

* Does it surprise you that the gospel accounts are not eyewitness reports of Jesus' life? Does this affect how you understand them?

* Do you think it is possible for a catechist to be "all things to all" as St. Paul says? Does this saying express an ideal towards which catechists should strive?

Notes

## Interplay between Community and Message

*Notes*

_____

_____

_____

_____

_____

_____

_____

_____

_____

_____

_____

_____

In the last section, the Bible itself emerged as a model for good religious education. The process of revealing God's word always begins with an appreciation for the unique needs and circumstances of the audience one is addressing.

The interplay between community and message runs throughout Scripture. In fact, it is part of the nature of inspiration: God speaks through human beings to address specific people in specific historical, cultural, and social circumstances. An appreciation for this aspect of the Bible is an invaluable asset to the catechist, who must also develop a teaching style that reflects the needs and learning capacities of the audience. The general term for this sort of approach is "relevance": the task of the catechist, like that of the authors of the Bible, is to make the Word of God relevant for an audience by knowing what's on their minds and what their religious questions are.

To refine your understanding of how the biblical message was always relevant for the community it addressed, try the following exercise based on the Book of Jonah. Jonah is an example of a literary category sometimes called "religious fiction." It's a fable, a "tall tale," told to communicate an important idea to its audience.

- Read the Book of Jonah (it is found among the prophets, towards the end of the Old Testament canon). You can read it quickly; it's only four chapters!

- Answer the following comprehension questions:

**1.** What does God call Jonah to do?

_____

_____

**2.** How does Jonah respond? Why do you suppose he acts in this way?

_____

_____

**3.** How do the people of Nineveh respond when Jonah finally speaks God's word to them?

_____

_____

**4.** How does their response make Jonah feel?

_____

_____

**5.** What does God say to Jonah?

_____

_____

• List what you consider to be the central ideas and themes of Jonah.

_____

_____

_____

• What sort of attitudes or behaviors in the community do you suppose the author of Jonah was addressing in this story?

_____

_____

_____

▲ _Try reading the Book of Jonah aloud, as if you were reading a story over the radio. Make it come alive; the many odd parts of the Jonah story can help us laugh and examine our own motives at the same time._

If you said that the author of Jonah wanted to address attitudes of hostility or superiority towards foreigners (non-Israelites), you're absolutely correct. Jonah was written after the return from Exile, probably in the fifth century B.C. Ezra and Nehemiah were the great leaders of the Jewish community after the return from Exile. Under their influence, many Jews became suspicious of foreign cultures. Ezra and Nehemiah had stressed the uniqueness of Israel's covenant with God because the immediate post-return community was small, and in danger of being overwhelmed and assimilated by its larger and more powerful neighbors. Over time, however, this emphasis became distorted into a narrow and vindictive nationalism, which held that God could care only about the fate of the Jewish nation.

The author of Jonah chides people with such attitudes, pointing out that God's mercy can extend to foreigners, even to traditional enemies of the Jews such as the Assyrians. God's love is not restricted by national boundaries, and Jonah shows the absurdity of complaining about those to whom God shows favor. God loves all people, so that disdain for others is entirely out of place.

Jonah, therefore, is more than an amusing (and often misunderstood) story. It is also not an allegory setting out a complicated theological doctrine. Instead, it holds a mirror up to its audience and invites them to examine their values and attitudes. Jonah accomplishes this by knowing its audience, and knowing how to evoke the desired response. Such awareness is a central goal of all catechesis.

## Pause a Moment . . .

• Jonah hesitated to accept God's call. Are there moments when you have doubts about accepting God's call to be a catechist? How do you deal with these doubts?

• Under what circumstances do you think studying Jonah might be helpful for your students?

# Moving into the Modern World

You have seen how the authors of the Bible spoke to the circumstances of their original audiences. The relevance of Scripture, however, was not exhausted in the first communities that heard its message. Over the centuries that people of faith have cherished the Bible, God's word has always had meaning for them. As times change and culture evolves, Scripture speaks to us in fresh ways, challenging us and offering us new perspectives on our lives.

## The Quest for Justice

Good illustrations of the continuing relevance of Scripture in the modern world are the various movements within Christianity which stress the duty of Christians to work for economic, political, racial, and social justice. These movements take various forms. In the third world, they're often called "liberation theology." In North America, such movements are sometimes known as the "social gospel." Whatever one calls them, these movements draw inspiration from biblical passages which speak of God's special love for the poor, as well as God's insistence that proper worship includes a commitment to justice.

It is no accident that many of the leaders in the American Civil Rights movements have come from religious backgrounds, often having served as ministers and preachers. Dr. Vernon Johns, Dr. Martin Luther King, Jr., and the Rev. Jesse Jackson are all examples of men whose calls for justice arise from scriptural convictions. In Dr. King's famous "I Have a Dream" speech, his eloquent pleas for racial tolerance often alluded to biblical passages. For example, Dr. King quoted the prophet Amos:

> *Let justice surge like water, and goodness like an unfailing stream.*
> (Amos 5:24)

Such words have not lost their power with time. Passages such as this one from Amos continue to challenge modern society, just as much as they did in ancient Israel. Christians today who have joined the struggle to create a more just, loving world draw strength from such biblical statements.

## A Message of Consolation

The ongoing relevance of Scripture is not simply a matter of challenges and demands, however. God's word as revealed in the Bible also offers modern people messages of peace, hope, and consolation for their suffering.

The theme of consolation is especially clear in Old Testament passages such as Second Isaiah, originally written to provide hope and optimism about the future for the Jews living in Babylon. This text has been applied throughout the years to offer similar words of comfort to suffering groups and individuals.

An example of such a group is slaves in nineteenth-century America. Blacks in the United States often drew strength from their Christian faith, and the most popular means of expression of their faith was the spiritual—a song with a religious theme. Studies of spirituals that developed during this period have shown that Second Isaiah was the most popular place in Scripture from which the spirituals drew themes and imagery. Passages such as the following help explain why.

*Do you not know, or have you not heard? The Lord is the eternal God, creator of the ends of the earth. He does not grow weary, and his knowledge is beyond scrutiny. He gives strength to the fainting; for the weak he makes vigor abound. Though young men faint and grow weary, and youths stagger and fall, they that hope in the Lord will renew their strength, they will soar as with eagles' wings; they will run and not grow weary, walk and not grow faint.* (Isaiah 40:28–31)

The theme that inner strength is offered to those who depend upon God is one that comforted slaves. A similar comfort is offered to all who suffer. For this reason, passages from Second Isaiah are among the readings used in the Church's liturgy for the Anointing of the Sick. The Church recognizes the power of this part of Scripture to speak words of comfort to individuals who need assurance of God's love and concern.

As a catechist, part of your function is to understand the ways in which your students needs to be challenged, consoled, or reassured by God's word and to know which parts of the Bible will accomplish these tasks.

## Pause a Moment . . .

- Describe a situation in your own life which you feel is directly addressed by a particular Bible passage.

- Can you think of a time when you needed God's words of consolation and comfort?

- How does knowing the original context of a Bible passage help make its words more meaningful?

### MAKING THE CONNECTION

Find modern situations which can be illuminated by the themes and concepts presented in Scripture. Read the text listed, identify its main themes, then note a modern community or situation for which these themes would be relevant.

**Exodus 3** Theme:_____

Modern Situation: _____

**Leviticus 18** Theme: _____

Modern Situation: _____

**Ruth** Theme: _____

Modern Situation: _____

**Revelation 17** Theme: _____

Modern Situation: _____

**1 Corinthians 12** Theme: _____

Modern Situation: _____

## The Church Teaches

The treasures of the Bible are to be opened up more lavishly so that a richer fare may be provided for the faithful at the table of God's word. In this way, a more representative part of the sacred Scriptures will be read to the people in the course of a prescribed number of years.

By means of the homily the mysteries of the faith and the guiding principles of the Christian life are expounded from the sacred text during the course of the liturgical year. The homily, therefore, is to be highly esteemed as part of the liturgy itself. *(Constitution on the Sacred Liturgy, # 51–52)*

# $\mathscr{P}$art IV $\mathscr{R}$esponse

## Meeting the Needs of Your Students

In the Discovery section, you saw that while the biblical authors always wrote with the needs of a particular community in mind, the relevance of Scripture is not restricted to these ancient communities. The Bible is as relevant for people today as it was for its original audiences. By determining the needs and experiences of your audience, you can help them to hear God's voice in Scripture, speaking to their own unique situation.

In order to accomplish this goal, the two dimensions of matching Scripture to your audience need to be clearly recognized:

- **Approach:** The manner of presentation must be suited to their aptitudes, experiences, and learning needs. In other words, your teaching methods must be appropriate to your audience.

- **Content:** The parts of the Bible you choose to present must speak to the experiences and interests of your students. Your selection must have them in mind.

## Approach

Part of creating an effective match between Scripture and the experience of your students is knowing how to communicate effectively relative to their age and developmental level.

1. **Kindergarten–Grade 1.** Students at this level have a natural appetite for story. The religious education curriculum often draws from biblical stories that show God's activity and concern for creation. These are kept simple and to the point, leading to student activities.

2. **Grades 1–3.** At this level, students are exploring their feelings for others, especially parents and friends. "God cares for us" is a theme that is frequently presented. God's love and concern are a consoling realization for young children.

3. **Grades 4–6.** As students begin to develop their own ideas and identities, Old Testament stories which deal with the formation of God's people are of great interest. Students at this age are beginning to develop a moral sense; they are particularly motivated by justice. New Testament parables which invite moral reflection and evaluation work well with this age group.

4. **Grades 7–9.** The Old Testament theme, "You shall be my people and I will be your God" parallels the students' need to feel that they belong to a particular group. The New Testament story of the growing Church (Acts of the Apostles) helps the students appreciate the faith community. Their growth in responsibility is also a frequent theme that focuses on the study of the Ten Commandments, the Beatitudes, and the Works of Mercy.

5. **Grades 10–12.** These students can handle the more complex Old Testament themes. They can explore in depth the themes of the

▲ *A person is never too old or too young to benefit from Scripture. The challenge is to offer the Bible appropriately, adjusting one's presentation to the age and ability level of the students.*

prophets (infidelity, justice) and even the Book of Job ("Why do bad things happen to good people?"). Especially effective is considering the value of believing in and living the Gospel values.

6. **Adults.** Adults come to the Bible out of their own needs and motivation. Some want to study it for knowledge, some for prayer, some for guidance, and some for comfort. Shape your approach to their needs. A mixture of serious study, group sharing, and fun activities are part of a well-rounded approach to the Bible.

The following chart provides a handy reference on when to use biblical themes.

| Age-Grade | Old Testament | New Testament |
|---|---|---|
| Pre-K | Stories that show God's concern for creation | Stories that show Jesus' concern for creation |
| 1–3 | Concern for God's people | Appealing qualities of Jesus found in stories |
| 4–6 | Faith—Abraham<br>Covenant—Moses<br>　　　—Commandments | Parables—moral values |
| 7–9 | The formation of God's people, "You shall be my people and I will be your God."<br>Responsibility—Commandments | Jesus as model to be followed<br>Church—Acts of the Apostles<br>Responsibility—Beatitudes<br>　　　—Corporal and Spiritual<br>　　　Works of Mercy |
| 10–12 and Adult | Apostasy—captivity—return<br>Prophets | Gospel study　　Gospel values<br>Implications for daily life |

## APPLICATION

1. Review the student text for the grade level that you teach. List the major Old Testament and New Testament themes that you find.

Old Testament themes _____

New Testament themes _____

2. Locate in your student text two examples of using the Bible. List them below. How are each appropriate for your grade level?

a. _____

b. _____

## Teaching Strategies

Because the Bible contains a variety of literary styles and different sorts of material, it can be presented in many different ways, based on the specific learning needs of your students. The list of activities and teaching strategies below provide some possibilities for you to consider.

**Activity Masters:** prepared carbon or blackline masters with creative activities that can be used to supplement a lesson.

**Audiovisuals:** some multimedia kits include charts and illustrations for overhead projectors, materials for individual thematic learning centers, worksheets, student handbooks, posters, videos, and audio-cassettes.

**Bible Reading:** reading from the Bible in various settings for different reasons is often more effective than merely referring to what the Bible says. Refer to the topic "Reading the Bible" for additional teaching suggestions.

**Bible Search:** have the students look through the Bible to find various passages.

**Bible Prayer Services:** Bible services, either with large groups or with individual classes, increase student participation.

**Computers:** consider using some of the Bible software being produced for teaching purposes.

**Felt-board Presentation:** words and figures of felt can be put on a felt-board and moved around. You or several of your students can tell a Bible story in this way.

**Games:** form your class into groups to compete in review exercises. Bible charades works with some ages. Check your local Christian bookstore for board games such as "Bible Pictionary" and "HolyWord Squares."

**Journals:** students can write their reflections about the Bible in a personal journal. Students should feel that the journal is a "safe" place to express their thoughts and emotions. Be sure to explain that the contents of each journal will be kept confidential.

**Lesson Review:** begin a lesson by reading a passage. Ask your students how the passage highlights the previous lesson. This can be an innovative method for review.

**Murals:** illustrate a Bible story. Draw various episodes of the story or passage on a large poster.

**Music:** use music based on Bible themes to enhance the lesson.

**Paraphrasing:** occasionally, paraphrasing can help the students to better appreciate the message of the passage.

**Prayer:** integrate the Bible into your class prayer.

**Reading Assignments:** ask parents to help their children locate and discuss the passages.

**Role-Playing:** dramatize episodes from the life and teachings of Jesus, as well as stories from the Old Testament. An often successful variation on this technique is to invite students to "update" the story by taking the same characters and plot, but placing them into a familiar modern context.

**Sunday Readings:** discuss the Sunday readings either in preparation for the weekend liturgy or as a review of it.

## Pause a Moment . . .

• Describe the age and developmental level of your students. What sort of delivery methods do you think would be most effective with them?

- Are there any good teaching strategies with which you're familiar that do not appear on this list?

## Content

Knowing how to make Scripture present to your students is only half the battle for the catechist. You must also know which parts of the Bible are most appropriate for your audience. This selection should be based on your sense of the experience your students bring to the learning situation, and the ways in which they need to be challenged and consoled.

### The Need to Challenge

One of the elements of Scripture that makes it essential for spiritual development is that it offers constant challenges for growth. The values and attitudes contained in the Bible offer benchmarks for people to evaluate themselves and their own life choices. Your students, like all people, need to be confronted with the challenges Scripture provides.

The key is knowing which specific challenges are most important for your students to experience. For example, if your students come from a predominantly affluent background, the Bible's words on social justice and care for the oppressed might be particularly appropriate. On the other hand, if your students are having difficulty with interpersonal relationships, sections of the Bible that have to do with respect for others should be addressed. As always, the key is beginning with the unique needs of the people with whom you're working.

Take a moment now to think about ways in which you believe your students need to be challenged by God's Word:

_____

_____

### The Need to Console

Human beings need to be challenged, but they also need to be comforted and reassured of God's loving concern. This is the duality that runs throughout Scripture: on the one hand, God loves people just as they are, without condition; on the other hand, God calls us to be more than what we are now, to develop into the loving, responsible people we can become.

Young people, because they do not have the life experience of adults, are especially sensitive to discouragement and despair. They can be emotionally turbulent, and prone to wide mood swings based on their most current experience. For this reason, they are often particularly responsive to passages that stress God's offer of peace and consolation. People also take great comfort in the psalms, especially Psalm 139.

Take a moment now and think about two areas in which God's offer of comfort and consolation may be important for your students.

_____

_____

---

### Helps in Using the Bible

1. **Bible Study.** *Catholic Study Bible (New American Bible),* Oxford University Press, 1990; *The New Oxford Annotated Bible with the Apocrypha (New Revised Standard Version),* Oxford University Press, 1991; *The New Jerusalem Bible,* Doubleday, 1985; *Christian Community Bible,* Claretian Publications, 1988.

2. **Locating Verses.** *Nelson's Complete Concordance of the New American Bible,* ed. Fr. Stephen J. Hartdegen. Liturgical Press, 1977; *QuickVerse 2.0,* Parsons Technology, 1990.

3. **Bible Dictionary.** *The Dictionary of the Bible,* John L. McKenzie, S.J. Macmillan, 1967; *Dictionary of Biblical Theology,* Xavier Leon-Dufour. Seabury, 1977.

4. **Biblical Information.** *The Collegeville Bible Commentary,* Liturgical Press, 1989; *The New Jerome Biblical Commentary,* Prentice-Hall, 1990.

5. **Compare Bible Verses.** *Let Each Gospel Speak for Itself,* Rhys Williams. Twenty-Third Publications, 1989; *The Complete Parallel Bible,* Oxford University Press, 1993.

6. **Bible Maps.** *Collegeville Bible Study Atlas,* Liturgical Press, 1990; *Atlas of the Bible Lands,* Hammond, 1984.

## *Pause a Moment . . .*

- Describe a moment in your life in which you needed to hear words of consolation. How can you use this experience with your students?

- How can you help students become more receptive to messages of comfort found in the Bible?

## *Prayer Response*

Get into a relaxed position. Recall the questions and struggles you have in your life. Then read each of the following Scripture passages. After each passage, pause to think about how the passage applies to your present search for meaning. Later this week, read and reflect on these passages a second time.

> *Blessed is the one who trusts in the Lord, whose hope is the Lord. This person is like a tree planted besides the waters that stretches out its roots to the stream: It fears not the heat when it comes, its leaves stay green; In the year of drought it shows no distress, but still bears fruit.* (Jeremiah 17:7–8)

> *"And I say to you, ask and you will receive; seek and you will find; knock and the door will be opened to you. For everyone who asks, receives; and the one who seeks, finds; and to the one who knocks, the door will be opened.* (Luke 11:9–10)

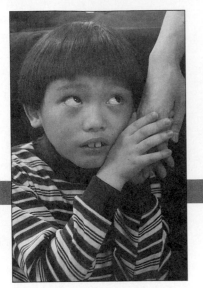

▲ *Use the Bible as a source of consolation for people who are hurting or who are afraid.*

## BIBLIOGRAPHY

Charpentier, Etienne. *How to Read the Old Testament.*

_____ *How to Read the New Testament.* New York: Crossroad Publishing Company, 1992.

Cronin, Gaynell. *Effective Teaching Methods.* Mahwah, NJ: Paulist Press, video.

*Flying House.* Mahwah, NJ: Paulist Press, video.

Furnish, Dorothy J. *Exploring the Bible with Children.* Nashville, Abingdon, 1975.

Gillespie, Mike. *Fun Old Testament Bible Studies.* Loveland, CO: Group Books, 1989.

Glavich, Sr. Mary Kathleen, S.N.D. *Leading Students into Scripture.* Twenty-Third Publications. 1987.

Lynn, David and Kathy. *4th–6th Grade Talksheets: 25 Creative, Easy-To-Use Discussions for Upper Elementary Students.* Grand Rapids, MI: Zondervan, 1993.

Lynn, David. *High School Talksheets: 50 Creative Discussions for High School Youth Groups.* Grand Rapids, MI: Zondervan, 1987.

_____ *Junior High Talksheets: 50 Creative Discussions for Junior High Youth Groups.* Grand Rapids, MI: Zondervan, 1988.

*Parables from Nature.* Nashville, TN, Ecu-Film, videos.

Reichert, Richard. *Teaching Tips for Religion Teachers.* Huntington, IN: Our Sunday Visitor, 1989.

Reichert, Richard and Westenberg, Michael. *Teaching Tips for Adolescent Catechesis.* Huntington, IN: Our Sunday Visitor, 1992.

Smith, Shawn Michael. *Strategies for Teaching the Hebrew Scriptures.* St. Mary's Press, 1990.

*Nihil Obstat*
The Reverend Gregory A. Banazak, S.T.D.

*Imprimatur*
The Most Reverend Kenneth J. Povish, D.D.
Bishop of Lansing
May 13, 1994

The *Nihil Obstat* and *Imprimatur* are official declarations that a book or pamphlet is free of doctrinal or moral error. No implication is contained therein that those who have granted the *Nihil Obstat* and *Imprimatur* agree with the contents, opinions, or statements expressed.

Send all inquiries to:
BENZIGER PUBLISHING COMPANY
15319 Chatsworth Street
P.O. Box 9609
Mission Hills, California 91346-9609

Second Edition

**ISBN 0-02-651213-0**

Printed in the United States of America.

1 2 3 4 5 6 7 8 9   BAW   98 97 96 95 94

**Benziger**

# Jesus and Discipleship

*We call him Jesus, a name that means freedom ... For two thousand years his name has been on the lips of the sick as they prayed for strength and in the hearts of the sorry as they asked to be forgiven. To this day some one thousand million Christians sing hymns in his honor and thank him for giving meaning to their lives.*

*Jesus of Nazareth: A Life Worth Living,* by Ronald Modras

**BOOK TWO**

## In this chapter you will:

- Recognize Jesus as both human and divine.
- Study Jesus' proclamation of the kingdom of God.
- Consider what it means to be a disciple of Jesus.
- Examine methods for appropriately presenting the life and message of Jesus to various age groups.

*Written by*
**Peter Ries**

*Consultant*
**David Riley**

Second Edition

# Part I  Experience

## Knowing from the Heart

Kim's parents were first generation immigrants to the United States from Vietnam. When they arrived in the States, they had no money and few prospects for the future, although they had been received warmly by the local Catholic community. Through hard work and self-discipline, however, they built a thriving retail business and succeeded in giving Kim a chance at a better life.

Kim deeply admired her parents, but she never shared their religious convictions. They carried with them a belief in a stern, authoritarian Jesus who despised laziness. Kim grew up regarding Jesus as an intolerant figure who threatened her with judgment for the slightest misstep. When she got older, she rejected Christianity, and decided that religion just wasn't for her.

Later, in college, Kim learned that her childhood impressions of Jesus were a little distorted. In a philosophy class, she compared the teachings of Jesus with other great figures from antiquity such as Socrates, Confucius, Buddha, and Gamaliel. Kim learned that Jesus actually preached a doctrine of love which had radical implications in social and political situations. Kim grew to admire what Jesus stood for, in the same way that she admired many other great religious and philosophical figures. Nevertheless, her intellectual admiration of Jesus did not translate into any kind of faith. Kim didn't believe that Christianity had anything to offer her personally.

A year or so after Kim had begun her legal career, she returned home for a vacation. On learning that a distant cousin had passed away, Kim gathered with the rest of her family for the funeral services. Kim had never met this cousin, but went with her parents to the funeral Mass because it was family.

When they arrived at the church, Kim noticed the obvious grief felt by people over this cousin's death. People were openly weeping and comforting one another. Such displays made her uncomfortable, so she retired to one of the side chapels to get away until the service began.

As she walked into the chapel, she saw an elderly man sitting quietly. She nodded to him and sat down. Kim struck up a conversation with the man, who seemed happy for the attention. They chatted amiably for a few minutes, until Kim asked how he was related to her cousin. "I'm his father," came the answer.

Kim suddenly felt ashamed. "I'm so sorry," she said. "I feel like an idiot, sitting here as if nothing's happened. Please forgive me."

"Not at all," the man said. "I'm glad for the company. But tell me, why did you come into the chapel?"

"I don't like funerals," Kim said. "They make me uncomfortable. I never know what to say or do. I came in here to get away, I guess."

"I understand," the man said softly, "but this is the wrong place to escape the funeral." He pointed to the large crucifix which dominated the chapel wall. "I came in here because seeing Jesus on the cross reminds me of what a funeral is all about: grief for your loss, but confidence in God's love and the resurrection to come." He walked over to Kim. "Don't worry about what to say. Just pray for me," he said, and then walked back into the main hall of the church.

Kim sat silently for a few minutes, studying the crucifix. What was it about his belief in Jesus that gave this man such amazing strength? She wrestled with the question a while longer. Then Kim knelt, and attempted something she hadn't tried since she was in grade school: she began to pray.

*Μεμο*

Have you ever been moved by another person's faith, as Kim was in this story?

## YOUR STORY

**1.** What images of Jesus did you form in your own childhood? How have these images been modified as you've become older?

_____

_____

**2.** How does a person's understanding of Jesus affect his or her experience of religion?

_____

_____

**3.** What is the difference between knowing about Jesus and knowing Jesus?

_____

_____

**4.** Complete the following statement: "For me, Jesus is . . ."

_____

_____

▲ *Kim went to the funeral as a gesture to her family. After studying the crucifix for a while she made an effort to pray.*

## Knowing Jesus

Most of us have an image of Jesus. It may be a picture we were presented in our childhood of a caring Jesus. Or it may be an image more recently acquired of Jesus, in his risen life, helping us to resolve our struggles. Some of us are finding that an old familiar picture of Jesus is no longer relevant as we ask new questions about ourselves and the meaning of life.

Jesus continues to have tremendous appeal for people. He is central to humankind's experience of God's revelation and to the message and effort of religious education. As catechists, we need to understand and appreciate Jesus. Through him and his Church, we are called to faith; with him as a model, we are called to live out our faith.

Jesus is certainly something of a paradox. On one hand, he is truly human, like us in everything but sin. On the other hand, he is truly divine, the second person of the Blessed Trinity. This paradox, this blessed mystery, is a central belief of our faith: the *Incarnation*, God becoming man.

> *Who, though he was in the form of God, did not regard equality with God something to be grasped. Rather, he emptied himself, taking the form of a slave, coming in human likeness; and found human in appearance, he humbled himself, becoming obedient to death, even death on a cross.* (Philippians 2:6–8)

This statement from Paul's letter to the Christian community in Philippi, written between A.D. 55 and 63, is among the earliest known writings we have that identifies Jesus as both human and divine. This passage is written in the form of a hymn or creed (it certainly is an exhortation). It reflects how the early Church felt about Jesus.

Over the centuries, two schools of Christology (the theological study of who Jesus was and what he did) have developed. One, called "high Christology," focuses its attention on Jesus' divinity. The second school, called "low Christology," emphasizes Jesus' humanity.

Both of these schools separate Jesus' humanity from his divinity to a degree. Church Councils (particularly Nicaea in 325, Ephesus in 431, and Chalcedon in 451) vigorously condemned this practice when taken to its extreme. It was at these councils that the doctrine that we profess was defined. Jesus is:

> *the only Son of God, eternally begotten of the Father, Light from Light, true God from true God, begotten not made, one in Being with the father. Through whom all things were made. For us men and for our salvation, he came down from heaven: by the power of the Holy Spirit he was born of the Virgin Mary, and became man.* (Nicene Creed)

To better understand the humanity and divinity of Jesus, it is helpful to consider each of these elements separately.

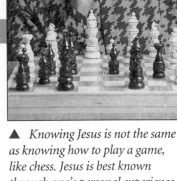

▲ *Knowing Jesus is not the same as knowing how to play a game, like chess. Jesus is best known through one's personal experience of him.*

## The Humanity of Jesus

Perhaps no figure in human history has ever been the object of a more exhausting or sustained historical inquiry. Scholars of all theological persuasions, including dedicated atheists, have pursued the study of the historical Jesus with an almost religious zeal. What can we learn from this focus on the historical Jesus? How does it affect us as catechists?

In biblical scholarship, the study of Jesus as a human being, who lived and died in a specific place and time, and who stood for certain values and ideas, is known as the "quest for the historical Jesus." While we can learn much from the Bible and other sources about Jesus and his times, we cannot learn everything we might like to know.

The gospel accounts were not meant to be biographies or historical records. Rather, they are works of theology. What they report about Jesus is shaped by the theological message they hope to convey.

- Matthew and Luke report on his miraculous conception and birth while Mark and John are interested only in his ministry. Do Matthew and Luke have information unknown to Mark and John? Possibly, but it seems more likely that Mark and John had other interests.

- Did Jesus go to Jerusalem only once in his life, as suggested by Mark, or did he go to Jerusalem regularly to worship in the Temple as suggested by John? We have no way of knowing. It's clear from Mark's account, however, that all of Jesus' ministry was pointing to the trip to Jerusalem resulting in his passion and death. Mark uses this one trip as a theological statement.

While there is much that we can't know about Jesus, there are a few things we can know.

1. **Jesus was a real person.** He was *born* of a woman named Mary. He grew up in Nazareth, a small village in Galilee, the northern part of Israel. Jesus was raised in the house of a carpenter and learned this trade.

2. **The Gospels show that Jesus lived a very simple life.** He held no official position in the religious or political circles of his day. Jesus owned no house or property. Often, he ate at other people's homes and enjoyed their hospitality.

3. **Jesus was extremely compassionate.** He understood other peoples' feelings. The Gospel shows that he effectively communicated with individuals as well as with large crowds of people. He was open and accepting of others, and never judged anyone.

At the same time, Jesus challenged the people of his day. He continually asked controversial questions and associated with social outcasts—sinners, prostitutes, the poor, and tax collectors. Jesus stated the truth as he saw it and was not swayed by public opinion. He was not afraid to challenge the status quo or to attack popular notions. Above all, Jesus called people to repent from their sins.

He did not know everything when he was born. The Gospels state that Jesus *grew* in wisdom and knowledge *(Luke 2:52)*. When people asked him when the kingdom of God would come in its fullness, Jesus answered that he *did not know (Matthew 24:36)*. Like each of us, he was called to follow God's will with faith and trust. And like us, his faith was tested.

Because he was truly human, Jesus experienced all that is characteristic of human nature (except for sin). He could not be in two places at the same

## The Church Teaches

Belief in the true incarnation of the Son of God is the distinctive sign of Christian faith: By this you know the Spirit of God: every spirit that confesses that Jesus Christ has come in the flesh is from God. Therein lies the joyous conviction of the Church from its beginning, as when it sings the mystery of its faith: He was revealed in flesh.

The unique and altogether singular event of the incarnation of God's only Son does not mean that Jesus Christ is partly God and partly man, nor does it imply that he is the result of a confused mixture of the divine and the human. He became truly man while remaining truly God. Jesus Christ is true God and true Man. (See the *Catechism of the Catholic Church*, #463–464.)

time. He knew hunger and thirst, warmth and cold. Jesus wept and laughed, got tired and excited, grew discouraged and anxious. He had friends who were important to him, and he counted on their support. Jesus knew that he would die one day.

These considerations are of tremendous pastoral importance. It is the human side of Jesus, the side that laughed, ached, felt sorrow and knew hope, that can console and inspire Christians today. People find it difficult to identify with a doctrine, such as the Incarnation; but they can readily understand the pain in Jesus' heart as he made his way up Golgotha.

When we focus on the awesome divinity of Jesus, the human side of his character can be obscured. Jesus was not solely the realization of an eternal plan; he was also a real person, who lived in space and time, and who demanded justice for those who shared the human condition with him. For this reason, it is critical that religious education not neglect the human dimension of Jesus.

## The Divinity of Jesus

Over the centuries, Catholic teaching has emphasized the divinity of Jesus at the expense of his humanity. In theology today, however, there is a danger of moving too far in the opposite direction and losing sight of the reality of who Jesus was. A non-divine Jesus gives just as impoverished an understanding as a non-human one.

In addition to being human, Jesus is also God. This statement is as mysterious as it is familiar. In what sense is Jesus "divine"? What sense does that make for Christians today? These are questions that religious educators are increasingly being called upon to answer.

Catholics believe that Jesus was the perfect revelation of the essence of God. Hebrews 1:2–3 expresses it this way:

> [h]e spoke to us through a son, whom he made heir of all things and through whom he created the universe who is the [reflection] the very imprint of his being, and who sustains all things by his mighty word.

The Greek word used here for "reflection" can also mean "stamp" or "seal." In other words, Jesus presents God to us in human form. The substance of God, God's essence, is present in the human person, Jesus.

**The Power of God.** Jesus shows the power of God through miracles. These were not random acts, but each a demonstration of some aspect of God's character. John calls them "signs" of the kingdom.

- When Jesus healed someone he revealed God's special love and concern for the suffering;

- The nature miracles showed God's awesome power as creator, and served as a reminder that the universe is purposeful and is moving toward the final realization of God's plan; and

- The exorcisms show us God's power over demons and the darker side of human nature.

Even more importantly, Jesus presents God to us through the perfect love which motivated him to accept death on the cross. We caught glimpses of this love in Jesus' warm acceptance of people, and in his genuine compassion for those who suffered, but it is perfectly revealed in Jesus' saving act on the cross.

**Seal of Approval.** The divinity of Jesus, as revealed especially in his death and resurrection, serves as the ultimate "seal of approval" on the kind of life he led. As a human being, Jesus exemplifies the qualities toward which we all strive: courage, compassion, and principle. Only through the awareness of Jesus as God, however, can we be assured that living this kind of life will ultimately bring us happiness. Through his death and resurrection, we have our assurance that striving to live like Christ is the true path we are to walk. Saint Paul referred to the risen Jesus as the "first-fruit" of the kingdom. All other fruit from this same vine—all Christians—should be like Jesus. Jesus is our model and our guide.

▲ *Those who follow Jesus serve others. The kingdom of God that Jesus preached centers around the idea of service to others.*

## Pause a Moment. . .

- Do you focus more on the humanity of Jesus or on his divinity?
- In what way(s) has reflecting on the humanity of Jesus been useful or inspiring to you?
- What does it mean to say that Jesus' humanity and divinity remain a mystery?
- What are the implications for faith in believing that Jesus is God?
- What are the implications for faith in believing that Jesus is human?

## Jesus' Message: The Kingdom of God

The central theme of Jesus' teaching was the kingdom of God. Sometimes today the word reign is used in place of the word "kingdom." Jesus used the word "kingdom," a familiar concept to his listeners, to denote a community marked by peace, love, friendship, reconciliation, and justice.

The kingdom of God could be seen in the person of Jesus, although it would not be fully revealed until the end of time. Jesus called each person to abandon motives of fear, selfishness, and hatred and to embrace the characteristics of God's kingdom. People were to repent and sin no more. Repentance, according to Jesus, meant an inner transformation of one's basic values.

Jesus' followers were to assist in the building of this kingdom by believing and living what he taught, performing dual roles as models and builders of this kingdom.

### Understanding the Kingdom

Certain elements of Jesus' message can be highlighted by comparing him to some of the recognized religious and political groups of his day.

1. **Jesus insisted that members of God's kingdom were to serve others.**
   The command to love one's neighbor took on a distinctly new meaning in the parable of the Good Samaritan, in Jesus' washing the feet of his apostles at the Last Supper, and in Jesus' words "[w]hatever you did for one of these least brothers of mine, you did for me" *(Matthew 25:40)*. This element of service put the message of Jesus at odds with the beliefs of the *Sadducees,* a group concerned with the Law of Moses. Jesus was not a member of this group. He insisted that service to others, not a prominent social position, made one closer to God.

2. **Jesus was not a legalist.** He said we are to obey the law but remember that the law was made to serve us; we were not made to serve the law. There is some disagreement among scholars today about the amount of similarity and difference between the teaching of the Pharisees and Jesus. Many scholars believe that Jesus was himself a Pharisee. The Pharisees had a sincere loyalty to the written Law and the more extensive oral law that had developed through tradition. However, Jesus always placed more emphasis on the person than on the law.

3. **The kingdom will come by peaceful means.** In this, Jesus opposed the Zealots; political revolutionaries motivated by religious convictions. The Zealots felt that only through violence could the Roman domination be ended. Jesus was not a Zealot. He told his followers they no longer had the option of hating anyone, going so far as to forgive his executioners. Jesus preached a radical nonviolence. He said we must love our enemies.

4. **The kingdom is now.** This part of Jesus' message contrasted with the beliefs of the Essenes, who lived separated from the world because they believed that it was evil. Jesus was not an Essene. He believed in the goodness of the world. He was constantly in the marketplace. He took risks and became involved with people.

These basic elements of Jesus' message give us a good idea about what God's kingdom is like. In addition, the person of Jesus is the clearest statement we have of what God is like. In Jesus, all the strands of meaning and glimpses of insight in the Scriptures come together. In him, the hopes of the prophets and the yearnings of the people were fulfilled beyond their expectations. Although there are still many levels of meaning to discover in the message and person of Jesus, it can be truly said that Jesus is the presence of God among us.

## Entering the Kingdom

While Jesus insisted that God's kingdom can be entered by anyone, living in the kingdom takes time and effort. It also requires accepting God's offer of grace: God's unconditional love. This realization that we are truly loved frees us to love others. Grace allows us to reject our sinfulness.

In reality, the only thing that has to be given up is selfishness. Instead of putting ourselves at the center of the universe and measuring everything by how it affects us, we can put the kingdom of God at the center and measure everything else by its effect on our experience of God and other people. In fact, that's what Jesus said eventually would happen to anyone who desires his kingdom.

Jesus said the kingdom begins for most people in small ways, then grows little by little until it embraces everything. Its growth is like that of a plant. You can't see the changes from one day to the next, but over a week it is obvious that the plant is larger and fuller. In Luke 13:18–19 and Matthew 13:31–32 Jesus compares one's growth in faith to the development of a mustard seed, which is very tiny, but grows into a large plant. Although a mustard plant doesn't actually get big enough for birds to nest in it, Jesus' exaggeration shows the tremendous fruitfulness—beyond all expectation—of the kingdom in a person's life.

Your tiny beginning might be anything—a single choice made with God in mind, or a small act of generosity for the sake of the Lord, or a shift in your thinking. You only have to respond positively to God's grace, choose a kingdom-quality life, and cooperate with God's action to help it happen to you.

## Living in the Kingdom Means New Attitudes

Jesus says the kingdom is always available to anyone who will accept it. That means one must adopt certain attitudes. By taking on these new attitudes, we allow the kingdom to operate in our lives.

One important area in which our attitudes need to change concerns material things. Especially in Western culture, happiness is often associated with how much one owns. Such an association promotes greed. When a person is greedy, who is the focus of attention? Is it God? Is it Jesus? Is it oneself? When a person is focused on him or herself, the kingdom is not treated as if it is worth more than anything else. Jesus says, "No one can serve two masters. He will either hate one and love the other, or be devoted to one and despise the other. You cannot serve God and mammon" *(Matthew 6:24)*.

What people ultimately are looking for by accumulating things is security—from need, from fear, from unhappiness. With the kingdom, Jesus says, there is one great surprise: Put the kingdom first, and everything else you need will be given to you! *(Matthew 6:33–34)*.

Life in the kingdom is secure. It is safe and free of anxiety over the future. No amount of money can give a person freedom from anxiety, because money can always be lost. But life in the kingdom will free a person from worry, because everything is in the powerful and loving hands of the Lord. That is one reason why Jesus' teaching was—and is—such good news.

That doesn't mean that Christians will not have problems. Jesus called us to take up our cross and follow him *(Matthew 10:34–42)*. We will experience difficulties along the way. Our security in the midst of these struggles is the knowledge that God is with us through Jesus. With Jesus, no burden will be too heavy or challenge too difficult to bear.

People of the kingdom forgive others. In Matthew 18:21–22, Peter asks Jesus how often a person is to forgive. Jesus answers, "Seventy-seven times." Symbolically, this number means that we should forgive *every time*. Anger builds a separation, like an inner wall, between the person and God. God cannot dwell where people's hearts are filled with grudges and bad tempers.

We have to remove ourselves from the center of our own universe, and allow the needs of others to take first place. This is easy to say, but challenging to live out on a daily basis. Through our awareness of the real, living presence of Jesus in our lives, however, we can take up the challenge with courage and optimism.

## Pause a Moment . . .

- What sort of meaning do you find in the message and person of Jesus? What helps and what hinders you in discovering that meaning?

- Jesus taught that the law was made to serve us. What are your beliefs and attitudes toward obeying laws?

- How can Jesus' attitude toward people influence the way family members treat one another?

## The New Commandment

Then he said, "What is the kingdom of God like? To what can I compare it? It is like a mustard seed that a person took and planted in the garden. When it was fully grown, it became a large bush and the birds of the sky dwelt in its branches."

Again he said, "To what shall I compare the kingdom of God? It is like yeast that a woman took and mixed [in] with three measures of wheat flour until the whole batch of dough was leavened."

(Luke 13:18–21)

## The Call to Discipleship

Jesus came not only to reveal the kingdom, but also to invite others to follow him. A follower of Jesus is called a "disciple," a Greek word which means "student." A disciple is one who studies the message and lived example of Jesus, and draws on his loving strength.

What does it mean to follow Jesus? In simple terms, it means to adopt Jesus' values in all areas of one's life. But what, practically, does that mean in terms of specific choices and directions in life? To get an answer, we can turn to the four gospels, each of which gives us a different, complementary picture of what being a disciple is all about.

### Discipleship in Mark: Suffering with Jesus

For Mark, discipleship is revealed through emphasis on the suffering of Jesus. The true disciple, according to Mark, is one who suffers along with Jesus. In Mark 8:34–35, Jesus says: "If a man wishes to come after me, he must deny his very self, take up his cross, and follow in my steps. Whoever would preserve his life would lose it, but whoever loses his life for my sake and the gospel's will preserve it." Being a disciple, therefore, means accepting the pain and disappointment that comes with discipleship. For Mark the true disciple is the one who takes up the cross and the suffering it implies in faith.

### Discipleship in Matthew: A Believing Community

Matthew presents Jesus as the fulfillment of the Law of Israel. In Matthew, Jesus appeals to the Law as the ultimate basis for his ministry. The Law, however, must be interpreted in light of human needs, which always take first place. Jesus is presented as the great teacher and interpreter of the Law for human beings.

For Matthew, discipleship means being part of a believing community. In that community, the Church applies Jesus' words about justice and the Law. The role of the disciple is to study and live out these teachings as a member of the wider Church community. A disciple supports the community, and makes decisions with the welfare of the community in mind.

### Discipleship in Luke: Spreading the Word

Luke's view of what it means to be a disciple is clear in several sections which are unique to his gospel. Luke emphasizes that being a disciple means spreading the good news about Jesus. Luke stresses many times that God will respond when the disciples present their needs in prayer.

Such gifts from God, however, mean that the disciples have a special responsibility to do God's will. Luke quotes Jesus as saying, "Much will be required of the person entrusted with much, and still more will be demanded of the person entrusted with more" (12:48). Disciples are obligated to use God's gifts positively. Further, in Chapter 17, Luke reminds his readers

▲ What does it mean to be a disciple of Jesus? A disciple will: show compassion for a person in need, participate in a believing community, and proclaim the Good News of Jesus. Disciples love one another.

not to expect tremendous honors or riches for their efforts; spreading God's word is no more than their duty.

For Luke, a disciple is one who does the work of God, spreads the good news about Jesus, and believes that God will provide the gifts needed to succeed. Luke reminds his readers that anyone, regardless of social status or past mistakes, may be a disciple of Jesus. All that is needed is a loving heart and confidence in God's protection.

## Discipleship in John: Loving One Another

More than any other gospel account, John is written with the specific needs of a particular community of believers in mind. So, it is not surprising that John provides guidelines for discipleship. In Chapters 13–17, John presents Jesus' last discourse before his arrest. In it, Jesus tells his followers what it means to be his disciple.

1. **Service.** Jesus washes the feet of his disciples, telling them that even though he is the master and they the servants, it is necessary for him to humble himself and serve them. In the same way, it is necessary for the disciples to humble themselves and serve others.

2. **Doing his works.** This involves teaching, healing, and revealing the Father to other people. God will provide the disciples with what they need to do Jesus' work, sending a Paraclete to them. In Greek law, a "paraclete" was like a defense attorney: someone who defends you and speaks for you before a judge. Jesus refers to this agent as the Holy Spirit, who will come to the disciples and guide them in following him.

3. **Living out the commandments he has given.** The most important of these commands, he says, is to love one another, even to the point of accepting death:

   *"This is my commandment: love one another as I love you. No one has greater love than this, to lay down one's life for one's friends. You are my friends if you do what I command you"* (John 15:12–14).

The true test of discipleship is love. If we love one another, then we are obeying Jesus' commands and living as his disciple.

John warns his readers that following Jesus will not be easy. The world will not support you, he says, and in fact people will persecute you. John tells his community to accept that they are not "of the world," and to endure being disciples no matter what. If they do this, he says, God will not abandon them when they are in need.

## Pause a Moment . . .

- Which of these four understandings of discipleship is closest to your own? Which is most unfamiliar to you?

- Do you think these four views of discipleship are valid today? Why or why not? In what ways might they need to be supplemented?

- What particular challenges does each understanding hold or entail for you?

# Considerations for Daily Life

When Jesus said that the law was made for us and not us for the law, he was not just removing the burden of law, but was indicating a radical new approach to life and to relationships. The morality that Jesus preached was one of gift and response. The basic notion is that God has first freely and completely loved us, with no strings attached. God's love is expressed by his creating each of us and by his continuing presence and care for us.

Each of us is called to respond to God in the light of God's total unconditional love. This concept of gift and response moves one beyond legalism in relating to God. Following laws will not help a person to answer the questions, "Have I done enough; have I loved enough?"

Realizing God's love and the call to live out one's response to it goes beyond fulfilling a set of laws. Such an attitude goes beyond a reward and punishment morality and results in a giving of self as Jesus showed during his life on earth. Motivation to give oneself spills over into relationships with others. The question changes from "What am I required to do for my neighbor?" to "What are the needs of my neighbor and how can I respond?"

Jesus was not satisfied with the way things were. He reacted to injustices and the needs of people as he experienced them. We must do the same. For us, it is no longer a question of what the law requires. For the follower of Jesus, human need becomes the barometer for Christian response. Human needs carry a greater weight of responsibility than human law.

## Pause a Moment . . .

- How do we show our love for God by following Jesus?
- What is the greatest responsibility of being a follower of Jesus?

## YOUR VIEW

The following exercise will help you refine and apply your knowledge of the concepts of discipleship in the four gospel accounts.

**1.** Mark emphasizes suffering as the prerequisite for a disciple of Jesus. What does it mean to suffer for Jesus today? (See *Mark 8:27 to 10:52* for guidance.)

_____

**2.** Read Chapter 18 of Matthew's gospel account. What could modern Christians do to better promote the idea of community?

_____

**3.** Read Luke 9:1–10:20. List two ways in which you have made an effort to spread the gospel to others through your life.

_____

**4.** Read John 13–17. What do you think Jesus meant when he called us to "love" others?

_____

# Part IV Response

## Teaching Discipleship

Jesus is at the heart of all catechesis. The transmission of the Christian faith is centered in proclaiming Jesus crucified and raised from the dead. As catechists, we set forth the fullness of God's plan of salvation in the person of Jesus and seek to understand the meaning of Christ's words, actions, and signs.

Catechesis aims to put people in intimate communion with Jesus, "who alone can lead us in the Spirit to the Father's love and enable us to share in the life of the Holy Trinity" *(Catechesi Tradendae, #5)*. Everything that is taught is taught with reference to Jesus. Everyone who teaches, does so as a representative of him. (See *Catechism of the Catholic Church, # 425–428.*)

Jesus himself is the one who issues the invitation to discipleship. As catechists, our role is to help students to appreciate this call and to think about what it means for their lives. The primary resource for teaching discipleship is the life and word of Jesus, as they are reflected in the four gospel accounts. The way we direct our students to apply this material, however, will vary with age and grade level.

▲ *Catechists hope to put people into intimate communion with Jesus. As students reflect on their lives they should see that Jesus is making the journey with them.*

### For Primary Grades

The emphasis here should be on stories, especially those about Jesus or those told by him featuring memorable characters and a relatively simple plot. Examples include the parable of the Good Samaritan *(Luke 10:25–37)*, and the story of Jesus and blind Bartimaeus *(Mark 10:46–52)*. Students find these stories easy to remember and can grasp the point of the story with ease.

In presenting these stories, two goals should be paramount:

1. To ensure that students understand and retain the story, and

2. To ensure that students can apply the point of the story in their own lives.

To accomplish these goals, experiment with a variety of ways of having students interact with the stories. Some possibilities include:

- dramatic readings,
- skits,
- an artistic response (paintings, songs), and
- role-playing exercises based on important characters.

When students have absorbed the context of the story, have them apply their understanding. Ask them what they would do in that situation, or have them point to a similar situation in their own experience. They should see that the story has some meaning for them beyond entertainment.

Be creative.

- Use felt cutouts of characters from Bible stories involving Jesus. As you tell the stories mentioned above, add and move figures on a felt board. The second time you tell the story, assign felt figures for students to move as appropriate.

## For Intermediate Grades

Students at this age level are able to tackle questions of values head-on. For this reason, material such as the parables and beatitudes works very well. Students can study the material, extract its important insights and values, and apply them in their own experience.

Generally, the more students can become actively engaged with the material, the more likely they are to absorb and retain its content. For this reason, catechists should search for creative ways for students to learn about the gospel accounts in a manner appropriate to their age level.

- Using a large map of the Mediterranean world and a detailed map of Israel, briefly explain the geography and history of Jesus' time.

- Write their own versions of a parable. For example, students might be asked to "update" the parable of the sower. Try this as a group assignment.

- Give each student a piece of paper and crayons. Ask them to write down three words that come to mind when they think of Jesus. Ask them to then draw a picture illustrating each word. Complete the exercise by having students describe their pictures.

- Work with parables. Form groups of four, each group with a Bible. Have them look up the parable in Luke 8:4–8 and:

  (a) figure out the point of the parable,

  (b) retell it in a way their peers would understand, and

  (c) state why the point of this parable is an important part of the teachings of Jesus.

Afterward, each group should report its findings to the class. Discuss any differences in their interpretation of the parable. You can also assign a different parable to each group.

## For Junior High

Students at this age are beginning to become aware of their moral sense. No longer just a matter of instinct, students are gradually learning to reflect on the values behind specific choices. For this reason, assignments in which students consider the values implicit in the stories and sayings of Jesus and apply them in their own experience often work very well.

- Have the students consider the following sayings of Jesus: (a) "your light must shine before others" *(Matthew 5:15)*, (b) "by their fruits you will know them" *(Matthew 7:18)*, and (c) "how much more important are you than birds!" *(Luke 12:27)*. Ask for examples of when they have heard a similar message.

- Ask students to take specific sayings of Jesus, such as his saying on divorce *(Mark 10:2–12)* or his instructions to the Twelve *(Luke 9:1–6)*, and to determine the value(s) upon which these instructions are based. Ask them to use the beatitudes as a checklist of values.

- Give students case studies of specific moral situations. Ask them to determine, in that situation, what decision a disciple of Jesus would make. Have students identify the specific value upon which they base their decision.

- In a prayer service, recall that God knows each of us by name. Ask the students to consider how special they feel when they are noticed in a crowd or when someone acknowledges them by name.

## For High School

First, students at this level should be introduced to the distinction sketched above between the "human" or "historical" Jesus and the divine side of Jesus. They should be led to consider why both dimensions of Jesus' personality are important for Christian faith. This might work well as the basis for class discussion, or for a group assignment.

Second, students should be asked to do some comparison of the four gospel accounts, noting differences in themes and content. The catechist should direct them in forming conclusions on the basis of these observations, focusing on the relation of our images of Jesus to our experience and outlook on life. In this context, students may want to consider the different images of Jesus from different perspectives, such as African theology, Latin American theology, and feminist theology.

Connected to this, students should be given numerous opportunities for prayer, cultivating an ongoing dialogue with the risen Jesus. In this relationship, students will discover the model for their own efforts at discipleship, as well as a source of comfort and strength as they struggle to practice what they learn. Use the following sayings of Jesus (*John 6:35, 8:12, 10:11, 11:25, and 14:6*) as part of a prayer service. What doubts and hope does each statement bring to mind?

Have the students keep a journal for their private use to help them explore more deeply their own relationship with Jesus.

▲ *Have the students keep journals for their private use. They can use the journal to keep track of how their relationship with Jesus is developing.*

### YOUR VIEW

- In your teacher's manual and student text, find examples that present Jesus as human, as divine, and as a model for our daily lives. Then list some possible methods for presenting each example to your students. Write your answers in the following chart.

| Examples of Jesus | Teaching Methods |
|---|---|
| Human _____ | _____ |
| _____ | _____ |
| Divine _____ | _____ |
| _____ | _____ |
| A model for daily living _____ | _____ |
| _____ | _____ |

## Memo

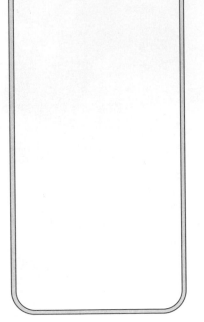

I want to keep the following considerations about Jesus in mind:

## Prayer Response

Take a few minutes to reflect on the place of Jesus in your life right now. What doubts or uncertainties do you have in this regard? Read and reflect on each of the following biblical passages. If you wish, jot down some of your thoughts.

- I am the bread of life *(John 6:35)*.
- I am the light of the world *(John 8:12)*.
- I am the good shepherd *(John 10:11)*.
- I am the resurrection and the life *(John 11:25)*.
- I am the way, and the truth, and the life *(John 14:6)*.

Go to a door or window through which you can see people at work or play. Ask Jesus for the ability to experience him in others and for the generosity to share his love through your attitudes and actions.

## BIBLIOGRAPHY

*Amie.* Los Angeles: Franciscan Communications, video.

DeSales. *The Living Gospels.* Los Angeles: Franciscan Communications, video.

Foley, Leonard. "Who Is Jesus?" *Catholic Update.* Cincinnati, OH: St. Anthony Messenger Press, September, 1985.

*God the Son.* Allen, TX: Tabor Publishing, video.

Heft, James L. S.M. "What Should We Believe About Jesus' Resurrection?" *Catholic Update.* Cincinnati, OH: St. Anthony Messenger Press, April, 1990

*Hey Janitor.* Mahwah, N.J.: Paulist Press, video.

*Jesus B.C.* Mahwah, N.J.: Paulist Press, video.

Modras, Ronald. *Jesus of Nazareth: A Life Worth Living.* Minneapolis, MN: Winston, 1983.

Mueller, Steve. "Four Ways to Follow Jesus," *Catholic Update.* Cincinnati, OH: St. Anthony Messenger Press, December, 1992.

National Conference of Catholic Bishops. "Chapter III, Revelation, Faith, and Catechesis." *Sharing the Light of Faith: National Catechetical Directory for Catholics of the United States.* Washington, DC: USCC Publications, 1979.

*Parable.* New York: Council of Churches, video.

*Resurrection.* Mahwah, N.J.: Paulist Press, video.

Senior, Donald. *Jesus: A Gospel Portrait.* Mahwah, N.J.: Paulist Press, 1992.

Smith, Virginia. "The Four Faces of Jesus," *Catholic Update.* Cincinnati, OH: St. Anthony Messenger Press, March, 1990.

*Nihil Obstat*
The Reverend Gregory A. Banazak, S.T.D.

*Imprimatur*
The Most Reverend Kenneth J. Povish, D.D.
Bishop of Lansing
May 13, 1994

The *Nihil Obstat* and *Imprimatur* are official declarations that a book or pamphlet is free of doctrinal or moral error. No implication is contained therein that those who have granted the *Nihil Obstat* and *Imprimatur* agree with the contents, opinions, or statements expressed.

Send all inquiries to:

BENZIGER PUBLISHING COMPANY
15319 Chatsworth Street
P.O. Box 9609
Mission Hills, California 91346-9609

Second Edition

**ISBN 0-02-651214-9**

Printed in the United States of America.

1 2 3 4 5 6 7 8 9   BAW   98 97 96 95 94

Benziger

# The Meaning of Church

*The Church is a mystery. It is a reality imbued with the hidden presence of God. . . . As a divine reality inserted into human history, the Church is a kind of sacrament. Its unique relationship with Christ makes it both sign and instrument of God's unfathomable union with humanity and of the unity of human beings among themselves. Part of the Church's mission is to lead people to a deeper understanding of human nature and destiny and to provide them with more profound experiences of God's presence in human affairs.*

*National Catechetical Directory, #63*

*Written by*
**Peter Ries**

*Consultant*
**David Riley**

BOOK TWO

## In this chapter you will:

- Recognize the Church as a living, growing community.
- Identify how the Church acts in the modern world.
- Explore effective ways of teaching about the Church.

Second Edition

## If Only It Were That Simple

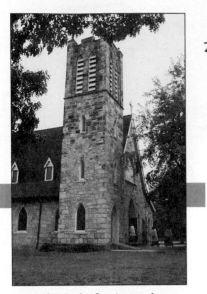

▲ *What is the first image that comes to your mind when you hear the word "church"? What are some other images that can also be connected to that word?*

Our job, our mission, was to put a man on the moon. If we were doing this project now instead of back in the 1960s we would be talking about putting a person, or an astronaut, or a man and woman on the moon. But back in 1960 it was definitely a man. No apologies needed, either. That's simply the way it was back then.

As I was saying, our mission was, as President Kennedy charged us, "to put a man on the moon by the end of the decade." We had a little more than eight years to accomplish this task, but we were ready for the challenge. We were all sure of ourselves, knew our abilities, and considered ourselves the most creative, the "best" scientists in the world. We proved ourselves up to the challenge when in 1969 Neil Armstrong took his "one small step for man, one giant leap for mankind."

That July night was the culmination of years of hard work and billions of dollars spent on research. To think what would happen if we put that kind of money and personnel into solving the problem of AIDS or world hunger, or even improving education in this country. . . . Oh, well, I've done it again. Every time I try to make a point I digress. Please forgive me if I wander a bit from the story.

I guess just about every person alive on this planet today knows that a man has walked on the moon. Heck, we are Americans, we even drove a "car" on the moon. But that came later. Like I was saying, most people know that we've been to the moon and back, but I would bet you that very few people truly understand the difficult challenges we faced to get there.

As you can well imagine, the task before us was very complex and full of problems. We had been working with rockets for nearly twenty years before we successfully put an object in space. They kept blowing up on us. We had just solved that problem for small rockets, but could we build ones big enough to get us to the moon? If we got them there, how would they get back? What would the astronauts wear? What would they eat? What would they do on the moon? That's just a few of the questions people asked. I became painfully aware that unless we could reach a common understanding of what we were really trying to do, we would fail miserably. That's when I called the meeting.

That meeting room in Washington, D.C. during the summer of 1961 was a total madhouse. We started on a Monday morning each with our own agenda. Although everyone in that room was supposedly working toward the same goal, you never would have guessed it from the first day's conversations. The rocket people wanted their needs to be the first priority, for without a propulsion unit the mission would never get off the ground. The life scientists argued that their needs took priority. What good would it do to get to the moon only to have the astronauts perish on the way? You even had the public relations people arguing that the most important aspect of the mission was selling it to the American public, for how else could political support be generated and funding approved?

By Wednesday, we had made great strides towards resolving our problems. The rocket engineers were talking with the life science people to determine maximum weights and minimum comforts. The public relations people were working with the practical science crowd to identify benefits that would result from this project.

There were many different ways of seeing this mission and each person had approached it from the viewpoint of his or her own specialty. They quickly realized that this approach would not get the project going. What they had arrived at was the understanding that each point of view was grounded in reality and was part of the whole picture.

Each was right; the project had no chance of succeeding without them. It also had no chance of succeeding with them unless they were willing to grant others the same understanding that they wanted for themselves. When they realized that their ideas and needs would be given a fair hearing, the bickering stopped, misunderstandings became less frequent, and people became extremely excited.

By Friday afternoon, we were heading home prepared to share our new-found attitudes with the people at work. This was a major change and it didn't happen all at once. We had to develop a communal sense of purpose and common values. We had to become a community united around our mission.

The meeting didn't solve all of our problems. There were still all of the technical, scientific, and engineering issues to address, but the first hurdle was past. Despite our different perspectives on our mission, we had agreed that only by working together could we be successful.

*Memo*

How would you define the mission of the Church?

## YOUR STORY

Just as there are many different aspects necessary to make a space launch successful, there are many different aspects necessary for the Church to fulfill its mission. Take a few moments here to consider what Church means to you.

1. What do you think when you hear the word church?

_____

2. How has your understanding of the Church changed over time?

_____

3. How do you see the Church working effectively to accomplish its mission?

_____

4. In a few words describe (a) joys, (b) a burden, (c) freedoms, and (d) responsibilities that come with belonging to the Church.

a. _____

b. _____

c. _____

d. _____

## The Church

*When Jesus went into the region of Caesarea Philippi he asked his disciples, "Who do people say that the Son of Man is?" They replied, "Some say John the Baptist, others Elijah, still others Jeremiah or one of the prophets." He said to them, "But who do you say that I am?" Simon Peter said in reply, "You are the Messiah, the Son of the living God." Jesus said to him in reply, "Blessed are you, Simon son of Jonah. For flesh and blood has not revealed this to you, but my heavenly Father. And so I say to you, you are Peter, and upon this rock I will build my church, and the gates of the netherworld shall not prevail against it."* (Matthew 16:13–18)

When asked to describe the Church many people would respond, "Some say the Church is an institution, others say that it is the People of God, while others call it a place for worship," in a way very similar to the disciples' responses to Jesus. Their responses name aspects of how they experience the Church. As the *Catechism of the Catholic Church (750–776)* points out, the word church is used to designate a wide variety of views:

* the liturgical assembly.
* the local community of believers.
* the universal community of believers.

The Church is, of course, all of these things. As the People of God, the Church draws its life from the liturgy (especially the Eucharist) and prayer. The Church lives in the world primarily through local communities, under the leadership of the Holy Spirit, as members of the universal body.

The word church comes from the Greek *ecclesia*, meaning "to call out of" into an assembly. Members of the Church are those who are called to "belong to the Lord." But even this definition isn't enough. The *Catechism* also refers to the Church as:

* A mystery, a complex and rich reality.
* The "People of God" united in Christ. (See *Lumen Gentium, The Dogmatic Constitution of the Church* 9–17.)
* A sacrament of Christ extending his life and ministry through history.
* An instrument of intimate union with God and unity with the whole human race.
* A body that exists to accomplish the Father's plan of salvation.
* A body whose mission is to proclaim and do the works of the kingdom.
* A sign pointing to the kingdom, not the kingdom itself.

### A Changing Reality

Throughout a lifetime, a person changes many times. And yet there is always a thread of continuity that makes the person unique and identifiable from birth to death. You are still essentially the same person you were when you took your first steps, first rode a bicycle, grew and changed through school and adolescence, and emerged into adulthood. You have been shaped continually by the many decisions you've made and the experiences you've had.

The Church is no different. Its understanding of itself, too, has grown and changed over the years, while continuing to be the Church founded at Pentecost. Language, practice, and customs have changed repeatedly, yet the Church's nature and mission remain the same. *The Church exists to preserve the authentic teachings of Jesus and preach the Gospel to the ends of the earth.*

The Church is always striving to grow in its understanding of God's will and in its expression of God's love. It is important to remember when reading history that contemporary knowledge and attitudes cannot be imposed on earlier times. The Church is the bearer of a timeless, divine message, but it presents that message so that it can be understood by each succeeding generation. Because the Church is made up of people who understand life and the Gospel according to their changing lives, the extrinsic parts of the Church—its mentality, choice of words, and customs—change with the times. But its intrinsic Spirit and mission never change.

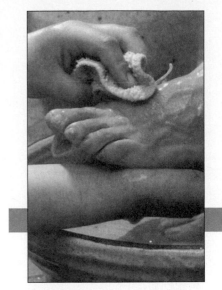

▲ *Members of the Church are challenged to preserve the authentic teachings of Jesus. One of these teachings is that we must be willing to serve others.*

## Marks of the Church

Each time you proclaim the Nicene Creed (usually at Sunday Eucharist), you profess a belief in those elements that describe the Church that we call "marks." We say that the Church is one, holy, catholic, and apostolic. These marks are not static achievements that show what the Church has done. Rather, the marks are signs that challenge us.

- **One.** The first mark is a plea for unity. The Church must constantly work to bring all people together in Christ.

- **Holy.** The Church is called to be filled with the grace of God both as a communal body and through its individual members. It is only to the degree that we are holy that we can hope to fully live the other marks of the Church.

- **Catholic.** The word catholic means "universal." This mark demands that the Church be open to people of every culture and tradition. As the author James Joyce is reported to have said about the Church, "Here comes everybody!"

- **Apostolic.** The Church holds firm to the witness and teaching of the apostles. It is from this solid foundation upon which the Church builds its tradition.

## Pause a Moment . . .

- How can the marks of the Church both point the way to holiness and still identify our imperfect Church today?

- Pick one of the ways that the *Catechism of the Catholic Church* describes the Church and explain what the description means to you.

## B.C. *(Before the Council)*

In the era immediately prior to the Second Vatican Council, the Church understood itself in terms quite different from those that we might choose today. The Church described itself as being a *visible, hierarchically structured society* that existed to pass on the *truths* by which we are *saved* and the *means to accept them* and *fulfill their ethical implication.* Its mission was to bring all people into union with Christ through the Catholic Church.

1. **A Visible Society:** an institution with government and law.
2. **Hierarchically Structured:** control was emphasized; people in authority (pope, bishops, priests) had the right to govern and the laity had the obligation to obey.
3. **Truths:** it alone was the "sole depository of truth."
4. **Saved:** salvation came through Christ's redemption and through the Church.
5. **Means to Accept Them:** through the sacraments and devotions, the Catholic Church provided its members with the means which would bring salvation.
6. **Fulfill Ethical Implications:** morality meant keeping the commandments and the laws of the Catholic Church.
7. **Bring all People into Union:** all people were called to salvation through the Catholic Church, which alone contained the truth.

Prior to the Second Vatican Council:

- The "body of Christ" and the "kingdom of God" were taken to be synonymous with the Catholic Church.
- The phrase "Catholic action" meant the work of the local bishop in which the laity participated.
- Emphasis was placed on a "heavenly reward." Little value was placed on an individual's role in the world.
- A high value was placed on uniformity. Diversity from the norm for any reason was frowned upon.

*Pause a Moment . . .*

- What do you know of the Church prior to the Second Vatican Council? How would you describe life in the Church then?
- In your opinion, what were the strengths and weaknesses in the Church's definition of itself prior to the Second Vatican Council?

## The Church in the Modern World

In 1961, Pope John XXIII decided to open the windows of the Church and let in some "fresh air." He announced the convening of a Second Vatican Council to begin the following year. The Council became the catalyst for a new awareness and insight into the meaning of being a Catholic in the modern world. It used different terms to describe the Church.

*Lumen Gentium, (The Dogmatic Constitution on the Church),* identifies the Church as a *mystery,* as a *community of people* called to *proclaim the Lordship of Jesus* which it does *sacramentally.* The Church's mission is to *bring about God's kingdom* by publicly acknowledging that Jesus is Lord and that the kingdom has been inaugurated in him. The Church struggles both to *bring about the kingdom* and to model the kingdom in its own behavior.

1. **Mystery:** the Church cannot be adequately defined. The Church continually grows in its understanding of itself.
2. **Community of People:** the Acts of the Apostles provides the model: people who organized their community around love and concern for one another.
3. **Proclaim the Lordship of Jesus:** Jesus is at the center of the meaning one finds in life. He gives life its basic sense of direction.
4. **Sacramental Profession:** ritual and sacramental acknowledgment that Jesus is the center of life. We are called to holiness *as a people*. Just as we come to faith through a community—our family and parish—we grow in faith the same way.
5. **Bring about God's Kingdom:** the material world is an important part of God's kingdom. The implication is that working for peace and justice is a vital Christian responsibility.

The "kingdom of God" cannot be used as a substitute for the word "church." The kingdom is more than a place or set of behaviors. It is the time when God's promises are fulfilled. God's kingdom includes all humanity and is not limited only to those who profess membership in the Catholic Church.

The Catholic Church is called to be: a **witness** to the kingdom—people should see evidence of what the kingdom is from the life of the Church—and the **means** of bringing the kingdom into existence on earth. Through both of these functions the Church is called to be a servant for others. As Richard McBrien says:

> It is the kingdom and not the Church which is at the heart of the preaching of Jesus and at the core of his entire ministry. . . . To the extent that men are reconciled one to another in Christ, the kingdom is in process. The Church exists to proclaim the rightness of this process, to cooperate in its realization here and now, and to offer itself as a model of genuine human community. (Do We Need the Church? p. 114)

## Pause a Moment . . .

- How does your understanding of Church change depending on the language used to describe it?
- How is the image of Church described by the Second Vatican Council different from the image described before the Council?

# Changes in Attitude

The Second Vatican Council returned to the ancient Church—back to the first several centuries—to recover aspects of the tradition that had become misplaced. The Church's teaching expanded as new emphasis was placed on these long-forgotten truths. The return to the ancient traditions also allowed the Church to escape from its attitude of "us against the world" to the new attitude of "a pilgrim people in the world." It's this change in attitude that is most clearly experienced in the Church today. Let's review other key points in the Church's understanding of itself.

## The New Commandment

The community of believers was of one heart and mind, and no one claimed that any of his possessions were his own, but they had everything in common. With great power the apostles bore witness to the resurrection of the Lord Jesus, and great favor was accorded them all. There was no needy person among them, for those who owned property or houses would sell them, bring the proceeds of the sale, and put them at the feet of the apostles, and they were distributed to each according to need.

(Acts 4:32–35)

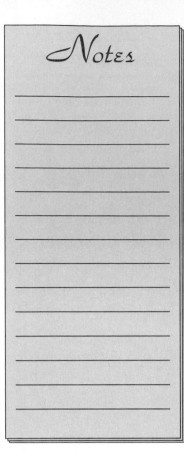

*Notes*

_____
_____
_____
_____
_____
_____
_____
_____
_____
_____
_____
_____

## Authority as Service

Authority in the Church exists to benefit the entire community, not just to control it. People in authority facilitate the growth of the faithful through their ministry and personal witness. First used during the Middle Ages, the title for the pope—"the servant of the servants of God"—describes the true purpose of authority in the Church.

## Collegial Organization

The Church may now be best described as collegial. The key terms are "co-responsibility" and "shared decision-making." The pope, as bishop of Rome, is first among equals with all of the other bishops. He shares with them the responsibility for teaching and directing the Church. He supports the bishops in their role and unifies them by his office of universal pastor. In turn, the bishops serve the priests, religious, and laity in their respective ministries. Each ministry involves a role important to the body of Christ and no one can do without the other.

The image used to describe this reality is the "People of God." All of the baptized are members of the People of God. Each is called to minister to others and to proclaim the Gospel according to his or her own ability and calling in life. Each shares equally in the life of Christ.

The wheel is an apt symbol to use here. A wheel is made up of many spokes (pope, religious, married people, bishops, priests, single people, lay ministers) all working in unison for the benefit of the whole. No one spoke is more important than the others. However, the entire wheel is weakened if it is missing any one of its spokes. The hub from which each spoke radiates is Christ. The wheel is held together by its rim: Scripture and tradition.

## The Role of Tradition

The tradition of the Church is both an inheritance handed down and a growing, living presence. Tradition and Scripture are the two sources of Revelation that we possess. In contrast to the canon of Scripture, which was finalized in the early second century, the Church's tradition is still being formed. Every generation will add something new to the Church's tradition, another way of understanding God's revelation.

Through its teaching ministry, the Church *preserves* the tradition of the faith and helps in its ongoing *development*. As the tradition is applied to contemporary issues, new ways of explaining it are developed. In this way the teaching ministry both protects and extends the tradition.

Every Christian shares in the Church's teaching ministry by reason of his or her baptismal call to share God's love through words and actions. Each of us, through the witness of our life or our role as parents, transmits God's Word to others. All parishioners have the responsibility for building up the parish and promoting the effectiveness of its teaching ministry, whether they are aware of this responsibility or not.

## The Importance of Diversity

The Church's understanding of itself has moved from a stress on uniformity to an emphasis on unity. Although these words are commonly used interchangeably in our society, they are quite different. Uniformity means doing things alike; unity means to be one as a collective of individuals, but not necessarily identical.

The Church recognizes the need for each culture to shape its own local community and local worship while holding firm to the universal aspects of faith. Such diversity is seen as a great treasure.

## Catholic Action

Catholic action is now commonly described as *Christian service.* Each Christian, by reason of Baptism, is called to serve the Christian community and the world at large.

While Catholics still look to the bishop or other members of the clergy for guidance for ministry, each person is empowered to live out the Gospel "works of mercy" on his or her own. Living out the Gospel message is the responsibility of all of the People of God. No one needs the permission of others to engage in ministry. However, the hierarchy can and does offer education and support regarding the most appropriate ways of giving service to others.

## Ecumenism

The Second Vatican Council's Decree on Ecumenism clearly states that Jesus founded only one Church. Therefore, we can speak about the "Church" of Christ and the Christian denominational "churches," one of which is the Roman Catholic Church. The points of unity among these churches are basic—we profess belief in the same God, the same Christ, the same Bible, and the same baptism.

The Council admonished Catholics, saying that too many of us do not live up to the splendor of our religion, causing the radiance of the Church's face to shine less brightly in the eyes of non-Catholics. The first ecumenical action for Catholics to consider, therefore, is to reflect more clearly the teachings of Christ in their daily life. We are called to pray for our separated brothers and sisters and work to inform them about the Church. We are also called to joyfully acknowledge and esteem the traditions and teachings of Protestant and Orthodox churches. The phrase "the Body of Christ" is to include all Christians, not only Catholics.

### REFLECTION

1. Describe your impression of the Church since the Second Vatican Council.

_____

_____

2. What is the vision of Church described by the Second Vatican Council?

_____

_____

3. St. Augustine said, "Many whom God has, the Church does not have; and many whom the Church has, God does not have." What does Augustine mean by this statement? How does it apply to the Church in our time?

_____

_____

---

## The Church Teaches

The restoration of unity among all Christians is one of the principal concerns of the Second Vatican Council. Christ the Lord founded one Church and one Church only. However, many Christian communions present themselves to men as the true inheritors of Jesus Christ; all indeed profess to be followers of the Lord but they differ in mind and go their different ways, as if Christ himself were divided. Certainly, such division openly contradicts the will of Christ, scandalizes the world, and damages that most holy cause, the preaching of the Gospel to every creature. *(Decree on Ecumenism, #1)*

## Understanding the Mystery

The full nature of the Church is truly a mystery. As is the case with all mysteries, no one definition or explanation can fully capture the entire message. In fact, direct language about the Church may often confuse the discussion and not enlighten the listener. As holographic images becomes more three-dimensional when looked at indirectly, so it is with the Church. Images may reveal the mystery better than a logical presentation.

*Lumen Gentium,* paragraph 6, says, "the inner nature of the Church is now made known to us in various images." The Church is:

- "a sheepfold, whose sole and necessary gateway is Christ."
- "a flock . . . at all times led and brought to pasture by Christ."
- "a cultivated field . . . planted by the heavenly cultivator."
- "the building of God" often called "the household of God in the Spirit, the dwelling-place of God," and "the holy temple."
- "our mother," the "spotless spouse of the spotless lamb."

There is another aspect of the mystery of the Church. Although it is guided by the Holy Spirit, the Church is still an organization involving human beings. As a human institution, the Church must wrestle with the many gray areas or problems that human organizations face. What, for example, should be the role of women in the Church? Or how should bishops be elected? These questions and many more like them are part of the Church's human heritage.

## Appropriate Models

Just as the Church itself uses images to try and explain itself, theologians have developed tools for understanding this mystery. Perhaps the most helpful of these tools was developed by Father Avery Dulles, S.J., in the book, *Models of the Church.* In this groundbreaking work, Father Dulles pointed out six ways or *models* that we can use to describe the life of the Church:

1. Institution
2. Mystical Communion
3. Servant
4. Herald
5. Sacrament
6. Community of Disciples

These models are not meant to define what the Church is or how it must be. Instead, they express how we experience it. None of the models is complete in and of itself. Each has various traits, assets, and liabilities. Let's look at each of these in more detail.

**Institution.** When we experience the Church as Institution we are most often in contact with its structure in some way. We may be grappling to

▲ *A wheel is an apt symbol for the Church as the People of God: many people working in unison around Christ the hub. No one person is more important than any other person.*

understand the Church's teaching about divorce and remarriage or trying to remember whether it has been an hour between eating and receiving communion. For many people, the Church as Institution is their strongest impression of the Church.

**Assets.** This model can be a source of support, providing stability and security in a changing world. This is the organizational—the parish office, diocesan chancery, and Roman Curia—side of Church.

**Liabilities.** When people think of the Institution, they tend to think of the "professional members," the clergy and professed religious. This can lead to clericalism, an uninvolved laity, and an overly legalistic view of the Church.

**Mystical Communion.** The Church as Mystical Communion model recognizes the Church as "the Pilgrim People of God" *(Lumen Gentium, VII)*. It is the body of Christ to which we belong. This model is biblically based, concerned with unity, and inclusive: everyone is invited, and so is ecumenical.

**Assets.** This model recognizes that the mission of the Church belongs to all of its members.

**Liabilities.** This model can seem wishy-washy. Because the Church's mission is everybody's business, everyone can escape responsibility for not acting because it is not any particular individual's responsibility.

**Servant.** The Servant Model of Church captures the side of the Church that is concerned for justice. Traits of this model include responding to a call from God, doing good works, and acting in service.

**Asset.** The challenge of justice upholds the Christian obligation to serve others, and thus fosters the idea of the family of God.

**Liabilities.** This can reduce the Christian mission to doing good works, and thus lose the sense of Christian witness and ministry. There may be little room for prayer or proclamation of the Word; a service provider without a religious purpose.

**Herald.** A herald is a messenger or proclaimer of the news. The Herald Model of Church is concerned with the proclamation of the Gospel. It is through the sharing of the Scripture story that people gather together into community; it is the Scripture that calls people to faith.

**Assets.** This model focuses on the Church's role as the announcer of the Good News of Jesus, calling people to a life of prayer and justice.

**Liabilities.** The danger is matching deeds to words. With such a strong emphasis on the importance of Scripture, the other font of Revelation—tradition—can be overlooked. The important role that legitimate authority has in the Church through tradition can seem to be replaced by appeals to the Bible.

**Sacrament.** Catholicism is very much a sacramental Church. In fact, the Church is the primordial sacrament of Christ from which all other sacraments flow.

**Assets.** This model presents the Church as an effective sign to the world: God is present with us through the sacraments. Through the sacraments, people concretely share in the Church's mission. The sacramental model projects a sense of vitality.

*Notes*

**Liabilities.** Although the celebration of the sacraments is always a communal activity, they are experienced by individuals. This model can lead to a personal understanding of salvation—"Just you and me, God"—ignoring the communal dimension of the Gospel entirely. What takes place within the church building—ritual—can become more important than living faithfully in the world.

**Community of Disciples.** At the center of this model is the ongoing relationship between Christ and the Church. Knowing Jesus' story and interpreting it for daily living are key elements.

**Assets.** This is a very inclusive model. With Jesus at the heart of the community, everyone has a responsibility to proclaim the Good News. To fulfill this obligation, every member of the community must also be a learner and continue his or her own personal growth in faith.

**Liabilities.** This model has the tendency to develop a bad case of the "warm fuzzies." The general "feel good" nature of this model can prevent many of the difficult day-to-day decisions from taking place. It cries out for its missing institutional side to handle the day-to-day management details.

## Where Do You Stand?

As you can see, there are many valid ways of thinking about the Church. Each of the models presented above offers an authentic but incomplete way of viewing the Church. The Church is everything described in each of the models *combined* and more.

Father Dulles's models provide us with important tools for understanding the Church. They help us recognize the "filter" we use when we think about the Church. Rarely does anyone see the Church only through one model; usually we recognize various aspects of the Church. However, it is not unusual for one model to dominate our thinking at times. For example, if you primarily think of Church in terms of authority and rules, you may be operating out of the Institutional model. If you primarily look at Church as the center of worship and the celebration of the Eucharist, you are most likely operating out of the Sacramental model. Neither one is right or wrong, nor is one better or worse than the other. They are both incomplete ways of understanding the Church, but they are a start.

How you fulfill your role as a catechist will undoubtedly be shaped by your model of Church. By recognizing this, you can seek balance in your lesson planning. For just as no one model can adequately describe the Church, no one model can adequately meet the learning needs of your students.

*Pause a Moment . . .*

- What are some additional images that you could use to describe the Church? List a few of them and explain why each image is important.

- These six models cannot fully capture the mystery of Church. What other suggestions would you have to describe how you experience the Church?

# Part IV Response

## Teaching about the Church

Your assumptions and beliefs about the Church will influence the spirit and tone of your teaching. Because you, as the catechist, are an important part of the students' religious education experience, you need to clarify your own understanding of the Church.

Your assumptions about the Church will also influence the religious education methods you use with your students. For example, if you believe that the laity should keep to a passive role in Church matters except to follow the directives of priests and bishops, you will probably tend to use the lecture/listen catechetical method. Conversely, if your idea of the Church is a community of people exercising their baptismal responsibilities, you may be inclined to use the inquiry/challenge approach.

Another important aspect of your students' religious education is their involvement in the parish. You should consider how the parish influences their attitudes about the Church and strive to build respect for the Church and a willingness to participate in the life of the community. Accept any complaints about the parish compassionately and help your students to find ways to build a better community by their involvement.

▲ *How might this person's work help to build up the Body of Christ?*

### Primary Grades

- Present the Church as God's family to which the students belong by their baptism. Help them to see that God's family lives and cares for them, and helps them to know and follow Jesus. Tell them that the parish is a gathering place for God's family, where we come together to be fed by Jesus' own body and blood, and to hear God's word.

- Ask the students to imagine their parish church on Sunday morning. When they open the doors, who do they see inside? Have the students put the name of each person they saw inside on a narrow strip of colored paper. Make a chain link of each piece of paper, then have the class connect them into one large chain.

- Display a large outline of a body, perhaps tracing the outline of one of your students. Put the outline on a bulletin board or on the door of your classroom. Invite your students to decorate the outline with snapshots of themselves, or pictures they draw of themselves, or outlines of their hands or their hand prints made with washable paint. Invite them to add the photos or names of other people who belong to the Body of Christ, such as their families, your pastor, their friends, and the pope.

- Write on a poster the various work that members of the Body of Christ do: teach, pray, take care of others, work for peace, and so on. Let the students find or draw pictures of these activities for the poster.

## Middle Grades

Students in these grades are interested in learning facts.

- Use vocabulary words and facts from each unit or class about the Church as questions for a tic-tac-toe game.

- Explain to your students that they are members of the Church, and that they have privileges and duties as members of this community. Tell them about the people who lead the Church and their roles, explain the organization of the Church, and tell them where important Church centers are located.

- Explain the corporal and spiritual works of mercy. Have your students make a large scrapbook, making a page for each of the works. Students are to be aware of events and activities in the parish that relate to the works such as a Thanksgiving clothing collection, soup kitchen involvement, or prison ministry. Students can report on what they have found and then record it in the scrapbook.

- Discuss with the students the main vocations or roles within the Church. Have them list the main activities for each of these vocations: marriage, priesthood, single life, religious life. Divide your class into four groups and have each design a shield or crest for a particular vocation. Be sure they divide their shield or crest into four sections. In addition to drawings, encourage the students to use various colors. Provide colored paper, scissors, paste, felt tip markers, and poster board. Each group should explain its finished shield to the rest of the class. Display the shields on the wall in the hallway outside your classroom.

## Junior High

These students may be at the stage where they begin questioning their involvement with the Church.

- Present the Church as a people set apart, called by the Father to live courageously and lovingly.

- Inspire them with stories of Christian heroes who made difficult choices and who changed their world for the better.

- Show them how they can become more involved in their parishes and church organizations to bring about change in their world. Arrange for opportunities in which small groups of your students can work along with adults in some of these activities.

## High School

You can begin to deal with the more subtle aspects of the Church at this age.

- Explain that members of the Body of Christ are born of water and the spirit, and are called to love and serve others.

- High school students are beginning to solidify their values regarding Church. This does not mean that all of them are actual church-goers, but the values developed now will influence how they participate in Church as adults. Point out how the Holy Spirit animates the Church and helps its members to fulfill their Christian responsibilities.

- Have your students develop a list of questions about some of the basic notions of Church presented in this chapter. Have them interview adults (parish council members, other parish leaders, catechists, and parents) about their understanding of Church. Have the students compare their findings with the rest of the class.

- Form the class into small groups to prepare for and debate two sides of a characteristic of the Church (e.g., uniformity verses diversity).

- Have your class read 1 Corinthians 12 and discuss what gift or contribution they feel they can make to the Church.

## Adults

Ask adults to think through the implications of the Second Vatican Council's vision of the Church and apply it to their families. How can they create the atmosphere of a "little church" to their careers? How do they give witness to Christ by the way they do business? through their civil relationships? Are they bringing the love and mercy of Christ to the groups to which they belong?

▲ *The Catholic Church often refers to itself as a part of God's family. In what ways is the Church like a family?*

### IMPLICATIONS

1. Reflect on your style as a catechist and the teaching methods you use. How is your catechetical style shaped by your preferred model of Church?

_____

_____

_____

_____

2. Review the various aspects of how the Church understands itself. Choose two aspects and describe how you would present them to your students.

_____

_____

_____

_____

3. Find two examples in your teacher's manual of how the Church is presented to your students. Describe the examples and the methods suggested for presenting those examples. What model of Church is reflected in this method?

_____

_____

_____

_____

# Notes

_____
_____
_____
_____
_____
_____
_____
_____
_____
_____
_____

## Prayer Response

Read this passage from First Corinthians to yourself. What does it mean for you to be part of the living body? How are you called to serve the body of Christ? Pray for God's blessing so that you may be faithful in your role.

*As a body is one though it has many parts, and all the parts of the body, though many, are one body, so also Christ. For in one Spirit we were all baptized into one body, whether Jews or Greeks, slaves or free persons, and we were all given to drink of one Spirit.*

*Now the body is not a single part, but many. . . . If the whole body were an eye, where would the hearing be? If the whole body were hearing, where would the sense of smell be? But as it is, God placed the parts, each one of them, in the body as he intended. If they were all one part, where would the body be? But as it is, there are many parts, yet one body.* (1 Corinthians 12:12–14, 17–20)

## BIBLIOGRAPHY

Diocese of Baker, Oregon. "Our Catholic Creed," *The DeSales Program.* Los Angeles: Franciscan Communications, video.

Dulles, Avery. *Models of the Church.* New York: Doubleday, 1974.

Flannery, Austin, O.P., ed. *Vatican Council II. The Conciliar and Post Conciliar Documents.* Grand Rapids, MI: Wm. B. Eerdmans Publishing Co., 1992. Confer "Dogmatic Constitution on the Church," "Pastoral Constitution on the Church in the Modern World," and the "Decree on Ecumenism."

Friedman, Greg, O.F.M. "What Does It Mean to 'Be Church'?," *Catholic Update.* Cincinnati: St. Anthony Messenger Press, May, 1985.

McBrien, Richard P. *Catholicism.* Minneapolis: Winston Press, 1980.

_____. *Do We Need the Church?* Harper & Row, 1969.

_____. "What Is 'The Kingdom of God'?," *Catholic Update.* Cincinnati: St. Anthony Messenger Press, September, 1980.

_____. *Where Is the Church Going?* Allen, TX: Tabor, video.

_____. *Who Is a Catholic?* Denville, NJ: Dimension Books, 1971.

National Conference of Catholic Bishops. "Chapter IV, The Church and Catechesis; Chapter V, Principal Elements of the Christian Message for Catechesis." *Sharing the Light of Faith.* Washington, DC: USCC Publications, 1979.

*What Catholics Believe About the Church.* Redemptorist Pastoral Communications, video.

"Understanding of Church," *What is Catholicism?* Allen, TX: Tabor, video.

*Nihil Obstat*
The Reverend Gregory A. Banazak, S.T.D.

*Imprimatur*
The Most Reverend Kenneth J. Povish, D.D.
Bishop of Lansing
May 13, 1994

The *Nihil Obstat* and *Imprimatur* are official declarations that a book or pamphlet is free of doctrinal or moral error. No implication is contained therein that those who have granted the *Nihil Obstat* and *Imprimatur* agree with the contents, opinions, or statements expressed.

Send all inquiries to:

BENZIGER PUBLISHING COMPANY
15319 Chatsworth Street
P.O. Box 9609
Mission Hills, California 91346-9609

Second Edition

**ISBN 0-02-651216-5**

Printed in the United States of America.

1 2 3 4 5 6 7 8 9   BAW   98 97 96 95 94

## Benziger

# Sacrament

The sacraments, symbolic actions which effect what they symbolize, celebrate the coming of the Spirit at special moments in the life of the community of faith and its members, and express the Church's faith and interaction with Christ. The Church celebrates the mysteries of God's presence through the word, bread, wine, water, oil, and the actions of the ordained ministers and the people.

*National Catechetical Directory, #114*

Written by
**Peter Ries**

Consultant
**David Riley**

## In this chapter you will:

- Consider the signs of God's presence in the world.
- Compare definitions of what "sacrament" means.
- Review suggestions for teaching the sacraments to students.

Second Edition

## A Symbol of Hope

▲ *What are some ways that you experience the touch of God in your life? How are these moments sacramental?*

On his daily trip to morning Mass at St. Anselm's downtown, Sonny passed St. Monica's parish. Even though St. Monica's was only a few blocks away from his house, Sonny never thought of it as his parish. It was way too "far-out" for his tastes. First Friday devotions had been replaced with "Prayers for Justice," and the stations of the cross had given way to a daily soup kitchen. A retiree, Sonny was not going to waste his precious time on foolishness like that. He'd had enough of "bleeding heart do-gooders" during his years in the construction business. People had to be willing to work; they couldn't expect handouts all of their lives.

In late January, St. Monica's opened its church basement as a sanctuary to the homeless people of the city, since the city shelter was overcrowded and nighttime temperatures were becoming dangerously cold. Sonny was furious that St. Monica's had invited such people into the neighborhood, and he let his family know how he felt. He quickly sent off an angry letter to the pastor (with a copy to the bishop and the diocesan newspaper) expressing his unhappiness at this decision.

When the fire happened, Sonny knew he had been vindicated. It had been a mistake, he told people, to invite the homeless into the church in the first place. "A disaster waiting to happen," he said, "that's what it was. I'm not surprised that someone fell asleep with a lit cigarette. Frankly, they were lucky the damage was confined to the church building and the rectory, and that nobody died." Sonny felt compassion for the people of the parish, but he also felt smug in his attitude.

A few weeks later, Joe, a friend from the construction business stopped by to visit. Joe had been asked by the parish council to convert St. Monica's old boiler building into a makeshift soup kitchen. People were still hungry and the parish wanted to continue feeding them.

Joe asked if Sonny, a darn good contractor in his day, might be willing to lend a hand. "We sure could use your expertise," Joe said.

> *"We have a lot of willing volunteers, but no one knowledgeable enough to oversee a job this complicated. You should see it, Sonny. This place is a pit. The only floor in the building is ten feet underground. They want to add stud walls from floor to ceiling, and add a floor at ground level. Sounds like the type of challenge you always enjoyed."*

Sonny thought to himself that this was "typical" of St. Monica's, always having its hand out. What he told Joe was that he really wasn't able to help just then because of other commitments. Joe persisted, however, and finally talked Sonny into inspecting the building and making suggestions about how the job might best be completed.

Sonny was not prepared for what he saw when he got to the parish. To his amazement, the place was alive with people able and willing to work. Several area supply companies had donated building materials. An architect was doing the plans *pro bono*. Someone had donated a walk-in cooler, and several workmen were donating their labor. Sonny met one man unloading a truckload of ceramic flooring tiles into the fenced-in storage area. His brother had been down on his luck, the man said, and had been treated with dignity at the soup kitchen. This was his way of giving something back for his brother.

Grudgingly, Sonny prepared his report and gave it to Joe. He had fulfilled his obligation and was now free from that crazy place. A few days later, though, Sonny found himself back at St. Monica's watching the construction. He never intended to help, but before he knew it, he was reading blueprints and directing workers. Before long he was working on the building every day.

People who knew Sonny saw a wonderful change take place in him as he worked on this project. When he described the kitchen to people, his eyes glistened and danced. He stopped making negative remarks about the work of St. Monica's. One morning, he opened the paper to see his face on the front page. A photographer had taken his picture as he worked on the building. Although he never would have sought this kind of attention, it was obvious that he was very proud of it.

Sonny was touched in ways he couldn't imagine by the generosity and selflessness this project awakened in people. To him, the boiler building became a symbol of God's involvement in his life and the lives of others. He couldn't help feeling that they were doing something more than putting up a building; they were participating in the work of God.

**MEMO**

Where and when do you recognize the presence of God in your life?

## YOUR STORY

The touch of God often comes when we least expect it, and almost always in surprising ways. God cannot be limited by our needs or controlled by our actions. Anytime we experience the touch of God, we are touched by grace and our lives are changed, just as Sonny's was. For Sonny, his work on this project was "sacramental," an experience of God through physical signs.

Answer the following questions.

1. What comes to mind when you hear the word sacrament?

_____

_____

2. What were you taught about sacraments as a child?

_____

_____

3. What does Sonny's story tell you about sacraments?

_____

_____

_____

_____

## Signs Everywhere

We mark our lives by important events: the birth of children, the giving and receiving of forgiveness, marriage, the reception of Holy Orders, times of sickness and times of healing. Catholics recognize God's special presence in these and other significant events. Sacraments both mark and deepen these key moments of Christ's actions among his people. Sacraments are the signs of Christ living among us. To understand this better, let's first look at the importance of signs in our lives.

### Give Us a Sign

Signs are everywhere around us. Billboards advertise cars, cigarettes, and liquor. Traffic signals direct our driving. Numbers show us where to find our destination. Sirens warn drivers to let emergency vehicles pass. Even the cover of a book contains a sign, the title. It tells us what we can expect to find inside the book, but is not, itself, the book. The same is true for traffic signals. A red light or a stop sign indicates that we should stop. When we see them as drivers, we know that we should step on the brake pedal. The signs do not themselves stop us, they merely alert us to the need to stop.

We use words, images, and sounds to indicate meaning. In fact, all communication takes place through signs. As people learn the meaning of signs, they can respond appropriately to various situations.

There are several types of signs. Some, like the traffic signal are arbitrary. Other signs not only point to something, they are actually part of the message they indicate. For instance, not only does a kitchen aroma indicate the presence of food, the aroma is a vital part of one's experience of food.

There is also a third group of signs that is quite different from the other two groups. This group is known as *symbols*. Symbols are both indicators of a reality and expressions of the very reality they indicate. A handshake can be a sign of an agreement between friends, but more significantly, it can be an aspect of that agreement or friendship happening now.

### More to Life than Meets the Eye

The world of symbols is grounded on the belief that there is more to life than what meets the eye; what you see is sometimes *not* what you get. Symbols are our "windows" into the world of the sacred. Through symbols we can experience God's presence and understand God's love.

Symbols function like metaphors. They allow us to take something we know and understand, like the warmth of fire, and use that meaning to express a more complex reality, like the warmth of friendship. Symbols mean something to us because they are familiar; we are comfortable with them.

Symbols are also ambiguous: they can have multiple meanings. Fire can both protect us from freezing and destroy us as we sleep. Water can wash us clean and satisfy our thirst—we cannot live without it—yet it also can wipe out years of labor in a flash flood.

▲ *Signs are everywhere: traffic signals, billboards, even junk mail. Some signs, however, carry a greater significance than others. They become symbols for us of a greater reality.*

Understanding symbols is important because sacraments belong to this group of signs. In Baptism, not only does water point to cleansing and new life; cleansing and new life happens as the sacrament is celebrated. In the Eucharist, the meal not only indicates spiritual nourishment and union with Christ and the community; it really does it.

## Pause a Moment . . .

- Discussions about signs and symbols can sometimes be very confusing. Take a moment to think about how you understand these two words.

- Make a list of the many signs you see during the day. How many of the items on your list are symbols? Discuss your list with a friend.

## Symbols in Our Tradition

Scripture tells of the origins of sacramental signs. The power of Yahweh is never seen as limited. Yahweh is described as being with the Hebrew people even in a foreign land (Egypt). God expresses compassion for their plight, and acts to deliver them from their enemies. Yahweh's presence among the Hebrews was sacramental. Moses and Aaron were signs of God's leadership. In the many signs and wonders God worked through Moses and Aaron, the Hebrews came to understand God's will and experience God's saving power. This notion of God is expressed in the name "Emmanuel," meaning "God with us."

### A Life-giving Word

In ancient times, people regarded the author of a message to be present when his or her words were spoken by the messenger. To welcome the messenger and graciously accept the message was to honor the sender. Jesus is both God's messenger and God's message. Jesus is the ultimate sign of God's loving presence among people. Jesus is the ultimate sacrament of God: "Whoever has seen me has seen the Father" *(John 14:9b)*. In Jesus, through his words and deeds, we experience God directly. Jesus is the true living image of the Father.

After his death and resurrection, the early Christians experienced the presence of Christ in the coming of the Holy Spirit, in their loving communities, in serving the needs of others, in their liturgies with the reading of the Scriptures and the letters from the Apostles, and in the breaking of the bread. The Church became a symbol of Christ continually present in the world. We can truly say that the Church is the sacrament of Christ!

The Church is the sacrament that makes Christ present in the world for all time. This sacramental reality has one final step. Each of us as members of the Church is called to be a sign of Christ's presence in the world today. In that sense, each of us is a sacrament as well.

### Mysteries of Faith

Symbols help us "peek" into the world of mystery. There are several senses to the word "mystery," but it is the Greek sense of *mysterion* that is important to our discussion of the sacraments. Mysterion means *something*

## Expressing God's Greatness

In order to appreciate the sacraments, a person has to have a faith in the sacramentality of all of creation. The world is not evil, as some would have it. The world is full of God's glorious love seen and experienced in creation.

> *The world is charged with the grandeur of God.*
>
> *It will flame out like shining from shook foil.*
>
> (Gerard Manley Hopkins *God's Grandeur*)

Two books recently translated into movies attempt to capture the power of God working through the normal things of creation. In both *Babette's Feast* by Isak Denison and *Like Water for Chocolate* by Laura Esquivel, God's power is experienced through food, especially through the love put into preparing it for the table. In *Like Water for Chocolate*, a woman's passion is put into her cooking. Everyone who eats of her food is also aflame by her passion.

What would happen if we allowed ourselves to fully partake of the Lord's grace through the sacraments. Would we not truly drown in the waters of Baptism only to be resurrected by God's power. Would not the gifts of the Spirit send us boldly forth on mission? Would not the healing power of God bring people new hearts, new limbs, and new lives?

*that is partially hidden and yet, partially revealed as well.* Our word sacrament takes its meaning from this Greek word.

Because sacraments bring us into contact with the divine life, their full meaning is partially hidden. What is revealed is that in each sacrament God is present through the ritual action that embodies the people's faith.

The effectiveness of the sacraments begins with God's reaching out to us through symbolic actions. Through these actions we are offered the gift of God's loving presence grace. But to be fully realized, a sacrament's effectiveness depends upon our capacity to understand and enter into it, and our ability to respond to it appropriately. Sacraments cannot magically effect a change in a person's life; the person must also act in response to the sacrament.

The reality and understanding of the sacraments are basic to everything we are as Catholics. We are a sacramental Church. We believe that we experience God directly through ordinary symbols. Catechists, particularly, need a clear grasp of these basic principles about sacraments in order to maintain a balanced view of revelation, the nature and role of the Church, and the content of religious education.

## *Pause a Moment . . .*

• How are you called to be a sign of Christ present in the world?

• What does it mean to say that Christ is the sacrament of God and that the Church is the sacrament of Christ?

# Seven Sacraments

Jesus said and did many things during his life, many of them having to do with aspects of everyday life. After his death and resurrection, the Church continued to remember the Lord's words and actions and celebrated them with believers at special times. Over several centuries, the Church recognized seven of these occasions to be signs of God's grace essential to Christian life. These signs have become known as the seven sacraments.

Although the sacraments come from Jesus' words and actions as found in Scripture, the seven sacraments, as we know them, were not formalized until the thirteenth century. All seven mysteries of Jesus have been celebrated from the earliest days of Christianity, but it was only at the Second Council of Lyons in 1274 that a profession of faith expressing belief in the seven sacraments was formally accepted by the Church.

The Council of Trent (1545–1563) restated that there were seven, and only seven sacraments. These sacraments, moreover, conferred the grace they signified in virtue of the rite itself and not solely because of the faith and trust of the recipient. This means that neither the sinfulness of the priest nor the sinfulness of the recipient can interfere with God. When a person celebrates a sacrament (even unwittingly), God's grace will be given and will act in some way upon the receiver.

The Second Vatican Council called for the renewal of all of the sacramental rites. Each has now been revised. The revised rites have reintegrated Scripture readings into the celebration of each sacrament, along with the understanding that sacraments are our response to a relationship with God.

## A Brief History

The seven sacraments are:

1. Baptism
2. Confirmation
3. Eucharist
4. Penance (also known as the Rite of Reconciliation)
5. Anointing of the Sick
6. Holy Orders
7. Marriage

Sacraments are sometimes grouped according to their function. The sacraments that *initiate* a person into the faith community are Baptism, Confirmation, and the Eucharist. The sacraments that bring *healing* are Penance and the Anointing of the Sick. The sacraments of *vocation and commitment* are Holy Orders and Marriage.

**Sacraments of Initiation.** Baptism, Confirmation, and Eucharist are called the sacraments of initiation because it is through the celebration of these three sacraments that a person becomes a full member in the Christian community. (See *Catechism of the Catholic Church,* #1212–1412.) A person states their belief and is baptized, is confirmed as a member of the community, and shares the common meal around the altar of the Lord.

Through the symbolic action of immersion in water, we ritually celebrate the death and resurrection of Jesus. In Baptism, Christ joins us to himself as members of his Church. Through Baptism, Christ forgives all of our sins and gives us a new life of grace. We are pledged to the Christian community by this sacrament and the Christian community commits itself to us. Baptism is celebrated only once. Through Baptism we share in the priestly, prophetic, and kingly nature of Jesus. We are obligated by Baptism to live out our share in the kingdom of God.

Confirmation is a ratification of the Spirit given in Baptism, signified by the bishop anointing a person with oil. One is "sealed with the gifts of the Spirit" through the sacrament. Christ gives a fuller outpouring of the Spirit so that a person has a deepened power to maturely understand and profess one's faith. Confirmation strengthens an individual to live out his or her baptismal promises, and prepares one for the missionary dimension of the baptismal commitment.

Today, through the *Order of Christian Initiation of Adults,* Confirmation and Baptism are celebrated during the same ceremony for adults and children of catechetical age. For people baptized as infants, Confirmation is generally celebrated anytime from second grade to young adulthood, depending on the diocese. Confirmation is celebrated only once.

Eucharist completes the act of initiation. In the Eucharist we share fully in the Body and Blood of Christ, really present to us. The consecrated bread and wine may still look and taste like bread and wine, but they are truly Jesus. We receive both the Body and Blood of the Lord whether we receive just the consecrated host or cup. The fullest sign is receiving both.

The Eucharist is more than the consecrated bread and wine, however. Jesus is present in the assembly, in the ritual prayers and gestures, and in the readings. Each time we share in the Eucharist we give thanks to God and reconfirm our commitment as disciples of Jesus. We leave the

## The Church Teaches

The purpose of the sacraments is to sanctify people, to build up the body of Christ, and finally, to give worship to God. Because they are signs they also instruct. They not only presuppose faith, but by words and objects they also nourish, strengthen, and express it; that is why they are called "sacraments of faith." They do indeed impart grace, but, in addition, the very act of celebrating them disposes the faithful most effectively to receive this grace in a fruitful manner, to worship God duly, and to practice charity.

It is therefore of capital importance that the faithful easily understand the sacramental signs, and with great eagerness have frequent recourse to those sacraments which were instituted to nourish the Christian life. (*Constitution on the Sacred Liturgy, #59*)

## The New Commandment

"Amen, amen, I say to you, no one can see the kingdom of God without first being born from above." Nicodemus said to him, "How can a person once grown old be born again? Surely he cannot reenter his mother's womb and be born again, can he?" Jesus answered, "Amen, amen, I say to you, no one can enter the kingdom of God without being born of water and Spirit."

(John 3:3–5)

Eucharistic table (the altar) dedicated to proclaiming the Good News and extending the Lord's ministry to those we meet.

The Eucharist may be received daily (twice in special situations). There is no need to receive the sacrament of Penance prior to receiving the Eucharist unless one is guilty of serious sin. The Eucharist itself forgives all other sins.

**Sacraments of Healing.** Penance and Anointing of the Sick are the two sacraments of healing. (See *Catechism of the Catholic Church,* #1420–1532.) Both of these sacraments can be celebrated as often as needed. Although commonly referred to today as the sacrament of reconciliation, the Church still officially calls it the sacrament of Penance celebrated through the Rite of Reconciliation.

The sacrament of Penance brings about the forgiveness of sins committed after Baptism. Through the sacrament the penitent both obtains God's forgiveness and is reconciled with the community which has been injured by that person's sin. The priest acts as a representative of the forgiving Christ and of the reconciling community.

Anointing deepens our trust in God, strengthens us against temptation and anxiety, and may even restore physical health. The sacrament asks the sick to associate themselves with the passion and death of Christ, offering their suffering for the good of the community. Although anyone who is sick may receive this sacrament, it is usually only celebrated when one is seriously ill.

**Sacraments of Commitment.** Marriage and Holy Orders celebrate the commitment that people make to a way of life, but they do more than that. The *Catechism of the Catholic Church* calls them "sacraments in service to communion." (See #1533–1666.) By celebrating these sacraments, those consecrated to the common priesthood through Baptism and Confirmation receive a special consecration to a particular way of life:

- Orders, to feed the Church in Christ's name, and
- Marriage, the partners are fortified for the dignity of family life.

As with all of the sacraments, but particularly with these two, people celebrate God's call to be of service to others.

## Nature of the Sacraments

**All revelation is sacramental.** In union with the early Christians, we affirm today that the seven sacraments are various manifestations of the one sacrament—Jesus Christ.

We cannot control the sacraments nor their effects on us. We can prepare ourselves and our students to be open to receive God's goodness in order to experience God most fully. The grace of the sacrament is always greater than our ability to receive it or act upon it. That is the true mysterion!

## Pause a Moment...

- Discuss with a friend how the celebration of the sacraments have changed during your lifetime.
- Which sacrament has the most personal meaning for you? Explain your reasons.

# $\mathcal{P}$art III $\mathcal{D}$iscovery

## Understanding the Sacraments

Most American Catholics who were alive before the Second Vatican Council studied religion from the *Baltimore Catechism*. Sacraments were defined in that catechism as "outward signs, instituted by Christ to give grace." Today the *Catechism of the Catholic Church* describes the sacraments as powers that go out from the ever-living and lifegiving Body of Christ, actions of the Holy Spirit at work in his Body which is the Church (See *#1116*).

Definitions present only summary statements of something's meaning. There are many other things to consider when looking at the sacraments.

### Beyond Description

The experience of God through the sacraments defies description. One always has to say, "It is this, but so much more!" The sacraments, to be understood, have to be experienced and lived—nothing less. The descriptions of the sacraments that are being offered here, can in no way fully describe the essential mystery of our sacramental encounter with God. However, just as maps can help us find our destination more easily, words and ideas about the sacraments can help us to form the right attitudes that will predispose us to fully experience the grace God gives through the sacraments.

### Relationship with God

One idea highlighted today is that the sacraments express our relationship with God. Sacraments make Jesus present in a special way and as part of our relationship with God. Each sacrament reflects a specific aspect of that relationship: *new life in Baptism, responding to mission in Confirmation, nourishment through the Eucharist, forgiveness in Reconciliation, and healing love in the Anointing of the Sick.*

Sacraments are also described as *times of meeting which produce change.* A meeting with Christ is an opportunity for growth through his freely offered gift of grace. Our part in the situation is whether or not we accept the gift and allow that growth to happen within us.

### Witness of Jesus

The sacraments are manifestations of the basic *values of Jesus.* During his public life, Jesus often spoke of the need to be born again and receive new life (**Baptism and Confirmation**), to forgive and be forgiven (**Reconciliation**), to celebrate the covenant with God and nourish one's relationship with the Father (**Eucharist**), to commit oneself to one's spouse wholeheartedly (**Marriage**), to teach the Good News, lead God's People, and serve others (**Holy Orders**), and to pray for physical and spiritual healing (**Anointing of the Sick**).

We have the sacraments because of what Jesus did. We recognize the importance of these actions because we see the power of God witnessed through them. When we celebrate the sacraments we continue Jesus' ministry.

$\mathcal{N}$otes

_____
_____
_____
_____
_____
_____
_____
_____
_____
_____
_____
_____
_____
_____

## Celebrations

Sacraments are *celebrations of important human events.* For example, Baptism ritualizes the meaning of birth and the decision to become a member of God's Family; Marriage ritualizes the meaning of committed love; Reconciliation, the meaning of forgiveness; Holy Orders, the meaning of service; Anointing of the Sick, the meaning of suffering and death. By celebrating God's presence in each of these events, we grow in faith, hope, and love.

Sacraments are *community celebrations,* not just transactions between individuals and God. They are Christ united with his body, celebrating life.

The community element of sacrament creates difficulty for some people today. They do not see how sin needs to be considered anything more than private. They cannot understand why the baptism of infants is dependent on the lived faith of the parents. Without an experience and understanding of community, much of the significance of these celebrations is lost for the ordinary Christian.

Because of the communal element of the sacraments, the family may be the most appropriate place for sacramental preparation. It is usually in the family that people learn best about relationships, experience forgiveness, celebrate a meal, express love, and are nurtured. Our understanding and communication of the sacraments should start with these common, familiar experiences. In addition, the more the family is involved in preparing for the sacraments, the more effective the catechesis will be.

## Moments of Transition

Sacraments are not something that happen once and then are finished. Sacramental life is, instead, very much an ongoing process, just as any other relationship would be. Sacraments are not *received* as if they were some type of holy thing. Sacraments are not things. Rather, sacraments mark transition points in our relationship with Jesus and the Church, the beginning of a new dimension of our life with Christ. They are grace-filled moments that we live continually.

The sacraments never bless the *status quo,* however. They always mark moments of major transition. In this way they are counter-cultural. When we celebrate a sacrament we admit to needing the something more we find in Jesus. We make a commitment to making a difference in the world by proclaiming the "Good News" of salvation.

### *Pause a Moment . . .*

- How do sacraments express something about your individual relationship with God?

- How are we called to ministry through the sacraments?

## *Symbols and Rituals*

A birthday party is full of symbols that communicate how we feel; not only about the guest of honor, but also about life itself. Signs of a birthday celebration are a cake with candles, balloons and streamers, the singing of

"Happy Birthday," and maybe even funny looking hats. These signs remind you of the sweetness of family and friends, the special love you share together, and the gift of life itself. With minor variations, this ritual is celebrated many times every day in essentially the same way all over the world.

Rituals, like birthday parties, help people to celebrate. They give people a familiar feeling that helps them to join in with the fun. Rituals use symbolic action—words, movement, objects, and space all woven together—to express our experience of the unseen or the otherwise inexpressible moments of life. Certainly, in celebrating our experience of God, words alone cannot convey all we know, feel, or mean to say. We use symbols to convey our real experience of God.

For example, the ritual for the sacrament of Baptism includes:

- a prayer of exorcism,
- flowing water,
- the presentation of a lighted candle,
- clothing the newly baptized with a white garment, and
- anointing.

Christ is present in the entire experience, but we specifically identify his presence through the symbol of water. The water is a symbol that the person is dying to the sin of his or her old life and rising to a new life in Christ Jesus. The baptized person is both washed clean and reborn. Water is truly a powerful symbol.

▲ *Families come together to celebrate important times in our lives: birthdays, weddings, graduations, funerals. As a Church family we celebrate those same events through the sacraments.*

## *Pause a Moment . . .*

- What are some of the normal rituals that you do everyday (e.g., when you get up in the morning what do you normally do?). How is this ritual different from religious rituals?
- How have sacramental celebrations led you to realize the value of the faith community in your life?
- How do you experience the reality of a sacrament beyond the moment you receive it?

### REFLECTION

1. Where and how do I experience Christ in my daily life? What helps me to perceive his presence? What hinders me from this presence?

_____

_____

2. How do I experience Christ's presence in my worship and celebration of the sacraments?

_____

3. How do I experience Christ in my parish community?

_____

_____

## Suggestions for Teaching the Sacraments

The sacraments are basic to the Christian life and are taught at most grade levels. Religious educators often talk about *remote* and *immediate* sacramental preparation. Remote preparation recognizes that all catechesis should prepare one for the sacraments. In immediate catechesis, catechists address a particular sacrament prior to its reception. Students also need to continually review the meaning of the sacraments. As they grow older, students acquire a greater capacity for understanding the deeper significance of the sacraments.

Taking its lead from the catechetical process developed in the *Order of Christian Initiation of Adults,* sacramental catechesis is usually separated into two periods: pre-sacrament and post-sacrament. Pre-sacrament is the catechesis that takes place before a person celebrates the sacrament. Post-sacrament is what occurs after receiving the sacrament.

Pre-sacrament catechesis intends to help the students understand what it means to have a special relationship with Christ and how that relationship is celebrated in the sacrament. Post-sacrament catechesis helps the students express their experience of the sacrament and then understand more about that experience. While this model works most effectively with adults, it is also the model used in the Children's Catechumenate.

### Effective Methods

What follows is a presentation of methods for presenting the sacraments. Each method relates to a particular aspect of an individual sacrament. The approaches described may not be appropriate for your students. You may feel that ideas suggested for one sacrament and age level will work well for you with another sacrament and age level.

**Baptism.** Baptism calls for a variety of objects when it is celebrated. Bring into your class the candle, white garment, holy oils, and book of prayers used in the sacrament. Read to the class the prayers that accompany the use of these articles. For the primary grades, ask students to bring in their baptismal certificate and candles and celebrate their baptismal days. For older students, teach the order of ceremonies in a baptism and then role-play the ceremonies. As you go through the ceremonies, explain the meaning of the objects used. If you are not sure about the meaning of the objects, have the sacristan at your parish or a priest give an explanation and demonstration of these materials for your students. Older students and adults can analyze and discuss the implication of their baptismal promises.

The theme of belonging can be used at any age level. To explore the meaning of belonging, direct various exercises that have some students as part of a group and others trying to get into that group. Ask older students to compare the fact that God invites everyone into the Christian family besides the fact that certain people are sometimes excluded from their groups at school.

▲ *In many cultures, special bread is baked to celebrate a particular season of the year. How can you use this tradition to catechize about the Eucharist?*

**Confirmation.** Confirmation can be used as an occasion to talk about the Holy Spirit received in Baptism. To little children, present the Holy Spirit as the way God is present with us since Jesus returned to the Father. For teens, describe God's Spirit as a friend to guide them through the difficult situations of daily life. Teens can analyze how Confirmation is both a final "yes" and a first "yes" to Jesus' invitation to follow him. If possible, have an older student who has received Confirmation talk to younger students about the sacrament. Adults can discuss the unpredictable ways the Holy Spirit leads them and presents opportunities for growth.

Confirmation is a sacrament of empowerment. It challenges people to accept the call to discipleship that comes with baptism. Students particularly need opportunities to witness their faith through service to others.

**Eucharist.** Stories about Jesus wanting to be with his friends can be very satisfying for younger students as well as for teens. To describe the meaning of Jesus' presence in the Eucharist to young children, give the example of a child coming home from school to find a plate of cookies with a note from his or her parent. For older students, use the example of receiving a gift with a letter from a friend. In each of these examples, we experience the presence of another person in some way.

Nourishment is another theme of the Eucharist. Students can describe the various ways they need Jesus' help. Older students can discuss the value they see in their friendship with Jesus. Adults can discuss various aspects of nourishment and how each applies to the Eucharist.

**Penance.** Reconciliation touches everyone's life in some way. You can compare Jesus' constant willingness to forgive with the difficulty we sometimes have in forgiving others. Have the students mention examples of how they need forgiveness. Use films or videos that deal with the idea of sorrow and forgiveness. Students might enjoy a tour and explanation of the Reconciliation Room.

**Anointing of the Sick.** Anointing of the Sick gives occasion to teach about the meaning of suffering. Although suffering cannot be totally explained, you can include in your discussion the fact that we are part of a developing creation that God has given us a free will. Describe what a communal celebration of this sacrament is like. You might bring in and display the Holy Oils used in this sacrament. For teens and adults, the prayers used with the sacrament can be good discussion starters.

**Orders.** Holy Orders is one of the sacraments of vocation and commitment. Perhaps you can have your parish priest describe what drew him to the priesthood and what his ministry is like today. You might have your students make a collage depicting the various activities of a priest. Often, this sacrament is used as an occasion to present the vocation of religious life for men and women.

**Marriage.** Marriage is the other sacrament of vocation and commitment. Have your students describe the various ways Christ showed concern for his people. List these on the chalkboard. Then ask the students to describe similar ways married people care for each other.

Have married people come to your class to describe the meaning of this sacrament from their experience. Show how married love is a form of ministry. Have your students analyze the marriage vows to see how they manifest the idea of commitment and ministry. Because of the prevalence

*Notes*

of divorce, you will need to deal with your students' questions about the inability of some people to have a lasting marriage.

## Age-Appropriate Suggestions

The following are some additional ideas for presenting the sacraments to various age levels. Check off the ones you think might be useful with your students.

**Primary Grades.** As you teach about any of the sacraments during these early years, bring in the symbols that express them. Let the children touch the oil, hold a baptismal candle, eat a piece of bread, and take a sip of wine. These concrete signs will make it easier for younger students to retain what they learn.

Have the students make dictionaries of these signs, with each entry including a picture of the sign, the word that goes with the sign, and, on the back, the sacrament that uses the sign.

Another way to work with these signs and learn about the sacraments is to have each student make a sign of their choice out of clay. Have them explain their sign to the class. Have the class say in which sacrament the sign is used.

**Upper Elementary.** Prepare a worksheet for your students with one column listing the seven sacraments and a second column listing a major symbol for each. Randomly mix the items in each column. Then have your students draw a line between each sacrament and the symbol that pertains to it.

When teaching about a particular sacrament, use a bulletin board to illustrate some main ideas about it. Put up, in large letters, the name of the sacrament. Have your students make drawings that depict major signs used in the sacrament.

Have your students look in magazines for pictures that might relate to the meaning or signs of the sacrament. Have them add their pictures to the bulletin board. At the end of class, or at the beginning of your next class, use the bulletin board as a tool for reviewing the main point of the lesson. Repeat this process for several of the sacraments.

**Junior High.** Use a pair of dice to review the sacraments. Assign a number from 1 to 7 for each of the sacraments. An 11 or 1 equals a 1; 2 or 12 equals a 2; 8, 9, and 10 do not count. Pass the dice to the first student. The number that student throws indicates the sacrament he or she must say one thing about. Pass the dice on to the next student, and so on.

Prepare a learning center for 4 different sacraments in the 4 corners of your classroom. Collect any articles or chapters of religious education textbooks, posters, pictures, and a copy of the ritual prayers used in the celebration of the sacrament. Divide your students into 4 groups. Have each group spend 15 minutes in each learning center listing as many things as they can about each sacrament. Every 15 minutes call time so all the groups can switch to the next corner (sacrament). Have the group bring their reports to the next class and use their material as an approach to the study of each of those sacraments.

**High School.** Have each student interview several adults in the parish about their earliest recollection of specific sacraments. Adults could be parish council members, education commission members, other catechists, parents. Have the students give a class report on what they heard.

Have these students talk to younger students about Confirmation or have them help young students in some aspect of their preparation for First Reconciliation or First Eucharist.

Ask the students, in groups, to work on the following question: "If God asked you to create an 8th sacrament, what part of life would you relate it to?"

## *Pause a Moment . . .*

- What other approaches do you use for teaching the sacraments? Share one of yours with a friend.
- What do you think is the importance of separating sacramental catechesis into pre- and post- phases? How would this change affect your teaching?

▲ *The exchanging of vows and rings are several of the symbols of the sacrament of Marriage. How could you use these symbols to teach about the sacrament?*

### PRACTICE FOR YOU

**1.** Locate in your teacher's manual and student text two examples of how a sacrament is presented to the students. Record these examples here.

| Sacrament | Methods Used to Present It |
|-----------|---------------------------|
| _____ | _____ |
| _____ | _____ |

**2.** Select one sacrament and design an approach for presenting it to your students. Feel free to refer to your teacher's manual, student text, and other resources to formulate your design.

Parts of Presentation: _____

Methods: _____

Materials Needed: _____

Time Available: _____

**3.** Describe what the sacramental presence of Jesus might mean to each of the following people:

**(a)** Seven-year-old or ten-year-old _____

**(b)** Fifteen-year-old _____

**(c)** Young adult _____

**(d)** Parent _____

**(e)** Senior citizen _____

## Memo

In light of what I have learned about sacraments, I want to keep the following considerations in mind:

## Prayer Response

Read the following Scripture passage. Reflect on the people, places, and situations that bring you the presence of Christ. Ask for the help you need to make Christ present in the world.

*As they approached the village to which they were going he gave the impression that he was going on farther. But they urged him, "Stay with us for it is nearly evening and the day is almost over." So he went in to stay with them. And it happened that, while he was with them at table, he took bread, said the blessing, broke it and gave it to them. With that their eyes were opened and they recognized him, but he vanished from their sight.* (Luke 24:28–31)

## BIBLIOGRAPHY

Bausch, William J. *A New Look at the Sacraments.* Revised edition. Mystic, CT: Twenty-Third Publications, 1983.

*Catechist Magazine,* Vol. 27, No. 4, January, 1994.

DeAngelis, William. *Seven Sacrament Workshops.* Mystic, CT: Twenty-Third Publications, 1989.

DeGidio, Sandra. *Sacraments Alive: Their History, Celebration and Significance.* Mystic, CT: Twenty-Third Publications.

Flannery, Austin, O.P. *Vatican Council II.* Grand Rapids, MI: Eerdmans Publishing Co., 1992.

Hill, Brennan. *Rediscovering the Sacraments: Approaches to the Sacred.* New York: Sadlier, 1983.

National Conference of Catholic Bishops. *Sharing the Light of Faith: National Catechetical Directory for Catholics of the United States.* Chapter III, "Revelation, Faith, and Catechesis;" Chapter V, "Principal Elements of the Christian Message for Catechesis;" Chapter VI, "Catechesis for a Worshipping Community." Washington, DC: USCC Publications, 1979.

*Religion Teacher's Journal,* Vol. 27, No. 7, January, 1994.

Sacred Heart Kids' Club. *Sacraments,* Don Bosco Multi-Media, videos.

*Sacraments for Children: An Introduction to the Seven Sacraments for Middle-Grade Children,* Liguori, MO: Redemptorist Pastoral Communications, video.

*Sacraments: Loving Actions of the Church.* New York: Ikonographics, videos for middle grade students.

*Nihil Obstat*
The Reverend Gregory A. Banazak, S.T.D.

*Imprimatur*
The Most Reverend Kenneth J. Povish, D.D.
Bishop of Lansing
May 13, 1994

The *Nihil Obstat* and *Imprimatur* are official declarations that a book or pamphlet is free of doctrinal or moral error. No implication is contained therein that those who have granted the *Nihil Obstat* and *Imprimatur* agree with the contents, opinions, or statements expressed.

Send all inquiries to:

BENZIGER PUBLISHING COMPANY
15319 Chatsworth Street
P.O. Box 9609
Mission Hills, California 91346-9609

Second Edition

**ISBN** 0-02-651215-7

Printed in the United States of America.

1 2 3 4 5 6 7 8 9   BAW   98 97 96 95 94

**Benziger**

# Preparing for Public Worship

['T]he liturgy is the summit toward which the activity of the Church is directed; it is also the fount from which all her power flows. For the goal of apostolic endeavor is that all who are made [children] of God by faith and baptism should come together to praise God in the midst of [the] Church, to take part in the Sacrifice and to eat the Lord's Supper.

*The Constitution on the Sacred Liturgy, #10*

Written by
**Peter Ries**

Consultant
**David Riley**

BOOK TWO

## In this chapter you will:

- Explore the nature of rituals and symbols and how they function in the liturgy.
- Describe the relationship between liturgy and catechesis.
- Outline ways to help students celebrate more fully as members of their parish assembly.

Second Edition

▲ *The family grieved at Grandpa's death. They did not know what to expect without him. But Grandma insisted on carrying on the family tradition. They would still gather, conduct the same rituals, and remember the stories that made them a family.*

## Continuing the Tradition

Everybody loved Thanksgiving at Grandma and Grandpa's house. Nearly eighty, they were so vital and loving that they lifted the whole family's spirits. After the meal, with turkey and Grandpa's special stuffing, people played games, watched football on TV, compared notes on the year that had gone by, and generally had a great time.

One Thanksgiving tradition that everyone looked forward to was having coffee from the special coffee service on Thanksgiving night. Grandma would put on the coffee, and everyone would gather in the living room. After the coffee was served, Grandpa would tell stories about the family. He would tell the grandchildren how their parents met, what they were like in school, and who they dated before they were married. He would describe distant relatives and their experiences. He also would talk about famous events from the past and how the family was touched by them. Grandpa was a great storyteller, and listening to him was part of what made Thanksgiving so special.

After the stories, everyone in the family was given an opportunity to share their plans for the future. This was the time when wedding plans were announced, investment ideas debated, and job opportunities critiqued. Grandpa never gave advice, although he never suffered foolish ideas either. Grandpa's favorite question at this time was "How will this make you a better person?" Everyone soon learned to include that answer in their announcement. If someone forgot, the rest of the family would ask it in unison.

When Grandpa died, Grandma missed him deeply, and grieved for him for most of the year after his death. The entire family felt a real sense of loss. As Thanksgiving drew near, the family wondered how they could possibly celebrate without him.

The oldest daughter offered to host Thanksgiving at her house, but Grandma insisted that they gather where they always had. So everyone arrived, ate the Thanksgiving dinner, watched football, and chatted. But there was a hesitancy in their conversation, a reluctance to mention anything about Grandpa or about past Thanksgivings that might muster new rounds of grief. It was as if the family had suffered a great injury to its foot, and was afraid to put too much weight on it for fear of reinjuring it.

No one had given much thought to what would happen at the end of the day. But as the sky grew dark and the grandchildren came in from their play, the adults started wondering what they would do when the time for coffee came. They knew that, more than anything else, time would summon memories of Grandpa, and no one was sure how they would handle them.

Before anyone could decide on a course of action, Grandma emerged from the kitchen carrying the coffee service. She had a smile on her face. "Sit down, everyone, and have some coffee," she said.

When everyone had a cup, the room feel silent, as if people were waiting to see what would happen next. After a few minutes, Grandma spoke. "I want to tell you a few things," she said, "about Grandpa." During the next hour or so, she brought Grandpa back to life for them through her stories. How they met at a USO dance, when he tried to impress her with his moves on the dance floor. She told them how Grandpa had once been a teacher in a one-room schoolhouse, something none of them had known. She told the story of how he once had faced down an angry crowd who wanted to run him out of town because of his race.

On and on the stories continued. The family's anxiety melted away in their retelling, and the family's grief gave way to laughter and happy memories. They were even able to share their plans for the coming year without too many people being asked Grandpa's question.

As the evening ended, Grandma made an announcement.

> *As much as I want to, I can no longer host the Thanksgiving dinner. But that won't stop this family from celebrating. Every year we will still gather, drink from the coffee service, and share our stories. We will continue to announce our plans and challenge our intentions. My wish is that long after I die, this family and its traditions will continue. When you share this special time together, remember who you are and how we got here.*

As the years went on, Thanksgiving continued to be a special day. The entire family would gather, share the meal, and tell their family stories. As they reminisced, it was as if Grandpa was right there with them. They could almost see him, sitting in his favorite chair, laughing along with everyone else, ready to ask, "How will this make you a better person?"

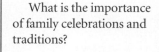

What is the importance of family celebrations and traditions?

## YOUR STORY

The family in this story enjoyed a special ritual on Thanksgiving day. What events do you celebrate with rituals in your family? For each event, tell how and why you and your family celebrate. Do you associate the celebration with any objects (like the coffee service in the story)? What are their significance?

**1.** Birthdays, anniversaries, or other events

How? _____

Why? _____

Symbolic objects? _____

Significance? _____

**2.** How are these family ritual celebrations similar to participating in the liturgy?

_____

_____

**3.** What are your expectations of the Eucharistic liturgy? What do you hope to gain from your participation in it?

_____

_____

## A Celebrating Community

If your pastor called and asked to visit you in your home, what would be your reaction? Most of us would probably agree to host him and then make every effort to prepare: housecleaning, planning menus, shopping for food and decorations, and perhaps even organizing some type of family presentation. Undoubtedly, you would want to celebrate, in some way, his visit to your home.

Human beings are social animals. We look for opportunities to gather with other people. Usually, these gathering will involve a celebration. Like the family in the opening story, we gather with relatives to celebrate special occasions, such as birthdays or graduations. In many ways, celebrations hold our families together.

Our celebrations are not limited to family occasions, national holidays, or sports championships. We also gather on a regular basis as a people of faith to offer communal worship and celebrate the greatness of God. We do this most regularly on Sundays when we assemble to celebrate the Eucharistic liturgy.

The National Catechetical Directory expresses it this way:

> *The Church is a worshipping community. In worship, it praises God for His goodness and glory. It also acknowledges its total dependence on God, the Father, and accepts the gift of divine life which He wishes to share with us in the Son, through the outpouring of the Spirit. Worship creates, expresses, and fulfills the Church. It is the action in and by which men and women are drawn into the mystery of the glorified Christ.* (#112)

It is worth examining the meaning of the above statements to arrive at a better understanding of the place of worship in the Church.

1. *We are totally and utterly dependent on God.* This is the primary attitude about worship upon which all subsequent conclusions rest. This is the reality that prompts our worshipful response.

2. *God invites us to share in the divine life.* Jesus commanded that the Gospel be preached to the ends of the earth and to anyone who would believe the Good News and reform his or her life.

3. *Those who accept God's invitation form a community of believers.* Jesus intended his followers to work together and worship together. The community of believers is called the *Church.*

4. *The Church is present where people worship God through Christ by the power of the Holy Spirit.* Jesus said, "Where two or three are gathered in my name, there am I in their midst" *(Matthew 18:20).*

5. *The Church acknowledges its total dependence on God in a spirit of thanks and praise.* The whole vision of life taught by Jesus is that one who surrenders to the Father's love and cooperates with others in building his kingdom on earth is doing God's will. Worship expresses the Church.

▲ *What are some of the ways your family celebrates special occasions? In what ways are these celebrations important to your life as a family?*

6. *The faith, hope, and love of individual members are built up through the worshipping community.* Only through other people do we first hear the Gospel message and receive the help necessary to follow Christ.

> *It is he who gave apostles, prophets, evangelists, pastors, and teachers in roles of service for the faithful to build up the body of Christ, until we become one in faith and in the knowledge of God's Son, and form that perfect man who is Christ come to full stature.* (Ephesians 4:11–13)

7. *Worship should prepare people for their work in the world.*

In the Church there is both private worship and public worship. Private worship is covered in more detail in the chapter on prayer. This chapter will look at the public worship of the Church known as liturgy. There are several forms of public worship which the Church considers liturgy:

1. **The Eucharistic celebration** (commonly called the Mass, from the Latin *missa*, which means dismissal, or better yet, being sent out);

2. **Celebrations of the sacraments** or any rites pertaining to a sacrament (such as the rites of the catechumenate);

3. **Funeral services;**

4. **The taking of religious vows;** and

5. **Praying the Liturgy of the Hours.**

For more information on this, see *The Constitution on the Sacred Liturgy,* Chapters III and IV.

In their document *Environment and Art in Catholic Worship,* #9, the American bishops describe liturgy this way:

> *Each Church gathers regularly to praise and thank God, to remember and make present God's great deeds, to offer common prayer, to realize and celebrate the kingdom of peace and justice. That action of the Christian assembly is liturgy.*

## Symbol and Ritual

Liturgy—Greek for "the work of the people"—involves:

1. gathering the community,

2. hearing God's word, and

3. performing the appropriate, necessary rituals.

Look again at the opening story of this chapter. The people in the story, too, gathered as a family, told family stories, and performed the prescribed ritual. Although their family celebration was important, it was not worship. Their intention was not to celebrate or offer praise to God, but to enjoy each other's company and reunite the family.

Obviously, not every celebration that uses ritual is an act of liturgy or worship. But to understand how and why we celebrate the liturgy as we do, it is important to start with an understanding of ritual.

Rituals play an important role in the lives of most people. As human beings, we have a basic need to express through ritual various aspects of our lives, including our experience of God. These rituals give meaning, movement, sound, and color to realities which often need more than words to describe them. They include things as mundane as where people sit around the dinner table, to how we welcome new life into the world.

---

### The New Commandment

*For I received from the Lord what I also handed on to you, that the Lord Jesus, on the night he was handed over, took bread, and after he had given thanks, broke it and said, "This is my body that is for you. Do this in remembrance of me." In the same way also the cup, after supper, saying, "This cup is the new covenant in my blood. Do this as often as you drink it, in remembrance of me." For as often as you eat this bread and drink this cup, you proclaim the death of the Lord until he comes.*

(1 Corinthians 11:23–26)

Ritual allows us to establish the proper climate for celebration, helping us feel comfortable when we are engaged in something greater than ourselves. It establishes that everything is okay, and we can now continue with the important event. Ritual also serves to connect the present with the past. Through ritual we can identify what it means to be family, we can identify with generations who have gone before, and we can relive memories, in a sense, making them come back to life. Ritual offers proven ways of expressing what we think, feel, or believe.

All cultures, in every age, have used rituals in this way. When the Jews settled in their new land after leaving Egypt, they remembered their experience of God freeing them from slavery and entering into a covenant with them. They celebrated these experiences with prayer, ritual, and the symbols of the Passover meal. The blood of the lamb on their doorposts had saved them in Egypt. The lamb in the Passover meal reminded them of God's continuing saving presence in their lives.

Jesus memorialized his life and death the night before he died in the prayers and ritual actions of the Jewish Passover meal that we have come to call the Last Supper. We celebrate through the same ritual in the Eucharistic liturgy. By referring to Jesus as the Lamb of God, offered for our salvation, we are ritually connected to the Jewish Passover event.

Through the ritual, many individuals can share in a communal event. Just as we have a need to concretely express our experience of God in worship, we need to do this as a community. Each of us can worship God individually and alone. Yet, we come most fully to appreciate our faith and experience God through other people. The faith of the community and of each individual within it is maintained and enriched through worshipping together. The ritual that makes communal worship liturgy bonds us as a people.

Liturgy allows each of us to get close to the meaning of life by getting close to God, the author of life. Our worship at liturgy always celebrates Christ's death and resurrection, drawing us nearer to the mystery of death and life. The meaning of Easter is that through the power of God death is not the end, but the beginning. Through liturgical ritual we are incorporated into that paradox of death leading to life.

These are complex realities. Words alone are not adequate to explain the depth of these mysteries. As human beings we cannot communicate about such realities without the help of symbols. In liturgy, symbols are used to express the deep realities which lie at the root of the meaning of death and life. (Symbols are discussed in the chapter, "Sacraments.")

In their ability to communicate, symbols such as water, fire, bread, wine, and oil express internal realities present to God's people. In their use these symbols cause new things to happen—awareness, questioning, growth in faith.

## The Liturgical Year

Family celebrations usually run in a yearly pattern. The year begins with a holiday on the first of January and continues on through birthdays, anniversaries, public holidays (Memorial Day and Fourth of July) until they end in December with Christmas. The flow of the year helps to regulate and even determine when we celebrate.

The Church's liturgy is also shaped by the flow of the year. The liturgy (especially the Mass and the Liturgy of the Hours) changes during the year to reflect the various season and feasts that are celebrated. This is known as the "liturgical year."

- The liturgical year starts with the first Sunday of Advent, a season which lasts for four weeks.
- This is followed by Christmas and the Christmas season which extends until Epiphany Sunday (approximately 12 days after Christmas)
- Ordinary time—the longest season of the liturgical year—follows the Christmas season and lasts until Ash Wednesday.
- Lent continues for six weeks, until the beginning of the Mass of the Last Supper on Holy Thursday.
- Holy Thursday, Good Friday, and Holy Saturday are known as the Triduum—the three high holy days.
- Easter is the most important feast in the liturgical year. All of Lent and the Triduum leads to the celebration of the Resurrection, the initiation of new members, and the renewal of our baptismal promises.
- The Easter season lasts 50 days until Pentecost.
- Ordinary time begins once again the Sunday after Pentecost. It will last until the first Sunday of Advent begins the year all over again.

Various colors are used during the liturgical year to indicate the season of the year or feast being celebrated (e.g., green—Ordinary time, white—Christmas and Easter, purple—Lent). In addition, various parts of the liturgy change during various seasons (e.g., the Gloria and Alleluia are dropped during Lent). The music played during the liturgy usually changes with the seasons as well (e.g., during Easter and Christmas special joyous hymns are sung, during Lent more somber music is played).

## Pause a Moment . . .

- What is the role of ritual in the celebration of the liturgy?
- How does the liturgical year reflect the rhythm and flow of the seasons?

### REFLECTION

1. How does the liturgy make present God's past actions?

_____

_____

_____

_____

2. Describe how the Church's ancient rituals and symbols help you to deepen and strengthen your experience of God.

_____

_____

_____

_____

---

### Special Feasts

In addition to the liturgical seasons, there are many special feasts celebrated throughout the year.

- Feast of the Holy Family (Sunday after Christmas)
- Solemnity of Mary (January 1) Holyday of Obligation
- The Annunciation (March 25)
- Ascension Thursday (forty days after Easter) Holyday
- Assumption (August 15) Holyday
- All Saint's (November 1) Holyday
- Immaculate Conception (December 8) Holyday

There are also many other celebrations of feast days both on Sunday and during the week.

## Regulations for Liturgy

▲ *We do not go to the liturgy to "hear the Mass," but to participate fully in it. Our bodies are needed to participate in the liturgy, not just our minds.*

The *General Instruction to the Roman Missal,* which can be found in the *sacramentary,* (the large book used at Mass that contains the liturgical prayers) contains the regulations for celebrating the Eucharistic liturgy. The following suggestions, adapted from the *Hymnal for Catholic Students* by Gabe Huck (Liturgical Training Publications, 1989), provide a simplified overview of these regulations. What Huck emphasizes for Masses with children is just as pertinent for adults:

1. **Repetition is not only okay, it is required.** Work to foster familiarity in the liturgy without stifling creativity. People like to sing the same songs, recite the same prayers, act out the same gestures.

2. **Those who minister come from the assembly to serve the assembly.** People should do the roles they are prepared to do. All who attend liturgies should also participate in them.

3. **Liturgy is something sung.** The liturgy is truly a hymn of praise. As much as possible, the entire liturgy should be sung, not just a few songs and responses. Some things in the Mass should always be sung:
   - Acclamations (Gospel acclamation—Alleluia; Holy, Holy; memorial acclamation; great Amen),
   - Responsorial Psalm (after the first reading),
   - Litanies (penitential rite and Lamb of God), and
   - Processionals (entrance, communion, and recessional).

   The music for each part of the Mass should vary from the other parts of the Mass.

4. **The liturgy is like a dance: the whole body must be used.** We are not a passive audience to be entertained or engage in private prayer. The assembled community is itself an essential part of the liturgy. Our postures and gestures are significant movements of the ritual. We *sit* to listen, we *stand* in respect, *we kneel* to adore and show contrition.

5. **Liturgy is handling and gesturing.** People should be comfortable with the gestures of liturgy: sign of the cross, folded hands, sign of peace, reception of the Eucharist, genuflection. Practice these with your students until they do them naturally.

6. **Liturgy is not about how we feel. It is about who we are and whose we are.** The liturgy is the Church's worship in which we participate. Huck says that "[Liturgy] rehearses me in the feelings I ought to have. . . . At liturgy, we play like we are in God's reign" *(page 21).*

7. **Liturgies are filled with processions.** The assembly gathers, the presider and other ministers process in, the Gospel procession, the presentation of the gifts, communion, and recession. These are all movements of the community, even if only done by one person.

8. **Liturgy has times of silence.** Most people have difficulty sitting still and being silent. Yet, the liturgy calls for just this after the readings and many

of the prayers. These are times of reflection and private prayer. We need to teach people how to be still.

9. **Comments should be few, brief, and prepared.** Don't overexplain what is happening. Use class time to teach about the experience.

10. **At Eucharist, the Word of God is to be a foundation.** The Scripture readings are our family stories of faith. They explain how we came here as a people. In Masses with children, the number of readings may be reduced; only the Gospel must be read. (See #41–49, *Directory for Masses with Children* for a full treatment of this issue.) The readings should never be paraphrased.

11. **The liturgy is celebrated in a fitting place.** The *Directory for Masses with Children, #25* says, "within the church, a space should be carefully chosen, if available, that will be suited to the number of participants. It should be a place where the children can act with a feeling of ease according to the requirements of a living liturgy that is suited to their age." If celebrated outside the church, the place "should be appropriate and worthy of the celebration." The space should fit the audience and not be too big or too small. It should also be conducive to worship.

12. **The objects and furnishings of the liturgy are to be worthy.** The following things are needed for liturgy:

    - Book of scriptures (lectionary),
    - Book of prayers (sacramentary),
    - Bread and its plate (paten),
    - Wine and its cup (chalice),
    - Table on which the vessels are placed (altar),
    - Ambo (podium or reading desk) where the scriptures are read,
    - Seating for assembly and presider, and
    - Processional cross and candles.

    These items should be worthy of their task and should be used with reverence. (See *Environment and Art in Catholic Worship* for complete details.)

13. **Liturgy does not happen in a void.** If we do not pray during the week, we cannot expect to pray well at liturgy on Sunday. As catechists, every lesson should revolve around the liturgy in some way. We prepare people to participate in liturgy, we teach them the skills to participate, we review in our lessons the themes developed in the liturgy.

14. **Liturgy in the school or (religious education) setting is to be in continuity with the parish liturgy.** Huck says on page 29:

    *The church's primary and normal existence is the parish. The liturgy of the parish, and that means above all else the Sunday Eucharist of the assembled parishioners, is the heart of parish life. All other celebrations of the liturgy are secondary to and dependent upon that Sunday liturgy.*

15. **Liturgy has dignity, clarity, and simplicity.** Avoid anything that seems casual or trivial. Take the time so that gestures are clearly seen. Don't add a lot of unnecessary words or gestures to the liturgy. Instead, perform the words and gestures that are part of the ritual with style and grace.

*Notes*

## The Church Teaches

Every authentic celebration of the Eucharist is directed by the bishop, either in person or through the presbyters [priests], who are his helpers. . . .

Within the community of the faithful a presbyter also possesses the power of orders to offer sacrifice in the person of Christ. He presides over the assembly and leads its prayer, proclaims the message of salvation, leads the people in offering sacrifice. . . . At the Eucharist he should serve God and the people with dignity and humility. . . .

In the celebration of the Mass the faithful . . . give thanks to the Father and offer the victim not only through the hands of the priest but also with him, and they learn to offer themselves. *(General Instruction of the Roman Missal, #59–61)*

## Pause a Moment . . .

- Which of the 15 principals presented above is most surprising to you? Which do you already incorporate into your ministry?

- How can you incorporate these principles to improve the experience of liturgy for your students?

## The Fourfold Mission of Christ

We find the following themes in Jesus' ministry. He came as a person of *prayer.* His mission was to announce the kingdom of God—*proclamation.* He was a *servant,* especially to the poor and those in need. *Communion,* the formation of community, was a manifestation of his presence. Christ's fourfold mission has become the mission of his Church.

Each of these aspects is related to worship. The Mass is a *prayer* of praise and thanksgiving. We hear the *proclamation* through the readings and the homily announcing the kingdom of God in our midst. The liturgy calls us to be of *service.* We are sent forth from the Mass to go and proclaim the Good News. Through the liturgy, a *community* of people gather and grow.

Liturgy is not something we attend, it is something we **do.** It truly is our work. Every member of the faith community, through the common priesthood we share through Baptism, is expected to fully participate in liturgical celebrations. In the liturgy, we will hear God's call to us and will be asked to respond in faith. Through the ritual, we remember what God has done for us, especially through Jesus, and we give thanks and praise. In the Eucharist, we experience the full presence of God.

### The Proper Attitude

A growing number of people move from parish to parish (and at times from one denomination to another) to find meaningful worship. They are no longer content to remain within their geographically assigned parish if the liturgy is uninspiring.

When people are asked to describe what they expect from a parish they often name the following: (a) a feeling of community—warmth and welcome; (b) good homilies; (c) meaningful liturgy; and (d) active parish life. Most of these are related to worship.

However, the liturgy is not only a resource. A person must *bring* something to liturgy to share with the community. To benefit from the liturgy, it is important that one has a positive attitude, a serious interest, and a willingness to participate.

Here are ways to improve one's experience of the liturgy:

1. Realize that other worshippers are there to support us in our growth in faith. The more we participate *with them* the more we benefit.

2. Participate at Mass as a proclamation of our membership in the People of God and not as an audience to be entertained.

3. Experience the celebration of the Eucharist as a special time to thank and praise God.

4. Come to the Eucharist willing to honestly forgive ourselves and those who have hurt us.

5. Prepare to listen to God's Word and to learn what it means to follow Jesus.

6. Offer yourself fully as a gift to God.

7. Accept the Body and Blood of Christ as God's greatest gift.

8. Use the grace we receive at Mass in everyday life.

Approaching the liturgy with these attitudes will ensure that one's worship is full of life and is not just words.

## The Relationship between Liturgy and Catechesis

Catechesis can help people to fully participate in the community's worship. The *National Catechetical Directory, #113* says:

> *There is a close relationship between catechesis and liturgy. Both are rooted in the Church's faith, and both strengthen faith and summon Christians to conversion, although they do so in different ways. In the liturgy the Church is at prayer, offering adoration, praise, and thanksgiving to God, and seeking and celebrating reconciliation: here one finds both an expression of faith and a means for deepening it. As for catechesis, it prepares people for full and active participation in liturgy (by helping them understand its nature, rituals, and symbols) and at the same time flows from liturgy, inasmuch as, reflecting upon the community's experiences of worship, it seeks to relate them to daily life and to growth in faith.* (#113)

Catechesis seeks to help people understand that worship flows from and renews their faith.

Catechesis guides people in reflecting on their experience of God and in relating their experience to the Church's tradition, including its ancient rituals and symbols. The student learns that the worship he or she shares with the Christian community today has its roots in the covenants with Abraham, Moses, and David, but even more significantly in the new covenant of which Christ is both the High Priest and the perfect offering.

Jesus invites us to worship in spirit and truth, giving us the symbols to do so. He is himself the gift we offer God in praise and thanksgiving. His whole life is the model of perfect worship; the liturgy itself reflects his four-fold mission.

Through catechesis, people prepare to meet God in worship. Having learned what God has done and promised, they are able to respond fully, receiving the full benefit of God's presence among them. The community, too, thrives when its members are informed and prepared. Religious education allows us to fully participate in and enjoy meeting with God.

## Pause a Moment . . .

• What are some of the attitudes you bring to the liturgy?

• How do you prepare to celebrate the Eucharistic liturgy? How do you take the liturgy with you when you leave it?

• In your own words, explain the importance of catechesis to worship and worship to catechesis.

*Notes*

## Preparing for Worship

One of your functions as a catechist will be to inspire students to worship and pray. To do this effectively, you must not only teach your students to understand what liturgy is about; you must also pique their interest in it. Students' interest in liturgy will grow in proportion to how involved they are in it. Regardless of their age, there is a number of ways you can help students actively, consciously, and authentically participate in liturgy.

1. **Consult the students.** Since the purpose of liturgy is to worship God and to reflect on one's experience of God, it is necessary to know the students' concerns, interests, thoughts, and fears. Bring student concerns into the liturgy. Accept their ideas for decorating the worship space. Have interested students participate as ministers of the word, as servers, as ushers and ministers of hospitality, and as gift bearers. This will ensure that the resulting liturgy is really theirs.

2. **Involve the students in a dialogue.** A good liturgy is a continual dialogue. Participation should be encouraged at every opportunity.

3. **Use the senses to draw students into the worship experience.** Liturgy should involve all of the senses; people should see, hear, smell, taste, and touch. Gestures, body movements, and processions involve students' bodies as well as their minds.

4. **Make everything simple, short, and clear.** Explanations should be limited. If your students are in grade school, use at most two readings (one being the Gospel) and a Responsorial Psalm in the Liturgy of the Word. Keep the readings brief. Use the children's lectionary.

5. **Make music an integral part of the celebration.** Familiarize students with the music used in the parish. Practice the sung responses of the liturgy. Make sure the rhythms are interesting, but not too difficult, and try to emphasize major keys instead of minor ones. Invite students to play instruments during the liturgy.

## Pause a Moment . . .

• What allowances does the parish make for students to be full participants in liturgy?

• How do you prepare students to participate in parish liturgies?

## Working with Your Students

The general concepts developed in this chapter can be applied to students of all ages. More specific ideas will apply to the students on your particular grade level. A few of these ideas are listed here.

▲ *Many people learn best when they are given the opportunity to do what they have learned. Your students will grow to love the liturgy the more they are actively involved in it.*

## Adults

Adults are the primary worshipping community and most liturgical services are planned for them. Many of the techniques that make adult liturgy meaningful can be used effectively with children. Adults will tune into liturgies that are in touch with real-life issues and situations. Brevity and simplicity will have a greater impact than lengthy and complicated ideas. Music should be familiar before being used in worship.

Encourage adults to participate at liturgy in all the ways listed below. Balance periods of activity, singing, or verbal input (the readings and the homily) with periods of reflection and quiet. Provide for silence or for instrumental music after the first reading, during the preparation of the gifts, and as a communion meditation.

## High School

From early adolescence on, teens should be encouraged to take active roles in the parish liturgy (as well as in any liturgy planned especially for them). Encourage students to participate at liturgy as acolytes (servers), ushers, song leaders, and gift bearers. Adolescent lectors and Eucharistic Ministers who have been commissioned should be used whenever possible. (Discuss with your parish director how you can prepare more students for these roles.)

These students tend to be more reflective than younger students. Some silence at liturgy is enjoyed. New experiences of liturgy are sought. In comfortable surroundings, and in groups that are predominately composed of peers, the students will express prayers that bring out some deeper feelings and, occasionally, real insight into life. Expressions of such feelings and insights should be encouraged, even though they may seem a little irrelevant at times. Encourage dialogue homilies, spontaneous petitions, and shared reflections at the communion meditation. Don't be afraid to include tastefully done popular songs, poems, slides, and sections of literature that are appropriate to the theme and nature of the liturgy.

Find ways for these youths to become more involved in the Sunday worship of their parish(es). Teach them the songs, sung responses, and prayers used at the adult liturgy on Sunday. Remember, Sunday worship is the norm.

## Junior High

These students are more verbal than younger children, but also more self-conscious. Worship services rooted in the group will appeal to them. However, very complex liturgies will be threatening. The students will worry about making mistakes and being embarrassed in front of their peers.

Group preparation removes some of this pressure. After the students have discussed and become familiar with the parts of the Mass, form the class into four committees: readings, music, environment, and prayer.

Freedom to discuss the main ideas in the readings, enhance the environment, and select music without criticism are positive experiences for this age group. The students' special interests should be honored as much as possible. Interest or concerns about upcoming games, tests, and special events can all be included in the celebration of the liturgy.

Using missalettes, have the students diagram the Mass. List the two main divisions—the *Liturgy of the Word* and the *Liturgy of the Eucharist*—then,

Notes

break each part into its smaller elements. Make a large posterboard diagram of the Mass using the proper name (and any common name) for each part.

## Upper Elementary

In addition to the ideas presented for the lower-grade levels which follow, fifth and sixth graders can make banners, posters, special tablecloths, attractive Bible or lectionary covers, a special vestment for the celebrant, candles, and flower arrangements. Take time to discuss with these students exactly what puts them in the mood to pray and celebrate. Some groups might prefer a highly decorated space for prayer while others might prefer simplicity in decor.

Use music at all opportunities. Explore the possibility of making "sound tracks" that the students record ahead of time to enhance the theme of the liturgy.

While these students will be less interested in using gestures throughout the Mass, you can readily interest them in dramatizing the readings and in participating in processions.

## Middle Grades

Plan class liturgies, including an occasional communal penance service each year. The students can familiarize themselves with the parts of the Mass and construct Mass booklets. Mass prayers should be practiced. Similarly, a penance celebration or sacramental reconciliation should follow a study and discussion of the personal and social aspects of sin and forgiveness.

Third and fourth graders can prepare the place and the materials for celebration, sing and play musical instruments, read the Scripture, dramatize the Gospel story, carry the Bible and Offertory gifts, make decorations, provide directions or commentaries throughout the service, and bake the liturgical bread.

The music used can include simple harmonies, echoes, and rounds. In using "Orff" instruments, have one child use two mallets per instrument. Teach the children countermelodies and harmonies to play while the rest of the class sings. You can use more than one harmony at a time or more than one kind of instrument at a time. Experiment with different rhythmic patterns and free improvisation.

Involve third and fourth graders in processions and recessionals, and in simple gestures. Be sure to substitute the Apostles' Creed for the Nicene Creed, and use a children's Eucharistic Prayer in place of the regular ones for adults.

Walk through the parish church with the students. Let the children explore all of the spaces—sacristy (priest's dressing room), sanctuary (where the altar is), altar, baptismal font, presider's chair, reconciliation room, choir area, and so on. Show them vestments, altar cloths, and sacred vessels. Explain the various books used during the Liturgy.

## Primary Grades

For the most part, these years will consist of "liturgy readiness" rather than actual liturgy experience. During these years, expose the children to some of the rituals of the Mass in class prayer services. For example, offer the children opportunities to listen to (not just hear) Scripture readings, apply the message to their lives, make gifts and offer them to Jesus, share food and drink, compose very simple prayers, and sing songs and acclamations that are used in parish liturgies.

It is quite possible, on occasion, to celebrate meaningful liturgies with first and second graders. To do this, as many children as possible should have some part in the liturgy. Have the children prepare the place and materials for celebration, play rhythm and Orff instruments (xylophone, metallophone, glockenspiel), dramatize the stories, carry the Bible and offer gifts, make decorations, and bring flowers, food, and other objects.

The music used should be so simple that no written words are needed. Keep the melodies and harmonies very simple.

Students should be part of the entrance and offertory procession, and the recessional. Teach them simple gestures for the Responsorial Psalm, Memorial Acclamation, Lord's Prayer, and Rite of Peace. If using a creed, substitute the Apostles' Creed for the Nicene Creed. In place of the regular Eucharistic Prayers, use one of the three approved for children (*Eucharistic Prayers for Masses with Children*).

▲ *Think about the major celebrations that take place during the liturgical year. What does your parish do to make each of these events special? What can you do to help students be better participants at these celebrations?*

## Pause a Moment . . .

- What suggestions listed above can you use immediately with your students? How will you implement those ideas?

- How do you prepare your students to participate in the liturgy? Share some of your ideas.

## IMPLICATIONS

Look through this topic again. Think about the students on your grade level and then jot down ways that you can effectively involve them in the planning, preparation, and execution of any given worship service. To help organize your thoughts, fill in the following chart.

|  | Environment | Readings | Music | Prayer |
|---|---|---|---|---|
| **Planning** |  |  |  |  |
| **Preparation** |  |  |  |  |
| **Execution** |  |  |  |  |

## Memo

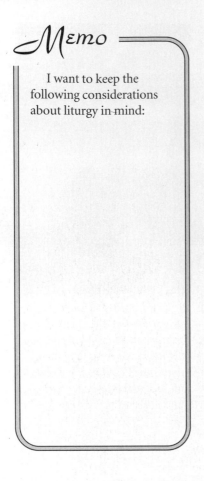

I want to keep the following considerations about liturgy in mind:

## Prayer Response

Read the following Scripture passage. Then reflect on your attitude toward worship, how it could improve, and how your developing attitude could help you as a catechist.

*What care I for the number of your sacrifices? says the Lord. I have enough of whole-burnt rams and fat of fatlings. In the blood of calves, lambs, and goats I find no pleasure . . . Wash yourselves clean! Put away your misdeeds from before my eyes; cease doing evil; learn to do good. Make justice your aim: redress the wronged, hear the orphan's plea, defend the widow.* (Isaiah 1:11, 16–17)

## BIBLIOGRAPHY

Berglund, Mary Catherine. *Gather the Children: Celebrate the Word With Ideas, Activities, Prayers and Projects.* Cycle A, B, C, The Pastoral Press, 1987, 1988, 1989.

Bernstein, Eleanor and Books-Leonard, John. eds. *Children in the Assembly of the Church.* Chicago: Liturgy Training Publications, 1992.

*Come Together: An Adult Catechesis On the Eucharist.* Allen, TX: Tabor, video.

Cronin, Gaynell and Rathschmidt, Rev. Jack. *Celebrating the Church Year for Children.* Mahwah, NJ: Paulist Press, video.

DeGidio, Sandra, O.S.M. "How 'All of Us' Celebrate the Mass," *Catholic Update.* Cincinnati: St. Anthony Messenger Press, September, 1987.

*Directory for Masses With Children.* Washington, D.C.: United States Catholic Conference, 1973.

Foley, Leonard. "Ten Reasons for Going to Mass," *Catholic Update.* Cincinnati: St. Anthony Messenger Press, August, 1986.

Huck, Gabe and others. *Hymnal for Catholic Students, Leader's Manual.* Chicago: Liturgy Training Publications, 1989.

Jeep, Elizabeth McMahon. *The Welcome Table.* Chicago: Liturgy Training Publications, 1982.

*The Liturgy Documents.* Third edition, Chicago: Liturgical Training Publications, 1991.

Luebering, Carol. "Liturgy: The Church's 'Work' of Praising God," *Catholic Update.* St. Anthony Messenger Press, April, 1987.

Machado, Mary Kathryn. *How to Plan Children's Liturgies.* San Jose, CA: Resource Publications, Inc., 1985.

Richstatter, Thomas, O.F.M. "A Walk Through the Mass—A Step-by-Step Explanation," *Catholic Update.* Cincinnati: St. Anthony Messenger Press, August, 1989.

_____. "How to Participate More Actively in the Mass," *Catholic Update.* Cincinnati: St. Anthony Messenger Press, August, 1982.

*Understanding the Liturgy of the Mass.* Liguori, MO: Redemptorist Pastoral Communications, video.

*Understanding the Mass for Children.* Mahwah, NJ: Paulist Press, video.

Weber, Gerard. "The Mass: Finding Its Meaning and Getting More Out of It" *Catholic Update.* Cincinnati: St. Anthony Messenger Press, 1990.

*Nihil Obstat*
The Reverend Gregory A. Banazak, S.T.D.

*Imprimatur*
The Most Reverend Kenneth J. Povish, D.D.
Bishop of Lansing
May 13, 1994

The *Nihil Obstat* and *Imprimatur* are official declarations that a book or pamphlet is free of doctrinal or moral error. No implication is contained therein that those who have granted the *Nihil Obstat* and *Imprimatur* agree with the contents, opinions, or statements expressed.

Send all inquiries to:

BENZIGER PUBLISHING COMPANY
15319 Chatsworth Street
P.O. Box 9609
Mission Hills, California 91346-9609

Second Edition

**ISBN 0-02-651218-1**

Printed in the United States of America.

1 2 3 4 5 6 7 8 9   BAW   98 97 96 95 94

Benziger

# People of Prayer

✤

The lover knocked at the door of his beloved.
   "Who knocks?" said the beloved from within.

"It is I," said the lover.

"Go away. This house will not hold you and me."

The rejected lover went away into the desert. There he meditated for months on end, pondering the words of the beloved. Finally he returned and knocked at the door again.

"Who knocks?"

"It is you."

The door was immediately opened.

*Song of the Bird*, Anthony de Mello

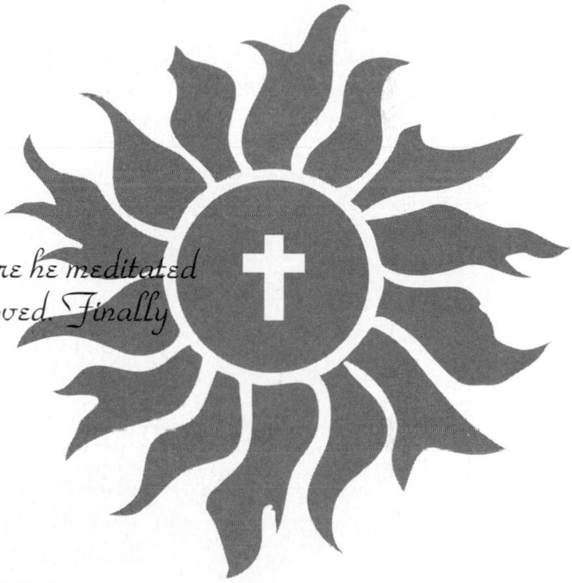

✤

Written by
**Peter Ries**

Consultant
**David Riley**

## In this chapter you will:

- Recognize prayer as part of one's personal relationship with God.

- Learn the value of prayer for ordinary people.

- Consider various techniques for teaching students to pray.

Second Edition

## The Gift of Love

▲ *What does it mean to give someone the gift of love? What are appropriate ways of responding to such a gift?*

Diana and Roberto had moved to New York City with great hopes for the future, along with a lot of trepidation. Diana grew up in a small town in Montana. Despite what you might think, she had never really yearned to leave her home and family and escape to the "big city." In fact, after high school she had been quite content to attend the junior college in the next county and stay close to home.

All that changed, however, when Roberto came to town. He was a member of a wildcatting crew working on an oil rig. They met at the high school basketball game. Roberto was at the game, he later confessed, because his motel did not have cable and he was desperate for something to do. Through some strange fate, he sat in the seat right in front of Diana's.

Before too long, Diana and Roberto had struck up a conversation about the joys of high school basketball. Before the evening was over, Diana had reluctantly agreed to go with Roberto on a date. Roberto took her to the library, where he read the poetry of e.e. cummings aloud in a wonderfully entertaining voice. Eight months later they were married.

Roberto was not your regular oil field roustabout. He had big dreams of becoming an actor. Because of this dream, Diana agreed to leave her home for New York, with the hope that Roberto could break into the theater there. Diana would be able to finish her college degree in two years and then get a job as a teacher.

Roberto had saved his money over the years, but they knew that times would be tough for awhile. They managed to find a cheap apartment that wasn't too rundown, and Roberto waited on tables, attended acting class, and went to auditions. Diana looked for part-time work, but couldn't find anything worthwhile that didn't interfere with classes at CUNY. As a result, they had to make it on Roberto's salary alone. Making do on Roberto's salary and savings would just last them until she finished school.

When Christmas of their first year together drew near, Diana was deeply depressed. She had always loved Christmas, but their budget did not allow for presents that year. She knew the sacrifices that Roberto was making to keep her in school, and she longed to be able to give him something. The money, she realized, just wasn't there, but that didn't make her longing go away.

Gradually, a plan formed in her mind. She had brought one thing of value with her from Montana. Her grandmother had given her a prized doll. Diana knew that a collector would pay quite a bit for it. She took the doll off the rickety bookshelf and sold it at a nearby doll shop for over $100.

Diana decided to buy Roberto the one thing she knew he would appreciate above all: an engraved glass case for his prized baseball, the one signed by his namesake, Roberto Clemente. She knew that ball meant the world to her husband, and that a display case would make him very happy.

On Christmas eve, Diana nursed a secret pleasure from the knowledge of her gift. After eating the special dinner she had prepared, Roberto and

Diana went into the living room. "Robbie," Diana said, "I know I wasn't supposed to, but I have a gift for you."

"I have something for you as well," Roberto said. He smiled as he handed her a large package.

Diana was surprised as she accepted the present from Roberto. As she opened it, her eyes filled with tears when she saw what it was: a silver stand with a glass cover for her grandmother's doll. "How . . ." she stammered. "How did you afford this?"

Roberto failed to hear the question, because he was exploding with laughter. He had opened his gift and saw the display case for his baseball. The funny part was, he no longer had the baseball. He had pawned it to buy the stand for Diana. He realized that they had both sacrificed things dear to them to purchase now-useless gifts.

As Diana realized what had happened, she began to cry. "How can you laugh?" she demanded.

"Because it's funny," Roberto said, as he wiped the tears from Diana's face. When she had quieted down, Roberto continued. "Anyway, this case means far more than that baseball ever could, because it's a symbol of what you really gave me for Christmas, yourself."

Diana embraced Roberto, and realized then that the case and stand hardly mattered at all, none of it mattered, because she had given and received the only gift of real value: love.

(With apologies to "The Gift of the Magi" by O. Henry)

## YOUR STORY

The gift of love is a precious thing, a deeply intimate response that often goes beyond any logical explanation. In our relationship with God, prayer can be that gift of love. Reflect for a few moments on the story above and your relationship with God.

**1.** Explain what motivated Diana and Roberto to give the gifts that they exchanged.

_____

_____

**2.** How is prayer a gift from God?

_____

_____

**3.** How is prayer a response for all of God's gifts?

_____

_____

**4.** What motivates us to respond to God in prayer?

_____

_____

*Memo*

What is the greatest gift of love you have ever received?

# $\mathcal{P}$art II $\mathcal{M}$essage

## Our Relationship with God

- *"How grown-up is your prayer life?" the priest asked his adult retreatants. The answers were as varied as the faces in the group. One man in his forties confessed, "I still pray the way I was taught as a child. Somehow, it doesn't feel right." A college student told of his "natural high" that resulted from prayer. A mother of four added, "I really don't pray, except at Mass, maybe. I don't have much imagination when it comes to that." A common remark among the retreatants was how hard and how often they tried to pray, and yet nothing happened.*

- *For me, prayer means launching out of the heart towards God; it means lifting up one's eyes, quite simply, to heaven, a cry of grateful love, from the crest of joy or the trough of despair. (St. Thérèse of Lisieux)*

Prayer is part of our personal relationship with God just as honest communication is part of marriage. God's love and eternal faithfulness are at the heart of both the Old and New Testaments. Over the centuries, people have responded to God's overtures of love in many ways, but most prominently through prayer. Prayer takes many forms, but it is always a natural response to the experience of God. No matter what the era or culture, people have tried to communicate with God in their own way.

## Prayer in the Old Testament

When Solomon completed the Temple in Jerusalem he offered this prayer:

> *Lord, God of Israel, there is no god like you in heaven or on earth; you keep your covenant and show kindness to your servants who are wholeheartedly faithful to you . . . Can it indeed be that God dwells with mankind on earth? If the heavens and the highest heavens cannot contain you, how much less this temple which I have built! Look kindly on the prayer and petition of your servant, O Lord, my God, and listen to the cry of supplication your servant makes before you. May your eyes watch day and night over this temple, the place where you have decreed you shall be honored; may you heed the prayer which I your servant offer toward this place. (2 Chronicles 6:14,18–20)*

Solomon's prayer shows a deep and abiding reverence for God. Solomon prayed as a subject addressing the king who holds the power of life and death over him. In Israel, even the king humbled himself before the one God.

Prayer in the Old Testament reflected the real concerns of the person praying. For example, in the Book of Tobit, Sarah pours out this prayer to God at a time when she was distraught with the circumstances of her life:

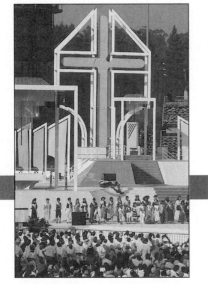

▲ *Throughout history, men and women have responded to God's goodness, to suffering, and to death in prayer.*

*Blessed are you, O Lord, merciful God! Forever blessed and honored is your holy name; may all your works forever bless you. And now, O Lord, to you I turn my face and raise my eyes. . . . I am my father's only daughter, and he has no other child to make his heir, nor does he have a close kinsman or other relative whom I might bide my time to marry. I have already lost seven husbands; why then should I live any longer? But if it please you, Lord, not to slay me, look favorably upon me and have pity on me.* (Tobit 3:11–12,15b)

There is nothing pious about Sarah's prayer. It is the cry of a person in anguish calling out to her creator for help. Sarah pleads with God because she knows her fate is in God's hands.

## How Jesus Prayed

The image of Jesus painted by the gospel accounts is of a man who prayed deeply and often. At times Jesus withdrew from the activity of daily life to pray in solitude. Jesus also prayed in the busyness of daily living. He prayed before the important events and decisions of his life: before beginning his public ministry, before choosing the twelve Apostles, before his transfiguration, and before his suffering and death. He also encouraged others to pray. He taught his disciples to pray (see *Matthew 6:5–14*), encouraged them to ask for what they needed (see *Matthew 7:7–11*), and begged them to pray with him in the garden of Gethsemane *(Matthew 26:40–41)*.

A devout Jew, Jesus prayed each morning, at every meal, and in the evening. At the synagogue and at home in the morning and in the evening, Jesus prayed by himself or with others, asking God for the basic things of life and thanking God for the many blessings of creation.

Jesus taught that if people were conscious of God's presence and love for them, they would naturally pray in response. He encouraged everyone to persevere in prayer, to pray always and never lose heart. He emphasized God's goodness and called for his followers to feel confidence and love when they prayed. Jesus warned people not to come to the altar of worship without first reconciling with their neighbor.

When his disciples asked Jesus to teach them to pray, he taught them the "Lord's Prayer." This prayer reveals the attitudes and behavior that should characterize a person's response to God's love.

*Father, hallowed be your name, your kingdom come. Give us each day our daily bread and forgive us our sins for we ourselves forgive everyone in debt to us; and do not subject us to the final test.* (Luke 11:2–4)

Perhaps the most beautiful prayer in the Bible is Jesus' prayer for his disciples the night before he died. In it, he describes a covenant relationship with God.

*Father, the hour has come! Give glory to your Son that your Son may glorify you. . . . I pray for them. I do not pray for the world but for the ones you have given me, because they are yours, . . . Holy Father, keep them in your name that you have given me, so that they may be one just as we are. . . . I pray not only for them, but also for those who will believe in me through their word, so that they may all be one, as you, Father, are in me and I in you.* (John 17:1b, 9, 11b, 20–21a)

## The Church Teaches

"If you knew the gift of God!" The wonder of prayer is revealed at the edge of the well, where we, like the Samaritan woman, come to seek water: there, Christ comes face to face with each one of us. He makes the first move and asks us for a drink. Jesus thirsts; his seeking and asking arise from the depths of his Father's desire for us. In prayer, whether we realize it or not, God's thirst encounters ours. God thirsts that we might thirst for him." (St. Augustine) *Catechism of the Catholic Church,* # 2560

The Lord's Prayer also reveals a method of praying. Use this method to write a prayer pertaining to this moment in your life.

## *Pause a Moment . . .*

- There are many examples of prayer in the Old Testament, in particular the Psalms. Leaf through the Bible and find several other examples of prayer. Begin a notebook of biblical prayer references that you can use with students. Share your findings with another catechist. To start, find Sirach 36:1–17.

- What do you think were the key elements of Jesus' prayer life? How can these shape your prayer?

## *Prayer for Ordinary People*

Prayer is really a matter of giving your best to God. Giving yourself to someone or something is really quite natural. For example, you can observe in parents loving relationships with their children the qualities that make for good prayer: they give them *attention*, they are *commited* to their well-being, they have *confidence* in their integrity, and they *persevere* in loving them in all circumstances.

Prayer is a personal response to God's presence in one's life, even though it may be shared with others. Prayer reflects a desire to be close to God. Through prayer, one's whole being responds to God: mind, feelings, will, and body. It is the offering of one's full attention and devotion.

### Types of Prayer

We can pray in three ways: individually, with a group, and in liturgy. The Mass, the celebration of the sacraments, and the Church's daily prayer—the Liturgy of the Hours—are all kinds of liturgical prayer.

Traditionally, prayer has also been placed under four categories: adoration, thanksgiving, contrition, and petition.

1. **Adoration.** When you praise, express your love for, or profess faith in God, you participate in an act of adoration. Here is an example:

   *I will extol you, O my God and King, and I will bless your name forever and ever. Every day will I bless you, and I will praise your name forever and ever. Great is the Lord and highly to be praised, his greatness is unsearchable.* (Psalm 145:1–3)

2. **Thanksgiving.** When you express your gratitude for God's generosity and love, you are offering thanksgiving. Here is an example:

   *I will give thanks to you, O Lord my God, with all my heart, and I glorify your name forever. Great has been your kindness toward me; you have rescued me from the depths of the nether world.* (Psalm 86:12–13)

3. **Contrition.** Prayers that express sorrow for sin and ask for forgiveness are prayers of contrition. An example would be:

   *I acknowledge my offense, and my sin is before me always: against you only have I sinned, and done what is evil in your sight.* (Psalm 51:5–6a)

4. **Petition.** When you ask God for something, you are offering a prayer of petition. A recent *Life Magazine* Poll conducted by the Gallop

Corporation reported that 98 percent of Americans have prayed for their families. These are prayers of petition.

> *Incline your ear, O Lord; answer me, for I am afflicted and poor. Keep my life, for I am devoted to you; save your servant who trusts in you. You are my God; have pity on me, O Lord, for to you I call all the day.* (Psalm 86:1–3)

In addition to these four forms, some writers have described the *prayer of faith* as that which expresses one's belief in God or some aspect of revelation and the *prayer of love,* which expresses one's love for God.

## Vocal Prayer

At times, you may find yourself spontaneously praying because you are suddenly aware of God's presence ("My Lord and my God!" or "Thank you, God!") or because you are in serious difficulty ("Help me, God!"). Spontaneous vocal prayer is often an emotional cry of the heart.

Because emotions cannot be regulated, and periods of creativity and composition are unpredictable, memorized traditional prayers such as the Our Father, the Hail Mary, the Glory Be, the Angelus, and the Psalms are important to know. Popular devotions such as the rosary or the stations of the cross help us to focus on the lives of Jesus and Mary.

## Mental Prayer

Mental prayer implies focusing one's mind on God. Mental prayer can be formal—routinely setting aside time to be with God—or informal—when you think about God while you are working, playing, or relaxing. No external words are used, but the mind praises or thanks God, or meditates upon some mystery of the spiritual life.

Mental prayer is important for the development of one's spiritual life. Through mental prayer, a Christian learns to "put on Christ," as the Apostle Paul encouraged, and become "perfect as your heavenly Father is perfect," as Jesus commanded.

The results of persistent mental prayer are many: your confidence in God increases, you learn to bounce back from failures, your repentance is sincere, you learn to accept others as they are, your love of prayer increases, and gradually, you begin to see yourself and all life from God's viewpoint.

There are three traditional forms of mental prayer: meditation, affective prayer, and contemplation.

1. **Meditation.** This first form of mental prayer aims at strengthening one's faith and convictions. Meditation is thinking about God, becoming aware of God present in your life. You can prepare for meditation by reading Scripture or some other spiritual book, or by thinking about your own life. Meditation can also be spontaneously triggered. When the mind is properly focused, you can consciously address God. Be open to hearing God's response to you. Resolve to remember the insight you have gained and live out its implications.

2. **Affective prayer.** For those who are already firmly rooted in God and want to develop their friendship with God, affective prayer is appropriate. Affective prayer is simply being alone with God. Your relationship grows as you become better attuned and receptive to God's will.

*Notes*

## Praying

Try this model for contemplative prayer a few times. Evaluate your progress after each session. Don't hesitate to adjust it to your own needs.

1. Set a mood for prayer. Quiet your body and your mind. Take several deep breaths, making your inhaling and exhaling a prayer itself.

2. Read a passage from the Bible reflectively. You might want to start with Matthew 26:36–46.

3. See the event that you have just read occurring before your mind. Use all of your senses to actually become part of the event: smell the air, hear the noise, feel the tension.

4. Ask for assistance to understand this event more deeply.

5. When you come to the climax, stay with it as long as possible. Speak what comes to your mind.

6. Slowly, allow yourself to return to your surroundings.

3. **Contemplation.** In this form of prayer, you approach God with awe and reverence. You are so struck by God's wonder that all images and assumptions disappear. In contemplation, one experiences great peace and joy "bathing" in the divine presence.

## Pause a Moment . . .

- You may have seen the four categories of prayer described by the acronym ACTS (Adoration, Contrition, Thanksgiving, and Supplication). Write a prayer of your own that combines each of these elements.

- Prayer is an essential part of every religion of the world. Many religions use prayer aids to help with mental prayer (chants, prayer wheels, proper sitting position). The rosary is a Catholic prayer and meditation aid. Why are prayer aids important? How can you use them?

## FOR YOUR EXPLORATION

1. The Gospel according to Saint Luke offers three parables about the importance and power of prayer. Read these parables in your Bible and then briefly explain what they mean to you.

a. Luke 11:5–13 _____

_____

b. Luke 18:1–8 _____

_____

c. Luke 18:9–14 _____

_____

2. Using the insight you gained from the three parables above, write a one sentence directive about how or why you should pray. (e.g. "Never give up!")

_____

3. Write a short prayer for each of the following categories.

a. Adoration _____

_____

b. Thanksgiving _____

_____

c. Contrition _____

_____

d. Petition _____

_____

# Part III Discovery

## Responding in Prayer

Our understanding of personal prayer flows from our understanding of communal worship. The topic "Worship" describes in more detail the experience of community prayer and how it leads one to participate in the Church's mission of bringing about a world of love, justice, and reconciliation.

For many older adults, prayer is "the lifting up of the mind and heart to God" as they learned from studying the *Baltimore Catechism* as children. This definition suggests that it is not enough to simply say words from memory; prayer requires proper intent and feeling.

The *National Catechetical Directory (NCD)* defines prayer as "a deepening awareness of a covenanted relationship with God, coupled with the effort to live in total harmony with God's will" (# 140). This definition stresses one's awareness of his or her relationship with God and its importance on his or her life.

Prayer may also be described as simply "talking to God." This implies one is familiar and comfortable enough with God's presence to speak easily and often. Another definition, "putting oneself in the presence of God," describes the reflective side of prayer, a quiet, restful activity. This is what takes place in meditative prayer. By "listening to God" in prayer, one gives up the need for constant control and allows God to take the initiative.

### Personal Dimensions

Prayer can be a self-reflective lens. Just as a person's vision is corrected by looking through glasses, a person's perspective on his or her own life can become clearer through prayer. Prayer provides empathy, insight, and a greater understanding of God's will.

Each person's relationship with God is unique and so is each person's prayer. However, prayer always includes:

- A reaching out to God in trust.
- An openness to listen to God.
- A willingness to respond to God's request of us.

**Reaching Out to God in Trust.** Before we can reach out to God, God has already reached out to us. All prayer is in response to God's prior call. When we acknowledge God's initial touch we are in a position to pray. In prayer, we turn to God in trust. Because of this trust, anything we are concerned about, interested in, or anxious over can be mentioned in prayer.

Museums today often have telephones at exhibits. If you want to know more about what you are seeing, you can simply pick up the phone and listen to a prerecorded tape. Imagine that your life is like a museum exhibit. When you reach out to pick up the phone, God is on the other end, patiently waiting for your attention. Instead of a prerecorded message, however, you have God's personal attention.

**An Openness to Listen.** Some people are so concerned with telling God things in their prayers that they cannot hear God's response. It is important

▲ *A parent's relationship with each of his or her children is unique, differing from the relationship that exists with any other child. The same is true with prayer; each of us must develop our own relationship (and means to express it) with God.*

_____
_____
_____
_____
_____
_____
_____
_____
_____
_____
_____
_____

to tell God what is in our hearts, but there is an even greater need for us to hear what God has to say. As you grow in your prayer life, you will learn to be patient, to be quiet in God's presence, and to allow God to fill your heart. Like conversation, prayer is a two-way street.

**A Willingness to Respond.** You cannot honestly listen to friends share their hopes, dreams, and expectations without being moved to some type of response. The life and creativity of personal conversation with God moves us beyond the immediate moment and affects who we are and how we live. The inner transformation that comes from prayer leads to a life of service and to acts of justice.

## Being Ourselves with God

We don't need to put on an act with God; it's simply not necessary. God knows us exactly as we are, no matter how we hide our faults and failings. Once we realize this we can pray simply and honestly. We can respond to God without fear and share with God our mood of the moment or our great rush of emotion without worrying about what God will think. Just as good friends do not limit their conversation to only certain aspects of their lives, so, too, can we share everything with God.

## Making the Effort

Parents may experience a time in their lives when they watch their children miss an opportunity because of a lack of effort. If they try to make decisions for their children they will soon realize the futility of their actions.

Our relationship with God is similar. Others can share their experiences and encourage us to pray, but we need to form our own relationships. We can only come to know God by personally reaching out.

God always answers a sincere prayer, but not necessarily in the way we expect. We need not say too much; quality counts more than quantity. We need to spend as much time (if not more) listening instead of talking.

### Pause a Moment . . .

- Which of the definitions of prayer above comes closest to yours? Why is that definition meaningful to you?

- In what ways do you need to develop in your prayer?

- Take a few moments to reflect on your relationship with God. Close your eyes and speak freely to God in your heart about how you would like to improve it.

# Difficulties with Prayer

Prayer is not a form of escape. It is an effort to grow with God. Like many growing processes, it often requires great effort and struggle. View problems with prayer as opportunities for growth.

You may have experienced some of the following difficulties with prayer.

**How to Start?** Like a young person who feels awkward and out of place at his or her first dance, many of us do not know how to approach God. Remember that God loves and accepts us as we are. We don't have to impress

God with fancy words or displays of emotions. Simply be silent and think about God. Then, we can share any ideas or feelings we have at the moment. We can talk to God as we would to a person we admire and respect, pausing from time to time to listen to God's response in our heart.

**Will God Listen and Help?** When you pray, know that God is always with you and hears your prayers. Remember, our prayer is always sparked by God before we even think to pray. In many ways, it is the Spirit within us who prays through us. Silence may be a message forcing you to take responsibility for your life and growth in faith. Keep Saint Augustine's saying in mind: "Act as if everything depended upon you and pray as if everything depended upon God."

**Impatient for Results?** We live in a society that expects instant results. From this point of view prayer can seem to be a waste of time. You can be influenced by this pervasive attitude without realizing it. Remember that prayer is not a way of manipulating God to produce a desired, tangible result. It is part of our relationship with God. Focus on this relationship rather than on answers to requests. Even the most urgent pleas are best put in the context of this relationship. God won't magically remove the problem, but prayer can lead us to find the best attitude and course of action to take.

**Lacking Concentration?** We can pray anywhere, at any time, in any way we want. However, most people find that choosing a special time (6 A.M. before anyone else in the house is up) and a special place (your chair in the living room that faces East so you can celebrate the sunrise) improves both the quality and the quantity of their prayer. If you are tired, or if there is too much noise where you pray, you will easily be distracted.

No matter how many precautions you take, distractions will come; they are part of the process. They are like ripples in a pool of still water; if you try to iron them out, you only create more. Instead, relax and learn to coexist with them until they subside.

**Can't Find the Time?** If you try to fit prayer into your schedule when free time pops up, you probably won't pray. You need to make regular appointments with God and give them top priority. Start with a modest schedule for prayer and try it for three weeks. Then, evaluate your plan and make necessary adjustments. Try not to do too much too soon.

**Tempted to Give Up?** Learning to persevere in prayer is difficult. At times, the wait to find meaning or an answer to some problem seems endless. The temptation is to give up. In such situations, pray one day at a time. Such an approach can move one past a crisis in prayer or a spiritual dryness. The important factor is that you continue to pray and attempt to develop a pattern of prayer in your life.

## Pause a Moment . . .

- How does the definition of prayer from the Baltimore Catechism "lifting up the mind and heart to God" differ from the NCD's "a deepening awareness . . . with God and . . . the effort to live in total harmony with God's will"?

- How are these two definitions different ways of expressing the same reality?

- What does it mean to say that in prayer, "quality is better than quantity"?

## The New Commandment

"Ask and it will be given to you; seek and you will find; knock and the door will be opened to you. For everyone who asks, receives; and the one who seeks, finds; and to the one who knocks, the door will be opened. Which one of you would hand his son a stone when he asks for a loaf of bread, or a snake when he asks for a fish? If you then, who are wicked, know how to give good gifts to your children, how much more will your heavenly Father give good things to those who ask him.

(Matthew 7:7–11)

▲ *Instead of thinking of prayer as a burden, try thinking of it as our dance with God. There are times when our prayer can be a slow, cheek to cheek embrace, a wild, passionate tango, or even a traditional expression with every step dictated by culture. As long as you are on the dance floor, the Lord is waiting.*

Take a few moments to reflect on the following questions and then write your answers on the accompanying lines. If you'd like, share your answers with a friend.

1. Describe one difficulty you frequently have with prayer.

_____

_____

_____

2. What accounts for this difficulty?

_____

_____

_____

3. How have you tried to overcome this difficulty?

_____

_____

_____

4. How can this difficulty be an opportunity to grow closer to God?

_____

_____

_____

5. What have you learned from this topic that might help you improve your personal prayer?

_____

_____

_____

6. Write down your reflection and discussion with God about any difficulty you might have with prayer.

_____

_____

_____

7. Take a moment now for prayer. Close your eyes, clear your mind, shut down your thoughts and just be in the presence of your loving God.

# Part IV  Response

## Leading Students to Pray

You are called to grow in your communication with God, and share your faith with your students to help them to grow in their own faith. Pray with your students, and build in them a sense of wonder for the sacred. Help them to relax, listen, and recognize God's loving presence in every moment of their lives. Through your own verbal prayers, students will learn to pray, and develop a positive attitude toward prayer and its purpose.

Here are some things to keep in mind when planning lessons:

- The act of prayer should be an integral part of every lesson, not something merely tacked on to the beginning or end.

- Remember the age of your students; children do not pray as adults pray.

- While prayer is a necessary part of every religion class, the family remains the primary prayer model for students. If a family does not attend the Eucharist or pray together at home, you will have only limited success leading students to prayer.

- Prayer must be experienced. Meaningful prayer experiences will have far more impact on a student's prayer-life than any memorization or discussion.

- We are blessed with many ways to pray. Don't limit yourself to only one.

- Music, dance, and other forms of artistic expression can be powerful forms of prayer. Encourage your students to express themselves in prayer artistically as much as you can.

- While variety may truly be "the spice of life," repetition is necessary for people to grow comfortable with a prayer form. If you plan to introduce a new way of praying, use that method for several sessions until students feel comfortable using it on their own.

### Pause a Moment . . .

- What are ways that you can integrate prayer throughout your lesson, regardless of the topic? Do you feel comfortable praying in this way?

- What is the most creative way that you have ever prayed? What prevents you from praying creatively more frequently then you do?

## Age-Appropriate Prayer

Try these age appropriate prayer suggestions with your students. Refer to your religion program's teacher's manual for additional suggestions.

### Preschool and Kindergarten

Very young children can be led, over time, through various levels of participation in prayer:

- *Level One: Listen to Prayer.* Children listen as prayer is offered by someone else: "Dear God, thank you for the many friends here today. Friends make me feel very happy. Amen."
- *Level Two: Echo a Prayer.* The children repeat phrases after the catechist: "Dear God/ thank you/ for the trees,/ the birds,/ and the squirrels/ which are so much fun to watch./ Amen."
- *Level Three: Complete a Prayer.* The catechist begins a prayer and then invites the children to complete it using their own ideas: "Thank you, God, for giving us so many people who love us. Thank you for _____."
- *Level Four: Compose a Prayer.* The catechist suggests a topic for prayer and the children compose their own prayer: Catechist—"Thank God for your favorite toy." Student—"Dear God, I like to play with my puppy. Thank you. Amen." Refer to your teacher's manual for various ways of expressing prayer through hand positions, body motions, and finger play.

## Grades 1 and 2

Although they still respond more readily to the "Jesus-and-me" type prayer, these children are at the threshold of wanting to pray as a group. The students will be very interested in learning the words of prayers, while drawings and other objects will help them to focus their thoughts. Remember to keep meditations and periods of silence very short. Prayer services with first and second graders should include clapping, holding hands, singing, and dancing. Murals, mobiles, and other student-made crafts can be part of prayer services.

## Grades 3 and 4

Prayer can seem somewhat magical at this age: "I prayed every night, and I still didn't get what I wanted for Christmas!" Their "law-and-order" mentality requires strict adherence to rules ("Maybe I didn't pray hard enough..."). God is thought of in very factual (anthropomorphic) terms ("I guess God didn't hear me."). Expect their prayer to be simple and straight-forward, with few extra words. Use short, simple prayers in class.

- These students have a growing group consciousness that makes communal prayer possible. They enjoy planning and participating in prayer services.
- Encourage spontaneous prayer by starting a sentence and asking them to complete it: "Thank you, God, for _____." "Jesus, help me to _____."

## Grades 5 and 6

In addition to being more verbal, these students are more reflective than younger children.

- At times, include several minutes of silence each lesson during which students can think and pray by themselves. A period of silence before or after certain parts of a lesson can also prove useful.
- Introduce students to keeping a prayer journal. In a small notebook, have them make short entries completing the phrase: "Dear Jesus, I want to tell you _____."

## Grades 7 and 8

This age group will enjoy spontaneous petitions, as well as planning and participating in occasional prayer services.

- Study the Stations of the Cross. Take the students on a tour of the church, pointing out the various stations. Provide a list of Scripture quotes that pertain to Jesus' suffering and death. Have each student choose a station and write his or her own prayer for it. Then, pray the stations using the students' prayers.

- Introduce your students to praying with the Bible. Read a story from the life of Jesus and invite students to reflect on its meaning for them. Have the students pick a saying and write a short conversation with Jesus about how that saying is important to them.

## High School

Many of the methods of prayer mentioned above can be used with high school students.

- Retreats are particularly well received at this age, especially if they are set in a place other than the usual classroom surroundings.

- Popular music, films, and videos, along with selections from literature, and poetry help students reflect and meditate. Encourage them to keep prayer journals or diaries and to respect the prayers expressed by others.

## Adults

By varying the way you pray with adults, you can renew interest and inspiration in their prayer.

- Explore new ways of using old prayers—for example, invite your students to come up with their own mysteries for the rosary. Perhaps pray one of the hours in the Divine Office together.

- Challenge your students to examine their images of God or the meaning of Church, Christian values, and the role of sacraments in everyday living.

- Cultivate periods of silent reflection; play instrumental music that helps create a mood for prayer; use simple environment settings to help focus on a specific theme.

- Through journal writing, spiritual reading, and praying with Scripture, help your students to perceive the spiritual life as a lifelong journey and to discover how their faith is developing.

- Introduce prayer experiences that develop the skills of listening and observing. Day and weekend retreats are also very effective.

## Pause a Moment . . .

- Look through three lessons in your teacher's manual and student textbook. What types and methods of prayer do you find there?

- Which of the ideas above do you think will be most helpful with your students?

*Memo*

In light of what I have learned about prayer, I want to keep in mind the following considerations for the next time I meet with my students:

## Notes

_____

_____

_____

_____

_____

_____

_____

_____

_____

_____

_____

## Prayer Response

Reflect on the following questions: "What did prayer mean to you when you were ten?" "What has prayer meant to you during the past six months?" Close your eyes and ask for God's help as you grow in your relationship with God through prayer.

## BIBLIOGRAPHY

Costello, Gwen. *Praying With Children.* Mystic, CT: Twenty-Third Publications, 1990.

Cronin, Gaynell. *Effective Teaching Methods I and II.* Paulist Press, videos.

_____. *Holy Days and Holidays, vols I and II.* San Francisco: Harper & Row, 1985, 1987.

Darcy-Berube, Francoise, and John Paul Berube. *Someone's There: Paths to Prayer for Young People.* Notre Dame, IN: Ave Maria Press, 1986.

de Mello, Anthony. *Song of the Bird.* New York: Doubleday, 1982.

Dues, Greg. *Season Prayer Services for Teenagers.* Mystic, CT: Twenty-Third Publications, 1991.

*Experiencing Prayer.* Allen, TX: Tabor, video.

Glavich, Mary Kathleen, SND. *Leading Students into Prayer: Ideas and Suggestions from A to Z.* Mystic, CT: Twenty-Third Publications, 1993.

Hawkowski, Maryann. *Pathways to Praying with Teens.* Winona, MN: St. Mary's Press, 1993.

Hays, Father Edward. "An Invitation to Prayer: A Guide For Deepening Our Prayer Life," *Catholic Update.* Cincinnati: St. Anthony Messenger Press, February, 1992.

Jeep, Elizabeth McMahon. *Children's Daily Prayer.* Chicago: Liturgy Training Publications, 1993. Liturgy of the Hours adapted yearly for children.

Manternach, Janaan. *And the Children Pray: A Practical Book for Prayerful Catechists.* Notre Dame, IN: Ave Maria Press, 1989.

National Conference of Catholic Bishops. "Chapter VI, Catechesis for a Worshipping Community." In *Sharing the Light of Faith: National Catechetical Directory for Catholics of the United States.* Washington, DC: USCC Publications, 1979.

Pennock, Michael. *The Ways of Prayer.* Notre Dame, IN: Ave Maria Press, 1987.

*Prayer Starters.* Kansas City, MO: Sheed & Ward, 3 videos.

Sacred Heart Kids' Club. Series One: Faith/Creed, segment #23, "Prayer: God Speaks and Listens," video.

Schaeffler, Janet, O.P. "Praying Is Saying Thanks," *Religion Teacher's Journal.* March, 1984.

*What Every Christian Should Know About Prayer.* Scriptographic booklet, Channing L. Bete Co., Inc.

Wintz, Jack. "Pathways of Prayer." *Catholic Update.* Cincinnati: St. Anthony Messenger Press, March 1981.

*Nihil Obstat*
The Reverend Gregory A. Banazak, S.T.D.

*Imprimatur*
The Most Reverend Kenneth J. Povish, D.D.
Bishop of Lansing
May 13, 1994

The *Nihil Obstat* and *Imprimatur* are official declarations that a book or pamphlet is free of doctrinal or moral error. No implication is contained therein that those who have granted the *Nihil Obstat* and *Imprimatur* agree with the contents, opinions, or statements expressed.

Scripture passages are taken from *The New American Bible with Revised New Testament,* copyright © 1988 by the Confraternity of Christian Doctrine, Washington, D.C. All rights reserved.

Copyright © 1995 by Glencoe/McGraw-Hill. All rights reserved. Except as permitted under the United States Copyright Act, no part of this publication may be reproduced or distributed in any form or by any means, or stored in a database or retrieval system, without the prior written permission of the publisher.

This chapter may be ordered separately using the following ISBN number.

Send all inquiries to:

BENZIGER PUBLISHING COMPANY
15319 Chatsworth Street
P.O. Box 9609
Mission Hills, California 91346-9609

Second Edition

**ISBN 0-02-651217-3**

Printed in the United States of America.

1 2 3 4 5 6 7 8 9   BAW   98 97 96 95 94

## Benziger

# Christian Morality and Catechesis

*Following Christ is not an outward imitation, since it touches [us] at the very depths of [our] being. Being a follower of Christ means becoming conformed to him who became a servant even to giving himself on the Cross and thus the disciple is conformed to the Lord. This is the effect of grace, of the active presence of the Holy Spirit in us.*

Veritatis Splendor, #21

**BOOK TWO**

Written by
**Peter Ries**

Consultant
**David Riley**

### In this chapter you will:

- Recognize Jesus as the center of Christian morality.
- Review the Commandments and their implications for today.
- Consider Christian morality as a journey of conversion.
- Examine approaches to teaching Christian morality.

Second Edition

## The Last to Know

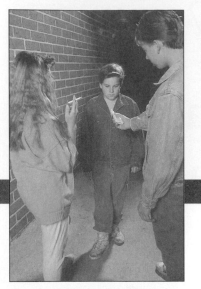

▲ *Luisa, the mother in this story, was unaware of the people at school who were influencing her daughter. How aware are you of the people and events who influence your children or the students you teach?*

As a child, Luisa Turza developed an acute sense of justice. Whenever Luisa saw what she considered oppression or injustice, she spoke out. In college, she was enraged by the maltreatment of minority students, and ran for student government president on that basis. Upon graduation, she pursued a law degree to fight for the rights of the underprivileged.

When she received her J.D. degree, Luisa went to work for the Mexican-American Legal Defense Fund. She won several landmark cases on behalf of people who often could not speak up for themselves in English. Luisa was honored several times by her colleagues for her courage and moral sense.

Luisa eventually married a classmate from law school, and they had a daughter whom she named Gabriella, after her grandmother. Luisa and her husband ensured that Gabriella went to the best schools and had many diverse cultural experiences, so that she would grow up to be a well-educated, self-reliant person. Luisa regretted not being able to spend more time with her husband and daughter, but she was very committed to her work.

One day, Luisa was called to Gabriella's high school. To her shock, she learned that Gabriella had been caught stealing items from other students' lockers. This meant automatic suspension and possible expulsion for Gabriella. Luisa was hurt, embarrassed, worried, and angry. The silence during the drive home was deafening and painful.

Luisa asked Sr. Frances, the pastoral assistant of her parish, to visit with Gabriella. Luisa had worked with Frances on a number of occasions and trusted her judgment. Frances agreed to meet Gabriella, but only if she spoke with Luisa first.

"Luisa," she asked, "what has been happening with Gabriella lately that might explain this behavior?"

"Nothing," Luisa said. "Her grades have been fine, she's been doing her work around the house, and her employer comments on what a good worker she is. I can't imagine what . . ."

"Excuse me," Sr. Frances broke in. "All that is good, in fact, very good, but it's also external to my question. What I mean is, what has Gabriella been thinking and feeling lately?"

Luisa realized that she couldn't answer Frances's question. It had been far too long since she and Gabriella had really talked. The same could be said about her relationship with her husband. "I guess I've been so busy with this tenant rights case and my other work that I haven't had time for Gabriella," she said. "But if she needed my attention, all she had to do was ask. I'm always there for my daughter."

"Well, she certainly found a way to get your attention this time, didn't she? My guess is that you have been too busy saving the world to hear your daughter's requests for help. Am I right?" Frances asked pointedly.

"Luisa, you are a courageous and heroic woman. What you have done for the poor and downtrodden of this community has been unbelievable. I can't thank you enough. But life has a way of interfering with our best laid plans. We get so tied up in what *we* have to do that we don't allow room for the needs of others. Making the right choices every day is difficult, but if we want our relationships to grow, we need to set our own plans aside and notice what the people in our life need in that moment."

Luisa was silent for a while. Finally, she said, "I was pretty satisfied with myself until today. I guess I have a lot to learn about relationships."

Frances smiled. "You have much to be satisfied with, Luisa. But to follow Jesus we must be willing to deny ourselves and take up his cross each day of our lives. You can never stop taking up the cross; in each moment, you have to ask what following Jesus means. Sometimes the answers will surprise you."

Luisa nodded slowly. "I think I'm beginning to understand," she said. Frances then headed upstairs to Gabriella's room.

Luisa let many important things get in the way of her relationship with her daughter. Her daughter misbehaved to gain her mother's attention. We can only surmise how many other ways she had tried in the past.

The same thing happens in our relationship with God. We get so busy that we no longer can hear God calling out for us. However, while Gabriella acted out to get her mother's attention, we act out—we sin—when we are not paying attention to God.

Take a few moments to answer the following questions.

1. How would you describe the basis of Christian morality?

_____

_____

2. Have you found this knowledge helpful or burdensome to daily living? Why?

_____

_____

3. How would you explain the value of Christian morality to a skeptical adult?

_____

_____

4. In what ways is Christian morality concerned with one's relationship with God?

_____

_____

_____

_____

> ## Memo
>
> What does it take to build a relationship and keep it strong?

## The Way, the Truth, and the Life

When Jesus saw the crowds, he went up on the mountainside and sat down. "How blest are the poor in spirit," he began. "The reign of God is theirs. Blest too are the sorrowing; they shall be consoled. Blest are the lowly; they shall inherit the land. Blest are they who hunger and thirst for holiness; they shall have their fill."

Jesus paused. He remembered the words of the prophet Hosea that described the heart of the law: "It is mercy I desire and not sacrifice." The words inspired Jesus. He stood up and continued: "Blest are they who show mercy; mercy shall be theirs. Blest are the single-hearted for they shall see God. Blest, too, the peacemakers; they shall be called children of God."

Jesus saw the hope in the people's eyes. He wanted them to know how much God loved them, that the covenant was not a one-sided affair. God would bless those who lived and loved according to the spirit of the law.

Jesus raised his hands in the air to hold the people's attention. He said in a loud voice, "Blest are you when they insult you and persecute you and utter every kind of slander against you because of me. Be glad and rejoice, for your reward is great in heaven."

The people looked at one another, amazed. "What does this mean? A completely new teaching given with such authority?"

Jesus let the crowd know his teachings were rooted in the Law of Moses and the message of the prophets. He quieted the crowd and said, "Do not think that I have come to abolish the law and the prophets. I have come, not to abolish them, but to fulfill them. Whoever breaks the least significant of these commands and teaches others to do so shall be called least in the kingdom of God. Whoever fulfills and teaches these commands shall be great in the kingdom of God."

Jesus spent the rest of the day explaining the Law of Moses. He breathed new life—a new spirit—into the law. It was a spirit of reconciliation with God and with neighbor, a spirit of justice, tolerance, and forgiveness.

When Jesus finished teaching, the people were spellbound. They felt refreshed and encouraged to learn that they could adhere to God's law and yet be so free. The people also felt challenged. God was doing something new and had asked for their help. To understand and act on Jesus' message, the people were called to see life in a new way. They were called to know the spirit of the law, to be a people of mercy and peace. They were called to see Jesus as the way, the truth, and the life, the leader and center of the new way, the mediator of a brand new covenant: "If you love me, keep my commandments."

This message Jesus preached (see *Matthew 5* and *Luke 6:20–49*) is at the heart of all Christian morality. The Bible offers us many more specific instances of how we are to behave than those offered in the Beatitudes, but the Beatitudes provide the core of Jesus' message. Morality is more than merely obeying laws, it is about living the life of the kingdom; living in a right relationship with God.

*Notes*

## Pause a Moment . . .

- What do you feel would be missing if you did not have Jesus' life and teachings to guide your moral decisions?
- What do you think the sentence "Morality is more than merely obeying laws, it's about living the life of the kingdom" means?

## What Is Morality?

In the past, the question "What is morality?" seemed to have a clear answer. There were lists of sins. If unsure about something, a person could go over such a list when examining one's conscience. This was basically an *act-centered morality.* Right and wrong were clearly defined. The emphasis was on obedience to Church authority and the role of individual conscience was minimized. This approach tended toward legalism—obeying the law without regard to intention. You didn't have to wonder about moral choices, they were made for you.

Today, the question is approached differently. Actions are seen as having two parts—the "what" and the "why." The "what" is the action itself. The "why" is one's reason for doing it. Morality is seen as more relational or intention-centered. Discerning right and wrong can be complex. Often clarity in moral decisions comes only after a long and strenuous search. At times, clarity is never reached. The emphasis is on knowing God's will for our lives through conscience formation within the nurturing presence of the believing community. If one is not careful and attentive to the wisdom of the faith community, this approach can lean toward subjectivism—"Right and wrong is what I say it is."

In this framework, "moral" is defined as that which improves one's relationship with God or other people. "Moral" is that which gives life or adds to the quality of life. "Immoral" is that which weakens one's relationship with God or other people. "Immoral" is that which takes away from life or the quality of life.

### Basic Concepts about Christian Morality

In general, Christian morality flows from three sources: Scripture, the teachings of the Church, and human reason and experience. Scripture, Church teachings, and human reason work together. For instance, the Book of Genesis reveals the equality of the sexes: God created Eve from Adam's rib. Church teaching understands and applies this revelation in various ways, condemning the maltreatment of women and affirming their rights. The Church has come to this understanding through human reason. From experience, we have learned how impoverished we are when the role and contribution of women are restricted.

### Motivation for Moral Decisions

From time to time Jesus said he always did the will of his Father *(John 6:38).* This was his one moral criterion. This was how he made his moral decisions. Jesus did his Father's will because of his personal relationship of love and not because of laws and punishment. Hopefully we Christians today

## The Church Teaches

In the young man, whom Matthew's Gospel (19:16–21) does not name, we can recognize every person who, consciously or not, *approaches Christ the Redeemer of man and questions him about morality.* For the young man, the *question* is not so much about rules to be followed, but about *the full meaning of life.* This is in fact the aspiration at the heart of every human decision and action, the quiet searching and interior prompting which sets freedom in motion. This question is ultimately an appeal to the absolute Good which attracts us and beckons us; it is the echo of a call from God who is the origin and goal of man's life.

*(Veritatis Splendor, #7)*

will make our moral decisions not out of legalism or duty alone, but because of our honest consideration of the question, "What does God want of me at this moment?"

This is a morality of *gift and response*. God has begun a relationship with us by the gifts of creation and love. Morality can honestly be seen as our response to God's gifts. Do we act out of love or do we reject God's gifts for our own desires?

As Christians we are called to live by the same standards as Jesus did. "This is my commandment: love one another as I have loved you" *(John 15:12)*. This may seem demanding. Its implications may even be frightening. Jesus is not asking for natural goodness. Nor is he asking for mere legalism which is impersonal and loveless. The call of Christian morality goes beyond legalism.

This type of morality is indeed a challenge. But Jesus promised that the Holy Spirit would always be with us to help us. We have his continuous presence in the Church, our faith community. We experience him through the sacraments and in prayer. We have his encouragement through each other.

## Foundation of Morality

The *Catechism of the Catholic Church*, in paragraphs 1691–2558, summarizes the Church's teaching on morality. In the first of these paragraphs, the Church offers us moral guidance.

1. Christian morality starts with human dignity. We can know good from evil because we are made in the image of God (1700–1715).

2. Christian morality is a free response to God's goodness. We shape our lives by our free choices. Because we are free, we must accept responsibility for our actions (1730–1737).

3. Freedom and dignity are injured through sin. By refusing to love God we deceive ourselves and become entrapped in the web of sin. It is only through grace that we regain our freedom (1739–1742).

4. The morality of human acts depends on: (a) the object chosen, (b) one's intention, (c) the circumstances. A morally good act presupposes that the object, intention, and circumstances of an act are good. Evil purposes can corrupt good acts, and evil acts cannot lead to good (1749–1756).

5. Through the moral conscience, every person is called to do good and avoid evil. Conscience bears witness to the supreme truth and judges the moral quality of an act. It is conscience that allows us to take responsibility for our actions. People have a right to act in conscience and freedom. They cannot be forced to act against their conscience (1772–1782).

6. Conscience is informed and enlightened in accordance with reason and divine will. Conscience is shaped from the earliest age through love, obedience to law, and learning to live the virtues (1783–1785).

7. Decisions made in conscience are not always moral. A conscience acting in error can lead one astray (1786–1794).

The *Catechism* continues on in its teaching of morality for nearly 800 more paragraphs. It offers in many of those pages a full treatment of the Ten Commandments as moral guides for our consciences.

- What do you understand by the words "moral" and "immoral"?
- How had what you have learned during the past ten years of your life influenced the way you make moral decisions?
- What is the significance of the statement that one cannot be forced to act against his or her conscience?

## The Ten Commandments: Covenant Roots

God showed Moses the way when he renewed the covenant he had begun with Abraham. He promised to guide the people, to hold them together, and to take them to a land of their own where they could at last settle. In turn, the Hebrews were to keep God's commandments. This covenant relationship was the Hebrew's identification badge; it was the glue that held them together—their constitution—and it was their guiding light into the future, into the world of their dreams.

The commandments were given to the Hebrews to preserve their relationship with God and to help them live in peace with one another. The first three commandments reminded the Hebrews that they were to hold God in highest esteem, and to revere and worship God. The last seven commandments reminded them to respect one another in every detail of their lives: in their relationships, in their property, in their speech, and in their actions.

The commandments still apply to us. Like the nomadic Hebrews, we look to our covenant with God as the source of our identity. When we keep the commandments according to the mind and spirit of Christ, we fulfill our part of the covenant.

### The Commandments and Their Implications for Today

The heart of morality is a consistent effort to know the will of God in one's life and to strive to follow it—to do always the will of the Father. Jesus reminded us that this is the task of every generation: To constantly reconsider, re-evaluate, and reinterpret their responsibility to God, other people and themselves in the light of their particular conditions and circumstances.

This does not imply that we can do whatever we want. "There are certain specific kinds of behavior that are always wrong to choose, because choosing them involves a disorder of the will, that is, a moral evil" (*Catechism of the Catholic Church, #1761*). (See also *Veritatis Splendor, #78*.) However, Christians are called to do more than avoid evil, they must also work for good. We are called to search out and discern the developing moral requirements of one's time and situation. Thus, the moral guidance provided by the commandments is necessary.

**I Am the Lord Your God.** *Basic Value:* There is but one God, who alone deserves our total and complete love. God's greatness is so overwhelming that nothing can substitute for God.

*Today's Issues:* False worship is not absent from modern society. Pleasure, popularity, and power are the primary foci for many people. Individuals sacrifice marriage and family for their job or success in business. Materialism or science is the only religion for many. Forms of idolatry will continue to

▲ *How are today's idols different from the gods of old?*

_____

_____

_____

_____

_____

_____

_____

_____

_____

_____

_____

change and we need to be aware of much more than graven images. How do people deny the living God today?

**The Name of the Lord.**  *Basic Value:* Prayer, worship, and reverence are means of praising God and acknowledging God's Lordship.

*Today's Issues:* People sometimes take this commandment too lightly. We need to be cautious about the mechanical use of prayers and sacraments as means to manipulate God to serve our needs. Are we aware that every prayer and approach to the sacraments is a direct meeting with God?

**Keep Holy the Sabbath Day.**  *Basic Value:* Regular, reflective, communal opportunities to open oneself to God's presence are essential to maintaining a healthy relationship with God.

*Today's Issues:* As human beings, we need a regular pattern for taking time for ourselves and for God. We need to celebrate the Sabbath as a community, for that is where we come to and grow in faith.

**Honor Your Father and Your Mother.**  *Basic Value:* A person's ultimate worth and right to respect are based on the fact that one is a creature of God.

*Today's Issues:* Honor, reverence, and respect are owed to every person, not because of one's talent, congeniality, or ability to contribute materially, but simply because of his or her unique dignity as a child of God. All Christians are to consistently promote, safeguard, and respect the dignity of every person.

**You Shall Not Kill.**  *Basic Value:* God alone (not individuals or society) is the ultimate Lord and Master of human life.

*Today's Issues:* Christians cannot avoid personal responsibility whenever human life is threatened. This commandment calls one to develop a *consistent* sensitivity and respect for life as a gift from God. Life in all its manifestations, your own and others, is a precious fragile gift from God. Ask yourself: Do I care for it, respect it, and assume my responsibility for it?

**You Shall Not Commit Adultery.**  *Basic Value:* Total fidelity in love and marriage, reflecting God's total fidelity, is essential to a responsible loving marriage and a healthy society.

*Today's Issues:* Since Vatican II the mutual personal growth of both spouses has been seen as an outcome of marriage, with procreation as a result of that growing love. Today, fidelity is seen as both a physical consideration as well as a manifestation of one's entire person. Fidelity reflects all aspects of a relationship.

**You Shall Not Steal.**  *Basic Value:* Depriving people of something that is rightfully theirs violates their God-given gift of freedom.

*Today's Issues:* Stealing in any form is an infringement on a person's freedom. There are many ways one can steal. For example, racism and sexual discrimination steal one's dignity and livelihood. The unfair manipulation and misuse of the world's resources keep nations in extreme poverty. Jesus considered indifference and unresponsiveness in the face of another person's urgent needs as grounds which could exclude one from the kingdom *(Matthew 25:31–46).*

**You Shall Not Bear False Witness.**  *Basic Value:* Respect for truth, especially as it affects one's reputation, is everyone's right and responsibility.

*Today's Issues:* The scope of this commandment extends to all situations of lying and dishonesty. We have become more sensitive to the subtle ways we can injure someone through racial prejudice and other forms of discrimination. Certainly, idle gossip and cutting remarks have a similar effect.

**You Shall Not Covet.** *Basic Value:* Genuine morality requires not only right actions but also right attitudes. Internal conviction is as important as external conformity in the area of sexuality and of property.

*Today's Issues:* These last two commandments are somewhat different than the first eight in that they point to another aspect of morality—the internal. The moral response is not merely external conformity; it also requires internal conviction. The heart of a person manifests itself in that person's actions (See *Matthew 15:19*).

These Commandments require a lifelong task of continuing openness and responsiveness to God's constant calling—the serious commitment to the often painful process of really getting to know oneself.

## *Pause a Moment . . .*

- What is the value of the Commandments today?
- How do the Commandments form the foundation of the Christian moral life?
- How can the Commandments help you develop a better relationship with God?

### REFLECTION

1. Which do you consider more important, love of God or love of neighbor? Please explain.

_____

_____


2. Read Matthew 5–7 (the Sermon on the Mount). Choose three points Jesus makes in those chapters and describe how each point applies to some situation in your life. Describe how each situation goes beyond actions and includes a consideration of attitudes and motives.

_____

_____


3. Leading a moral life involves struggle. There is a risk of error in our moral judgments. There is also the risk of personal failure. What is your attitude toward the struggle and failure of moral living?

_____

_____

_____

# $\mathcal{P}$art III $\mathcal{D}$iscovery

## Christian Morality—A Journey of Conversion

The Mind of the Church ◀

The Mind of the Church

The Holy Spirit also guides the Church through the faith of the community or *sensus fidelium.* The Second Vatican Council *(Dei Verbum, #8)* teaches that the living understanding of the deposit of faith grows through the contemplation and study of the faithful and their own perception of the spiritual things they experience. The mind of the Church is the mind of the believers in the ecclesial community. In this way, the Church's understanding is shaped by the lives of the faithful.

The Church is God's family on a journey to the Father. While the trip is full of wonders and surprises, it is also full of hazards, and so the Church stays united to Christ who is himself the way. Through the Holy Spirit Jesus leads his Church on the journey, guiding it safely through various difficulties and challenges along the way.

The Holy Spirit helps us on our journey of conversion, shaping us into Christ by teaching us to follow Jesus. The Spirit guides us in three important ways: (1) by opening up the meaning of the Scriptures, (2) by guiding the Magisterium in formulating moral teachings, and (3) by enlightening our reason with the gift of faith.

Christian morality is rooted in the covenant with God in Christ. We follow Jesus Christ who is himself the love of God. But following Christ does not come automatically. By our baptism we are freed from the slavery of sin to follow Christ. We study the Scriptures to hear the word of the Lord and to learn his will. We listen to the Church's moral teachings to know how to apply God's word in the modern world. Enlightened by our faith in Christ, we use our reason to personalize all these principles and act on them in our own ways. To live the new covenant in Christ, one must both do good and avoid evil. Christians focus their attention on the good they must do on their journey to the Father, but they try to avoid the sins that harm themselves, others, and their relationship with God.

Doing good and avoiding evil sounds simple, but it is a difficult maxim to live by. Saint Paul talks about the difficulty he had in accomplishing this simple task in Romans 7 when he says, "For I do not do the good I want, but I do the evil I do not want" *(Romans 7:19)*. Living a moral life is an ongoing process of sin and forgiveness, of good intentions and setbacks, of moving forward and moving back. While we must do our part, our hope lies in the goodness of God.

### Living a Virtuous Life

Virtues are good habits learned through practice. Saint Paul, in Galatians 5:22–23 offers several virtues as fruits of the Spirit: love, joy, peace, patience, kindness, generosity, faith, mildness, and chastity. By living these virtues constantly, we can grow as members of the Christian community and build a better world in response to God's will.

By practicing the theological virtues (faith, hope, and charity) and the moral virtues (prudence, justice, courage, and temperance), Christians learn to habitually keep the covenant law in Christ. Though the obligation to obey God's law remains, once a person habitually avoids evil, he or she is free to focus on creatively doing good.

Jesus showed us how to live. His description of the Last Judgment shows what it means to put the Ten Commandments and the Beatitudes into positive action.

*"For I was hungry and you gave me food, I was thirsty and you gave me drink, a stranger and you welcomed me, naked and you clothed me, ill and you cared for me, in prison and you visited me"* (Matthew 25:35–36).

The more we do good and work for justice, the more we grow in love, and our ability to do good and avoid evil increases. Eventually, our judgment about what is right and wrong is honed to reflect the will of God.

## Values as Challenges

Jesus did not leave us an answer key to all the moral questions in our lives. His values can conflict with ours when we attempt to apply them to concrete personal decisions. And there is a risk of failure in every decision we make. As a result, it may seem that Jesus was not too concerned with the risk of failure in our moral decision-making. However, he allowed more room for mistakes than he did for pride and dishonesty. All he asked was that we accept the challenge of these values and apply them honestly in our lives. We may dread facing the implication of these values, e.g. in the area of social justice, because we are not sure if we want to go in the direction these values are leading us. In these moments we can ask for the guidance and strength of the Holy Spirit.

The Commandments were initially given to define God's people. God's people were those who lived according to the values found in the Commandments. Their original purpose was positive and life-giving, not negative. Following the Commandments is the path to true happiness.

Jesus in the Gospels is not opposed to the Commandments. He is against the negative legalistic way in which some people were living them out. He continues the spirit of the Commandments but warns against the self-satisfaction that can arise when one merely fulfills the law. It is not enough to simply do good. We must also *love* God and *love* our neighbor. The commandments inner message is reborn and fulfilled in the Beatitudes and the social teachings of Jesus.

Judgment that has been fine-tuned to know the mind of Christ is an informed conscience. It is a learned skill developed by studying, reflecting upon, and practicing the Gospel in union with the whole Church. As we come to know Jesus better and allow the Spirit to work in our lives, we grow in conscience. As our conscience develops we move beyond the compulsions and fears learned in childhood. We become freer to love the Lord.

Moral questions are questions about our relationship with God and our relationships with people. A Christian considers friendship with God to be most important and so lovingly obeys God's commands. A Christian acts toward others with the same love and respect that he or she has for God. Law and love become one for the Christian because Jesus Christ is God's love and sums up in himself the whole law and message of the prophets.

## Pause a Moment . . .

- Why is Christian morality more than avoiding evil?
- What does it mean to be a virtuous person? How can you help someone develop virtue?
- Leading German citizens plotted to kill Adolph Hitler during a staff meeting. Others would be killed by the bomb as well. Was this a moral act?

## The New Commandment

*"What is your opinion? A man had two sons. He came to the first and said, 'Son, go out and work in the vineyard today.' He said in reply, 'I will not,' but afterwards he changed his mind and went. The man came to the other son and gave the same order. He said in reply, 'Yes, sir,' but did not go. Which of the two did his father's will?"*

Matthew 21:28–31

▲ *Help your students reflect upon their actions and begin to take responsibility for them.*

# Part IV Response

## Approaches to Teaching Christian Morality

No matter what grade you teach, keep the following things in mind:

1. Present Jesus as the center of Christian morality. Knowing right from wrong comes from following Jesus, specifically by studying and applying Gospel values in the light of Church teachings. Treat moral obligations as important and necessary for growing in our relationship with God and our relationships with others.

2. Present Jesus as the model of virtuous conduct and the Ten Commandments and the Beatitudes as guides to use in following Jesus.

3. Give your students the information necessary *for their age level* to help them develop their consciences.

4. Emphasize that the students not only must know what is right, but they also must *desire to do* what is right. Help them develop the proper attitudes by practicing the virtues.

5. Promote self-reflection in your students. The capacity for self-reflection will vary widely according to age. Challenge students to think for themselves so that they can learn the art of making moral decisions according to their level of development. This includes learning to take responsibility for their actions.

6. Have your students consider how they would want to be treated in a given situation. Children in the middle grades can understand the golden rule, "Do unto others as you would have them do unto you."

7. Ask your students to describe their choices as they see them. Help them see the consequences of these choices. Students learn to make moral decisions as they recognize their own situation and understand what their choices are. Encourage students to creatively apply Gospel values to the choices they make daily.

### Preschool and Kindergarten

These youngest of students can be taught basic attitudes upon which moral values can be developed.

- **Taking turns:** Have short lines of students take turns playing a game such as a beanbag toss or seeing who can build the tallest tower with blocks. After each child finishes, he or she should prepare the pieces for the next child.

- **Helping:** Invite the children to suggest ways they can help their families at home. Draw their ideas on the chalkboard with stick figures. Have students help straighten out and pick up the classroom before leaving.

- **Sharing:** Use a children's book about sharing (check with your DRE or your public library for examples). Tell the story about Jesus feeding the 5,000 hungry people. Use it as an example of how we should share with others.

- **Concern:** Help students learn to empathize with others. Ask, "How do you feel when that happens to you?" "How do you think it feels when you hit (say mean things to) her?"

## Lower Elementary

At the primary level, children need a strong sense that they belong to their families and to their parishes. You can't repeat enough that they are important members of God's family. Because of their level of moral development, they judge "rightness" and "wrongness" by the *consequences* of their actions rather than by their *intentions.*

- Children from ages six to nine generally perceive right and wrong in terms of reward and punishment. Stress obedience to Jesus and God's family as the virtue for these children to practice.

- Present the children with stories of saints and Christian heroes as examples of how people have followed and obeyed Jesus. Tell the students some of the parables that Jesus told (for example, the story of the Good Shepherd, the Widow's Coin, the Good Samaritan), and stories about Jesus to help them see the right way to act.

- Ask your students to name some simple rules they are asked to follow. List the rules on the board. Taking each rule in turn, ask what happens when the rule is not followed. Ask what happens when the rule is followed. Add these answers on the board next to the particular rule. Stress with your students that rules are intended to help us. Make the same point about the Commandments.

## Upper Elementary

During the middle grades, children have need for social approval through living by the rules. Stress the idea that as members of the People of God they are called to live according to the covenant with God.

- Tell the children unfinished stories with moral dimensions and allow them to create the endings. Or have them examine case studies to see which person acted in accordance with God's law and which person did not.

- Children from ages nine to twelve perceive right and wrong in terms of adult approval. Help the students to see that they are expected to obey their parents, teachers, and other people of legitimate authority.

- These students have a keen sense of justice. Explain that just as society has rules to keep things running orderly, the People of God have rules—the Ten Commandments and the Beatitudes—to help members love God and others. When people follow the rules of God's family, they grow as persons and build up the Church.

- Let students work with Bible stories to find the principles that guide God's family. Also, have them analyze contemporary situations—whether fictitious or real—to discover the motivations and behavior that should characterize members of God's family.

## Junior High

Most of these students are now beginning to understand principles of right and wrong. Their need for approval begins to shift from their parents to their peers. There is now the sense of "the right way" to think and behave. Tap into their natural moral development by showing them that the Church is a community that cooperates to improve the world. Jesus is God's Son who set out to build God's kingdom. We contribute to that task by loving and caring for others, by participating fully in the life of the Church, and by remaining faithful to the teachings of Christ and the Apostles.

- Respect for themselves and others is a key developmental issue at this age, especially in areas of sexuality. Use affirmation exercises to build a sense of self-respect. Have students discuss what they like about themselves. Have others say what they like about others. Praise students whenever the opportunity presents itself. Compliment them on their looks, their attitudes, their behavior.

- The students are now capable of researching and understanding the lives of saints and Christian heroes. Have the students analyze how, by living the right way, these Christian models bettered the world.

- Ask students to make a record of particular situations in their favorite TV shows when characters face decisions or make choices. Tell them to bring the results of their research to your next class. Discuss: What did the character decide? What were the consequences of that choice? Was this a good or bad decision? What would Jesus have done in a similar situation?

- Help students develop a sense of *media literacy.* Have them evaluate what they see and hear and discuss their findings in class. Develop with students criteria for judging the value of the media.

## High School

Many high school students are capable of wanting to do good for its own sake and not necessarily for the reward or approval of doing the right thing. They are developing a sense of self and a personal relationship with God. Help them to grow closer to Jesus as the model of unselfish love and the Church as the community reborn in God's love. The task of each Christian is to pattern one's life after Christ so that thoughts, words, and actions reflect God's compassion. All work, play, hobbies, and relationships are to be charged with faith and loyalty to Christ. One's very identity should reflect Gospel values; plans and commitments are made in harmony with Christ's teachings.

- In teaching about morality at this age level, help the student identify with Christ and commit him or herself to Jesus as a special friend.

- Specific discussions such as sexual responsibility, honesty in one's career, or loyalty to one's friends are best addressed in the context of one's committing to Christ and adhering to Gospel values.

- Pose situations that require analysis and moral solutions. In all cases, have the students relate the ideas and the discussion to their own lives. Challenge them to see where they need to adjust their lives to more closely identify with Jesus.

- Have students apply Christian principles to contemporary moral questions. Allow the students to wrestle with the perplexity of some contemporary moral issue to see that following the teachings of Christ and the Church does not mean that all uncertainties vanish.

- Have groups of four come up with a simple definition of peer pressure. Have each group report its definition while you record the main points on the board. Have each group come up with at least three to five suggestions about how to deal with peer pressure. After 20–25 minutes, have each group report on their discussion to the rest of the class. On a sheet of paper, have students complete the following: (1) The situation in which I am experiencing the most peer pressure right now is _____. (2) A suggestion I will use for dealing with that peer pressure during the coming week is _____. Have the students fill out their worksheets in silence. Conclude this exercise with a brief appropriate prayer service in which the students pray for one another in their efforts to deal with peer pressure.

- It is sometimes difficult to discuss sensitive topics because students may be insecure about sharing their feelings, opinions, or questions in front of the rest of the class. Have the students write out their responses anonymously to a question or scenario. Collect and shuffle the responses. Read the top one to the entire class. Do they agree or disagree with the response? Why or why not? How would they add to the response? Then discuss the next written response in the same fashion and so on.

- Have your class analyze various positive and negative values of youth culture. Some aspects of youth culture which could be considered are fashions/clothes, language/slang, heroes/heroines, or movies/TV.

*Memo*

In light of what I have learned about Christian morality, I want to keep the following considerations in mind:

## Pause a Moment . . .

- What particular questions do you have about discussing morality with your students? Discuss these with a fellow catechist.

- Students enjoy considering moral dilemmas. Think of one case study that you can use in your next class.

## IMPLICATIONS

1. Recall how you were taught about Christian morality.

a. What did you like about that approach?_____

b. What did you not like about that approach? _____

c. In general, how will you approach the subject of Christian morality with your students? _____

2. Which commandment is needed most by the students on your grade level? Why?

_____

_____

3. What are two ways you can help your students to form and use their consciences?

_____

## Notes

**4.** How can you *lead* your students to the insights of Christian morality rather than merely dictate to them what they should do?

## Prayer Response

As you think about your students, pray for the sensitivity and perception you need to gently lead them toward living out the values of Jesus. Read the following Scripture passages and consider how faithfulness to the values of Jesus sometimes involves struggle.

> *I cannot do anything on my own. . . . I do not seek my own will but the will of the one who sent me.* (John 5:30)

> *For whoever does the will of my heavenly Father is my brother, and sister, and mother.* (Matthew 12:50)

> *I came down from heaven, not to do my own will but the will of the one who sent me.* (John 6:38)

## BIBLIOGRAPHY

Auer, Jim. *Responsible Sex: What Every Teen Should Know.* Liguori, MO: Liguori Publications, 1990.

Haggerty, Brian. *Out of the House of Slavery.* New York: Paulist Press, 1978.

Hall, Robert T., "The Hard Line vs. The Soft Line": The Dilemma of Moral Education," *Moral Education: A Handbook for Teachers.* Minneapolis: Winston Press, 1979.

Heft, Jim, S.M. "Right or Wrong: How Can I Know?" *Youth Update.* Cincinnati: St. Anthony Messenger Press, June, 1986.

Lohkamp, Nicholas, O.F.M. "Your Conscience and Church Teaching: How Do They Fit Together?" *Catholic Update.* Cincinnati: St. Anthony Messenger Press, December, 1982.

McBride, Alfred, O.Praem. "Ten Commandments: Sounds of Love from Sinai," *Catholic Update.* Cincinnati: St. Anthony Messenger Press, September, 1989.

*McGee and Me.* Colorado Springs, CO: Focus on the Family. 9 videos.

Miner, Chalise. "Making Good Choices: A Process to Practice," *Youth Update.* Cincinnati: St. Anthony Messenger Press, July, 1989.

Pennock, Michael. *Choosing: Cases in Moral Decision Making.* Notre Dame, IN: Ave Maria Press, 1989.

Reichert, Richard. *Teaching Tips for Religion Teachers.* Our Sunday Visitor, 1989.

Reichert, R. and Westernberg, Michael. *Teaching Tips for Adolescent Catechesis.* Ft. Wayne, IN: Our Sunday Visitor, 1992.

Shelton, Charles M. *Morality and the Adolescent.* New York: Crossroad, 1989.

*The 10 Commandments for Teens: God's Game Plan for a Happy Life.* Liguori, MO: Redemptorist Pastoral Communications, video.

Wintz, Jack, O.F.M. "Guilt—A Tool for Christian Growth," *Catholic Update.* Cincinnati: St. Anthony Messenger Press, February, 1986.

*Nihil Obstat*
The Reverend Gregory A. Banazak, S.T.D.

*Imprimatur*
The Most Reverend Kenneth J. Povish, D.D.
Bishop of Lansing
May 13, 1994

The *Nihil Obstat* and *Imprimatur* are official declarations that a book or pamphlet is free of doctrinal or moral error. No implication is contained therein that those who have granted the *Nihil Obstat* and *Imprimatur* agree with the contents, opinions, or statements expressed.

Send all inquiries to:

BENZIGER PUBLISHING COMPANY
15319 Chatsworth Street
P.O. Box 9609
Mission Hills, California 91346-9609

Second Edition

**ISBN 0-02-651219-X**

Printed in the United States of America.

1 2 3 4 5 6 7 8 9    BAW    98 97 96 95 94

*Benziger*

CATECHISTS IN FORMATION

# Social Justice and the Catechist

*Action on behalf of justice is a significant criterion of the Church's fidelity to its mission. It is not optional, nor is it the work of only a few in the Church. It is something to which all Christians are called according to their vocations, talents, and situations in life.*

*National Catechetical Directory, #160*

BOOK TWO

## In this chapter you will:

- Discuss the foundations of Catholic social teaching.
- Compare the role of charity and justice.
- Examine new approaches to teaching social justice.

*Written by*
**Peter Ries**

*Consultant*
**David Riley**

Second Edition

# Part I Experience

## Making a Budget

▲ *Glenn's family ran a successful furniture store. Glenn found that he would have to change his lifestyle drastically to live on the budget he made.*

Glenn and his family lived in relatively prosperous surroundings. His grandparents had suffered through the Great Depression and World War II, but had become successful business owners. Glenn's father now owned the store, the "largest one-stop furniture store in northeast Kansas," Glenn had heard his father brag. Glenn enjoyed the benefits of his family's fortune and hard work and had a native faith that God would always reward people for their efforts.

Because of this faith, Glenn found the economic part of his Justice class at St. Michael's High School a waste of time. Glenn felt compassion for the poor, but thought that they could overcome their problems if they just worked harder. This certainly wasn't a religious question for him. "What's God got to do with this?" he wondered.

In place of the final exam, Mr. Rodriguez assigned a final project. Each student was to develop a budget for a family of four assuming a single, minimum-wage income of $180 a week. The budget was to include rent, groceries, insurance, transportation, taxes, and other expenses families paid.

Glenn thought the project was a waste of time and said just that to Mr. Rodriguez. "I make nearly $100 a week working part-time in my dad's store," Glenn stated. "I'm sure you do," Mr. Rodriguez responded. "I wonder how many of your father's employees work for minimum wage. I'll tell you what. Find out from your father, if you can, the average wage a full-time employee makes after two years with the company. Develop your budget from that." Glenn, seeing an opportunity to make points with his teacher and his father, agreed.

After two years, the average employee made $5.23 cents an hour—about $840 a month. The company provided one week paid vacation, paid half the worker's health care (but none of the family's), and five paid sick days per year. As he prepared his budget, based upon where and how he would live, Glenn found he needed twice the proposed income. The only way the budget would work was if the family lived in the part of town no decent people walked in after dark, took public transportation, and did without cable and eating out. Not a whole lot of luxuries here, Glenn thought, but livable.

But the project wasn't finished. Mr. Rodriguez asked one simple question: "What happens when your wage earner is mugged walking home from the bus stop and is laid up for two months with $15,000 in hospital bills?"

Glenn looked at his budget: health insurance was one of the things he had eliminated to make the budget add up. And there was no money in savings. "This is impossible!" he yelled at Mr. Rodriguez. "You're setting us up to fail."

Remember the anger you feel right now, Glenn," Mr. Rodriguez said. "How much anger do you think people who live on this budget feel? Where's the love of God for them?"

Glenn sat down. Even through his frustration, Glenn could see that his simple faith in God's blessing people who work hard didn't seem so simple anymore.

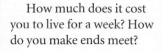

1. What areas of social justice touch your life? How do they affect you?

_____

_____

2. What is your attitude about the minimum wage or why people have financial difficuties?

_____

_____

3. Have you ever been the victim of injustice or an unjust system? Describe your experience.

_____

_____

4. When did you first become aware of the Church's involvement in social justice? How did this awareness affect your decisions and actions?

_____

_____

5. Think of a number of regular, not overly involved parishioners. How would these people respond to the statement that "Action on behalf of justice is something to which all Catholics are called"? What does this statement mean to you?

_____

_____

_____

How much does it cost you to live for a week? How do you make ends meet?

▲ *Education for justice begins in the home. What are some ways that a family can teach a concern for justice?*

## The Call to Justice

The 15-year period from 1978 to 1993 was a heady time for education in social justice. The American bishops wrote frequently to help focus Catholic thought, including: "Community and Crime," "Statement on Handicapped People" (78), "Brothers and Sisters to Us: A Pastoral Letter on Racism in Our Day," "Ratification of Human Rights Treaties" (79), "Statement on Capital Punishment" (80), "The Challenge of Peace: God's Promise and Our Response" (83) and "Economic Justice for All" (86). The world celebrated the centennial anniversary of "*Rerum Novarum*" in 1991, along with Pope John Paul II's encyclical "*Centesimus Annus.*"

One could conclude from these public statement that justice issues are suddenly "in." Such a conclusion would be mistaken, however. Catholics, as a group, are often unaware of the Church's rich tradition of teaching and involvement in the area of social justice.

It is important for Catholics to understand that a concern for justice and peace is integrally related to an authentic Christian faith-life. If students are to develop this concern, their catechists need to be familiar with the basic themes of justice and peace, how they have developed, and how these themes relate to some of the key elements of our faith. The catechist then has the responsibility of helping students respond in faith to the critical public issues that face us all.

▲ "*Hear this, you who trample upon the needy and destroy the poor of the land!. . . Never will I forget a thing they have done!*" (Amos 8:4,7)

### Old Testament Foundations of Catholic Social Teaching

Although the Church's modern social teaching began with Pope Leo XIII's encyclical, "*Rerum Novarum,*" (On Labor) in 1891, it actually reflects an ancient tradition with roots deeply embedded in the Bible.

Catholic social teaching is based on Scripture. Both the Old and New Testaments contain an urgent summons to justice and mercy. The precept, "You shall love your neighbor as yourself" (*Leviticus 19:18*), tells us that our relationships with others are to be characterized by justice, equity, and charity. Additional passages throughout the Bible tell us to be just, fair, and loving.

The Old Testament specifically commands the Israelites to respond to the problems of the needy. Deuteronomy 15:11 states, "I command you to open your hand to your poor and needy kinsman in your country." The Pentateuch instructs the Israelites to respond particularly to the needs of orphans, widows, and aliens (see *Deuteronomy 10:17–19*). The prophet Isaiah goes even further in specifying the extent of the Israelites' responsibilities.

> *This, rather, is the fasting that I wish: releasing those bound unjustly, untying the thongs of the yoke; setting free the oppressed, breaking every yoke; sharing your bread with the hungry, sheltering the oppressed and the homeless; clothing the naked when you see them, and not turning your back on your own.* (Isaiah 58:6–7)

These matters were placed in the Old Testament because the poor and oppressed—the *anawim*—were recognized as being special to God. The

Israelites were commanded to act justly to the poor because they had experienced oppression as slaves in Egypt. To reject this responsibility would be to deny their liberation by God's power.

The prophets of Israel, in particular, were concerned with questions of justice whether it was Amos (8:4, 7): "Hear this, you who trample upon the needy and destroy the poor of the land! . . . The Lord has sworn by the pride of Jacob: Never will I forget a thing they have done!" or Jeremiah (9:23): "in his prudence he knows me, knows that I, the Lord, bring about kindness, justice, and uprightness on the earth: for with such am I pleased." It is clear that the authors of the Bible believed that God's concern went beyond the spiritual welfare of the people, addressing their material needs as well.

## New Testament Foundations of Catholic Social Teaching

A basic theme in the Old Testament is the movement from slavery to freedom. In the New Testament, we find this same theme of justice described in the movement from death to life. In both cases, the movements show how God's freely given love leads people to leave behind their limitations and to grow into the fullness of their potential. The motivation for justice finds its ultimate source in the Paschal Mystery of Christ's living, dying, and rising. Jesus' obedience to his Father led him to give himself fully for the salvation and liberation of others.

Many themes of justice characterize the public life of Jesus. He showed *compassion* for the sick and poor, and he requested us to do the same (see *Luke 14:12–14*). Jesus characterized the purpose of his coming with the word *service;* he said he came to serve, not to be served. Those who follow Jesus must follow his example and serve the needs of all (see *Matthew 20:26–28*). In his life and in his teachings—especially the parables of the lilies of the field and the man who hoarded his riches—Jesus emphasized simple living and the sharing of extra possessions (see *Luke 12:15–34*).

In the New Testament letters, we read about the necessity of taking responsibility for justice. Saint John asks: "How can God's love survive in a person who has enough of this world's goods yet closes his or her heart to others when he sees them in need?" *(1 John 3:17).* For John, justice is a requirement, not a choice. Saint James is equally blunt in his letter summing up the relationship between justice and Christian living.

> *What good is it, my brothers, if someone says he has faith but does not have works? Can that faith save him? If a brother or sister has nothing to wear and has no food for the day, and one of you says to them, "Go in peace, keep warm and eat well," but you do not give them the necessities of the body, what good is it? So also faith of itself, if it does not have works, is dead.* (James 2:14–17)

Christian living must be characterized by a concern for social justice that is evidenced in action.

## Pause a Moment . . .

- Attempt to summarize what the Old Testament teaches about justice in one sentence. Share your sentence with a fellow catechist.

- According to the Bible, what are the consequences of not living justly?

# The Moral Basis for Social Justice

A fundamental concept in Catholic social teaching is the dignity of the human person, a dignity that is rooted in the fact that every human being is created by God in God's image and likeness. Flowing directly from one's humanity are certain rights and duties that safeguard and promote this human dignity. These are realized through the practice of justice.

According to Aquinas, justice is "rendering to each one his due" (*Summa Theologica, Q58, A. 1*). Justice is a moral virtue, a habit of the will towards creating or preserving equality.

- Quantitative justice is known as *commutative justice.*

- When concerned with individuals, commutative justice is known as *particular justice.*

- When owed to the community, it is known as *general justice.*

- Proportionate justice is called *distributive justice.*

- Social justice, as defined in the *Concise Catholic Dictionary for Parents and Religion Teachers,* means "respect for human beings because of their dignity as persons," and implies "concern for and actions for human rights to protect that dignity" *(p. 138).*

Justice is necessary to prevent personal desires from conflicting with the needs of others: it is the virtue that insures that people can live together in peace. Actions that attempt to make the material, social, technological, and economic aspects of creation better are servants to human dignity; they are not only praiseworthy but also required of Christians.

Groups as well as individuals have rights. Human beings are, after all, social by nature. Our happiness and fulfillment are found in community. We reach our individual potential through mutual cooperation. We come to faith and are nurtured in that faith through a believing community. As the *National Catechetical Directory* points out:

> Since societies are essential to human development, their organization and functioning—legal, political, economic, and cultural—raise important moral issues. Catholic social teaching provides principles by which the Church as an institution and Christians as individuals, can evaluate political, economic, social, and legal structures. (#158)

Our happiness also depends on a fundamental commitment to God: we are transcendent beings that have a life beyond this one.

The aim of such principles is to bring about the kingdom of God, which is the Church's mission. A sign of the kingdom is working for the common good. The common good consists chiefly in the protection of the rights and the performance of the duties of the human person. It is the sum of those conditions which allow not only groups but also individual members to achieve their own fulfillment more fully and more readily than they otherwise could. (see "Declaration on Religious Freedom," #6). The world and all that is in it and from it are gifts from God for the benefit of all. Although there is a right to private property and the wealth generated from it, this right is tempered. Owners are truly stewards with the obligation of preserving and developing these gifts for others (see *Catechism of the Catholic Church,* #2402–2404).

"Then the king will say to those on his right, 'Come, you who are blessed by my Father. Inherit the kingdom prepared for you from the foundation of the world. For I was hungry and you gave me food, I was thirsty and you gave me drink, a stranger and you welcomed me, naked and you clothed me, ill and you cared for me, in prison and you visited me.' Then the righteous will answer him and say, 'Lord, when did we see you hungry and feed you, or thirsty and give you drink? When did we see you a stranger and welcome you, or naked and clothe you? When did we see you ill or in prison, and visit you?' and the king will say to them in reply, 'Amen, I say to you, whatever you did for one of these least brothers of mine, you did for me.'"

(Matthew 25:34–40).

God's kingdom is one reality. It is not just otherworldly; it includes this world. It is very difficult for people to consider spiritual matters if their basic material needs are not being met. Involvement in specific social issues is necessary if one is to prepare the way for the fullness of the kingdom.

Although the Church has a clear responsibility for social justice concerns, Christ did not give us a political and economic blueprint. Instead, Jesus asked his followers to uphold certain values.

During the first five centuries, the most pressing problem was the great economic inequality within the Roman Empire. Church leaders responded to this problem by arguing that property be given to all, and that common ownership was more important than private rights to property. During the Middle Ages, Saint Thomas Aquinas described the virtue of justice as the protector of love. As Western civilization became industrialized, new social problems arose that prompted the writing of the first modern social encyclical, *"Rerum Novarum,"* by Pope Leo XIII in 1891.

Christians measure their success not by the fruit of their efforts, but by their fidelity to the process. That process must be executed with justice, in a nonviolent manner, and with love. This emphasis on style is very important in a world that has frequently seen the oppressed switch places with the oppressors.

The scriptural insight is not what economic system should be used but is having a thorough fidelity to human rights. Christians need not only be faithful to the goal of social justice but also to the process of social justice.

Each and every social encyclical calls for Catholics to both be aware of and act for justice. As *"Centesimus Annus"* (1991) says: "Today more than ever, the Church is aware that her social message will gain credibility more immediately from the witness of actions than as a result of its internal logic and consistency."

Although specific issues have changed over the centuries, six basic foundational principles exist that characterize the Church's teaching about justice:

1. Every human person possesses a basic dignity that comes from God.

2. Each person has basic rights and responsibilities that flow from his or her God-given dignity.

3. Each person has been called to support the family, form community, and participate in the life of society.

4. Work is part of the human condition; there is a dignity to work, and workers have rights.

5. In all cases, people are to be guided by a fundamental option for the poor and vulnerable.

6. As a goal, Catholics are to work for solidarity with the human family in search of world peace, global development, environmental protection, and safeguarding international human rights. (USCC Administrative Board, *Political Responsibility,* 1991.)

The Catholic social justice tradition has continued to our own day through many subsequent encyclicals and Church teachings, and is based on the Gospel call to love. Like love, social justice is at the very heart of Christian living.

*Notes*

## Papal Social Encyclicals

• 1891 *Leo XIII* "Rerum Novarum," "The Condition of Labor." Addresses problems created by industrialization for the laborer.
• 1931 *Pius XI* "Quadragesimo Anno," "The Reconstruction of the Social Order." Criticized unrestricted Capitalism and Marxism while affirming just wages and unions.
• 1961 *John XXIII* "Mater et Magistra," "Christianity and Social Progress." Recognized the need for global independence and identified the problem of the gap between rich and poor countries.
• 1963 *John XXIII* "Pacem in Terris," "Peace on Earth." Called for human dignity and rights to direct actions of the world.
• 1967 *Paul VI* "Progressio Populorum," Development of Peoples." Human development is to be seen in cultural, social, religious, and economic terms resulting in fair trade and international cooperation.
• 1971 *Paul VI* "Octogesima Adveniens," "A Call to Action." Confronts the problems of discrimination, misuse of the environment, and political power.
• 1981 *John Paul II* "Laborem Exercens," On Human Work." Criticizes both Marxism and Capitalism, affirms the rights of labor, states the primacy of people over things, and presents a spirituality of labor.
• 1987 *John Paul II* "Sollicitudo Rei Socialis," On Social Concern." Promotes collaboration for peace and a redirection of resources from weapons to alleviating misery.
• 1991 *John Paul II* "Centesimus Annus," "The Hundredth Year." Encourages a fresh enthusiasm for Church's social teaching.

## Pause a Moment . . .

• Find examples of how one or two of the six basic values that form the vision of Catholic social teaching are being violated. Do you see progress in any of these areas? Explain your answer.

• What is the relationship between peace and justice?

## A Comparison of Charity and Justice

When it pertains to matters of human need, justice is often regarded as a secular obligation that is established and monitored by law. Charity is regarded as a moral response that is determined by need and that, basically, remains optional. Some Christians think that they should respond in charity to human need but that their charitable response should not be mandated. The Gospel teaches that both justice and charity are part of the Christian's moral response. Justice, as the *National Catechetical Directory, (#165)* defines it, is the very foundation of charity: "It is impossible to give of oneself in love without first sharing with others what is due them in justice."

Therefore, justice and love cannot be optional if one's conduct is to be described as Christian. Both are good and necessary.

Although justice and charity go hand in hand in a moral response, they are not identical. One difference is the *circumstances* that elicit a response. Acts of charity often arise out of situations caused by natural disasters: floods or earthquakes. Charity can be thought of as acts of love shared with people who need help until they are back on their feet. Acts of justice arise out of circumstances that are not accidental or spontaneous but result from a series of economic or political decisions made over time. An example of this is the presence of substandard housing in some neighborhoods caused by *red lining,* the practice by some banks of refusing loans to people because of where they live. Justice involves making sure that these same people who have experienced discrimination have an opportunity to get back on their feet. Justice demands that people be treated fairly. Charity is concerned with acts of kindness.

Another difference is in the duration of the response. Charitable responses are usually temporary and short-lived. When the crisis is past, the response ceases. Working for justice usually requires a long-term commitment. A temporary effort will not correct a deeply rooted problem.

A final difference lies in society's acceptance of the acts. A charitable response is generally noncontroversial. Collecting food for starving people is acknowledged as a worthy undertaking. One person's charitable response is not perceived as a threat to another person's well-being or best interests. The response to a situation of injustice, however, is often controversial and sometimes even risky. The proposed solution may affect certain individuals monetarily. Responding to justice issues can cause divisions and personal repercussions.

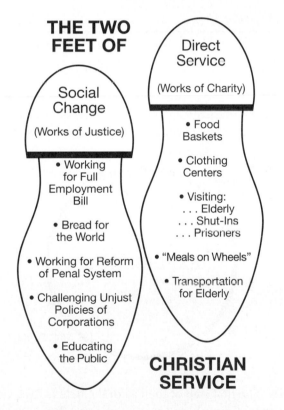

**THE TWO FEET OF**

**Direct Service**
(Works of Charity)

**Social Change**
(Works of Justice)

- Working for Full Employment Bill
- Bread for the World
- Working for Reform of Penal System
- Challenging Unjust Policies of Corporations
- Educating the Public

- Food Baskets
- Clothing Centers
- Visiting:
  . . . Elderly
  . . . Shut-Ins
  . . . Prisoners
- "Meals on Wheels"
- Transportation for Elderly

**CHRISTIAN SERVICE**

### A Story

Once there was a village by a river. One day someone from the village rescued a baby as it floated by. Assuming the baby had been abandoned, the village agreed to rear the child as its own.

The next day two babies were rescued from the river, which the village promptly adopted. The next day four babies, and the next day eight arrived. This quickly became too much for the villagers' charity. They could not simply let the babies die, however. So they sent people up river to see what was happening.

Several days later the upriver party returned. The babies were coming from a very large village that had lost its harvest in a fire. They were sending their babies down river as fast as they could make boats in order to save them from starving. The down-river village could help them solve their problems or it could continue to rescue babies.

- Which is the act of charity? Which is the act of justice?
- Which response will generate the longest-lasting results?

*Pause a Moment . . .*

- Describe a situation of human need with which you are aware. What is an appropriate charitable response to this situation? What is an appropriate justice response?

- How do the implications of social justice and charity affect your daily life?

# Part III Discovery

## A System of Analysis

Think back to the opening story. Glenn thought the teacher's assignment was pretty weak. Preparing a budget using the minimum wage would be a snap for a person of his intelligence. He quickly found out, however, that no matter how smart someone was, living on a near minimum wage job was terribly difficult.

As Glenn discovered, finding solutions to problems is often more difficult than it seems. What exactly is the justice issue in Glenn's story? Is his father's business taking unfair advantage of labor? Are rent and health care costs too high? Is the worker at fault for not going to college or learning a skill that draws a higher pay? There are no clear-cut answers to many of these questions. It's no wonder that many people simply ignore justice issues; they are just too complex.

### The Pastoral Circle

Peter Henriot, S.J. and Joe Holland, in their book, *Social Analysis: Linking Faith and Justice,* recognized how the complexity of justice issues caused many people to simply throw up their hands in defeat. Henriot and Holland proposed that people use a four-step process called the *Pastoral Circle* to both better understand justice issues and to devise a simple course of action that they could follow in order to respond to the issues.

**Awareness.** The first step of the Pastoral Circle is **Awareness.** What do people experience? Glenn found that people making more than the minimum wage would have problems surviving if they became ill for any length of time. That's the first step, simply recognizing that there is a problem.

**Analysis.** Once you know that there is a problem, the next step is to ask, "Why is this a problem?" Work at identifying the reasons behind the problem. (Don't try to solve the problem yet: it's too early in the process.) In many cases there will be numerous possible causes. List them in their order of importance. How much deeper do these causes go than what you see on the surface? This part of the process is also known as "Social Analysis."

▲ *Through the Pastoral Circle process we reach the point where we must act. One positive action you can take to resolve the issue of homelessness is to work with Habitat for Humanity (or a similar group) to help provide shelter for people who are willing to invest their "sweat equity" in order to have a home.*

**Reflection.** Why should Glenn care about people making $5.23 an hour? That's a fair wage in his part of the state. Many people are happy to have a job no matter what it pays. Glenn cares because he is a person of faith. He recognizes that something is not right.

The process of reflection (called theological reflection by Henriot and Holland) engages the results of analysis in a dialogue with how things ought to be. What is it that the Church teaches about justice? How about standards of fairness? Glenn believed that hard work solved all problems. When he found out that this wasn't true, he had to rethink his position under a new light.

### Action

> *For evil to triumph, it is only necessary for good men to do nothing.*
> (Edmund Burke, eighteenth century).

What steps can an individual take to make a difference? The key to succeeding at this point is to be realistic without being cynical. The cynic will say "I can't solve the problem so I won't even bother to try." The realist will say, "I can't solve the problem, but maybe I can do something to make a difference."

**Start small.** For Christians, acting for justice begins with prayer. Pray for God's help in resolving the issue, pray for the strength, wisdom, and patience to act for justice, and pray that others will join with you.

**Think Globally, Act Locally.** Recognize that while most justice issues are bigger than your local community, you can probably accomplish the most by addressing the problem at your local level. As an individual, Glenn could write his congressional representative about health care or the minimum wage law (easy steps to take). But he could also work with a local *Habitat for Humanity* group to build affordable houses.

## Using the Process

You must become familiar with using this process before you can begin to insert it into your normal thinking pattern. Consider the following problem and consider how the "Pastoral Circle" is used. Add your own thoughts where indicated. You do not have to agree with the conclusions reached, although you might find it helpful to discuss them with other catechists.

**Awareness.** In 1994, the Los Angeles area was rocked by a 6.8 earthquake, damaging or destroying 123 parish churches or other buildings. However, because of the size of the Los Angeles area, most of the parishes in the diocese were not harmed. A collection was taken up the week after the earthquake and the diocesan appeal would go to help pay for the damage. The diocese as a whole and the individual parishes will be responsible for paying for the damages. *What is the problem here?* _____

_____

**Analysis.** Why should it be the responsibility of the individual parishes to resolve their own problems? Won't they have enough to take care of without this added responsibility? Parishioners will face additional expenses rebuilding their homes, will need to find new places to live and work, and will be suffering from the trauma they experienced. The diocesan collections will help defray immediate needs (charity). What can be done to resolve the situation so that the parishes alone do not bear sole responsibility for replacing their losses? _____

_____

## The Church Teaches

The teachings in regard to social matters for the most part are put into effect in the following three stages: first, the actual situation is examined; then, the situation is evaluated carefully in relation to these teachings; only then is it decided what can and should be done in order that the traditional norms may be adapted to circumstances of time and place. These three steps are at times expressed by the three words: *observe, judge, act.*

However, when it comes to reducing these teachings to action, it sometimes happens that even sincere Catholics have differing views. When this occurs they should take care to have and to show mutual esteem and regard, and to explore the extent to which they can work in cooperation among themselves. . . . Let them also take great care not to weaken their efforts in constant controversies. Nor should they, under pretext of seeking what they think best, meanwhile, fail to do what they can and hence should do. *(Mater et Magistra, 236, 238)*

**Reflection.** The Church is one body. As Paul writes:

*For if eagerness is there, it is acceptable according to what one has, not according to what one does not have; not that others should have relief while you are burdened, but that as a matter of equality your surplus at the present time should supply their needs, so that their surplus may also supply your needs, that there may be equality. As it is written: "Whoever had much did not have more, and whoever had little did not have less." (2 Corinthians 8:12–15)*

The Church's social teaching holds that the right to private property is not absolute, but that it is held in stewardship for the benefit of all. "The right to property must never be exercised to the detriment of the common good" *("Progressio Populorum," #23)*. In justice, then, does not every parish in the diocese (state, country, world) have an obligation to help rebuild the parishes damaged by the quake? _____

_____

**Action.** If every parish in the United States would set aside 1% of its yearly income for the support of other parishes in need, the burden would be borne by all. _____

_____

### YOUR TURN

Use the "Pastoral Circle" for yourself. Choose a situation of possible injustice—local, national, or international—and work through it using the process. Write your answer on the lines that follow.

1. Situation:

    _____

2. Awareness:

    _____

3. Analysis:

    _____

4. Reflection:

    _____

5. Action:

    _____

### Pause a Moment . . .

* Consider the example presented above about earthquake damage in Los Angeles. Do you consider this an issue of justice? Explain.

* How can you envision using the "Pastoral Circle" as part of the catechetical process? (Hint: With what other four-step processes are you familiar?)

# Part IV  Response

## Approaches to Teaching Social Justice

How a catechist teaches and disciplines the students can be a basic approach to teaching social justice. Is classroom discipline maintained with fairness? Are corrections made in anger or with calmness and control? Is each student treated as an individual and shown respect and care?

When dealing with issues of social justice, distinctions do need to be made. Sometimes, the aim of teaching justice is simply to make people aware of the problem. However, awareness without the prospect of involvement does not hold student interest for long. A catechist must also take into account the grade level and concerns of the students.

### Primary Grade Students

Education for justice should occur at every age. Children in primary grades are highly impressionable. Care must be used so that adult concerns are not imposed on them or that they are not led to feel responsible for things beyond their control. The goal is to lead these students to adopt certain styles of behavior that prepare the way for justice later on.

- Focus on positive values such as peace and caring rather than on the horrors of war or hunger.

- Foster attitudes of respect, acceptance, and sharing as foundations on which the students can build an appreciation for justice.

- Review your teaching techniques. Balance cooperative learning methods with competitive ones.

- Use rivalries and moments of conflict among your students as opportunities for teaching methods of nonviolent problem solving.

- Develop a "Peacemaker Award." Give the award to individuals you notice making a particular effort at peacemaking.

### Upper Elementary Grades

Older students are able to consider the justice values of everyday situations. They can learn to make choices between mocking or respecting people of a particular racial background or physical characteristic, accepting or shutting out a new person at school, or not sharing with someone in need.

- Ask the students to make a list of some ordinary conflicts they experience at home, at school and at play. List the conflicts on the board, several under each heading. Form the students into groups of three, with each group responsible for developing several alternatives to resolve one of the conflicts. Discuss the alternatives in light of fairness to all.

- Have the students list their five favorite TV programs. Determine the top five shows, erasing all others. Have each student rate each show on a scale from 1–5 (5 = excellent) using the following factors: Promotes concern for others; Presents women in wholesome way; Treats violence

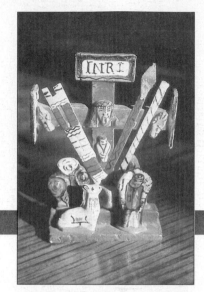

▲ *Christians are concerned with justice because of the love of Christ, not because they are liberal or do-gooders. What do you think this Latin American artist is trying to show in this cross?*

as evil; Promotes understanding between races. Discuss the value of each program in terms of Gospel values.

## Junior High

Junior high students need direct involvement in *group* activities (they like to do things together at this age). One group of students became aware of a poor African tribe suffering from a severe drought. The students learned of the many factors that trapped these people in a cycle of poverty. As an action step following their study, the students raised money to drill a well for these people. They became enthusiastic about this project because it counteracted the drought, gave hope for improved agricultural productivity, and did not demand a long-term commitment on the part of the students.

- Sensitize students to the importance of cultural diversity. Study the history and gifts of minority groups. Have students from minority groups share experiences of prejudice and stereotyping.

- Provide students with a sheet listing the beatitudes, corporal works of mercy, and spiritual works of mercy. Over a week's time, have them find examples in newspapers or magazines of how these works are carried out or ignored. They should bring all of their examples to class. Have them discuss and sort their examples according to each beatitude or work. On posterboard, have small groups of students develop collages for each beatitude and work of mercy.

## Older Adolescents and Adults

High school students and adults can analyze the many different values and issues involved in particular justice situations. These age groups have the understanding and stamina needed to research and understand such issues, as well as the ability to make the necessary subtle distinctions, highlight the values involved in the issues, and determine the relative worth of the available choices.

- Involve these groups in ongoing parish outreach efforts. Work in the parish soup kitchen or food center. Collect food and clothing for the poor. Arrange to help out in the neighborhood homeless shelter. Take part in Right to Life activities.

- Participate in an "Urban Plunge." Spend a day or more living and working with the poorest people in your community. (Check with your diocesan Justice and Peace office for details.) Prepare the students for what they will experience before each trip. Following the activity, ask these or similar questions: (1) What did they expect before they arrived? (2) How would they describe the actual experience? (3) What difference was there, if any? (4) Who received the most: the people they went to serve or themselves?

- Organize a 12–or 24–hour fast (either on its own or as part of a lock-in—make sure to get parent permission statements). During the fast, study the problem of local or world hunger. Contact your diocesan Catholic Charities office for more information. Debrief this exercise with a discussion of the experience.

- Have the students discuss the racism that exists in their school or community and how they would resolve these situations.

▲ *Students of all ages can benefit from an "Urban Plunge" experience. After spending a day learning first hand of the problems faced by the poor people in their communities, many adults have rethought what it means to work for justice.*

## Justice: A Commitment

Commitment to justice is not something that occurs only during religion class. Caring for other people and working for their just treatment is a full-time responsibility. Studying about justice should not be limited only to a particular course or chapter in a book. Justice questions should be asked in every class. Bishop Kenneth Untener of Saginaw, Michigan asked that each parish group ask the question, "How will what we do here benefit the poor and less fortunate?" before every meeting. A similar question could be asked before each lesson, "How will what we learn here help us respond to the needs of others?"

A popular method of bringing justice into every subject is called "Infusion." The method is actually quite simple. When teaching English, diagram sentences on a justice topic. ("Over 30,000 people have been killed in Bosnia since the civil war began.") For geography, consider who owns and benefits from the land.

### IN ACTION

1. Find two lessons in your student textbook that treat justice and peace concerns in some way.

Lesson # _____

Justice or Peace Issue _____

Method(s) Used to Teach It _____

_____

_____

2. How can you encourage your students to be responsive to one another's

needs and to promote justice and peace among themselves? _____

_____

_____

3. How can a catechist affect students' basic attitudes regarding justice?

_____

_____

## Pause a Moment . . .

- In light of what you have learned about social justice, what do you want to keep in mind for the next meeting with your students?
- What are additional activities that you do with students on the theme of social justice?

## Prayer Response

Ask the Holy Spirit for the assistance you need to be sensitive toward those who are oppressed in any way. Ask for the ability to deal justly and peacefully with your students. Then read the passage from John's Gospel. Reflect on how Jesus gave us, as a pattern for justice, his own attitude of total love and concern.

*"This is my commandment: love one another as I love you."* (John 15:12)

## BIBLIOGRAPHY

Bright, Thomas and Roberto, John, eds. *Poverty! Do It Justice.* New Rochelle, NY: Don Bosco Multi-media. 1993.

*Catholic Connections to Media Literacy.* Los Angeles: Center for Media and Values, 1993.

Condon, Camy and McGinnis, James. *Helping Kids Care.* New York, NY: Crossroads/Continuum, 1988.

Cronin, Gaynell and Rathschmidt, Jack. *Works of Mercy.* Mahwah, NJ: Paulist Press, video (grades 4-7).

Ekstrom, Reynolds and Rosemary. *Concise Catholic Dictionary for Parents and Religion Teachers.* Mystic, CT: Twenty-Third Publications, 1982.

Henriot, P. J., DeBerri, E. P., and Schultheis, M. J. *Catholic Social Teching: Our Best Kept Secret.* Maryknoll, NY: Orbis, 1985.

McGinnis, James. *Helping Teens Care.* New York, NY: Crossroads/Continuum, 1991.

McGinnis, Kathleen and Oehlberg, Barbara. *Starting Out Right.* New York, NY: Crossroads/Continuum, 1988.

Meagher, Laura. *Teaching Children about Global Awareness.* New York, NY: Crossroads/Continuum, 1991.

*National Issues Forum in the Catholic Community.* Dayton, OH: Kettering Foundation. Yearly.

O'Connell, Frances Hunt. *Giving and Growing: A Student's Guide for Service Projects.* Winona, MN: St. Mary's Press, 1990.

Overberg, Kenneth, S. J. "Guidance for a Troubled World: 100 Years of Catholic Social Teaching," *Catholic Update.* Cincinnati, OH: St. Anthony Messenger Press, 1990.

Untener, Kenneth. "How Should We Think About the Poor?" *Catholic Update.* Cincinnati, OH: St. Anthony Messenger Press, 1992.

*Nihil Obstat*
The Reverend Gregory A. Banazak, S.T.D.

*Imprimatur*
The Most Reverend Kenneth J. Povish, D.D.
Bishop of Lansing
May 13, 1994

The *Nihil Obstat* and *Imprimatur* are official declarations that a book or pamphlet is free of doctrinal or moral error. No implication is contained therein that those who have granted the *Nihil Obstat* and *Imprimatur* agree with the contents, opinions, or statements expressed.

Send all inquiries to:

BENZIGER PUBLISHING COMPANY
15319 Chatsworth Street
P.O. Box 9609
Mission Hills, California 91346-9609

Second Edition

**ISBN 0-02-651221-1**

Printed in the United States of America.

1 2 3 4 5 6 7 8 9    BAW    98 97 96 95 94

Benziger

# A Christian Perspective on Creation

God [is manifested] through creation . . . The first chapter of Genesis tells us that God spoke and created all things. Because it is "spoken" by God, creation is a great symbol of God. Because human beings are created in God's image and likeness (see Genesis 1:27), they are most capable of making God manifest in their lives. The more fully people live in fidelity to the image of God in them, the more clearly perceptible is the divine in human life.

*National Catechetical Directory, #51*

**BOOK TWO**

## In this chapter you will:

- Investigate the Scriptural perspectives on creation.
- Consider the implications of creation on working for justice.
- Examine ways to apply creation themes in your teaching.

Written by
**Peter Ries**

Consultant
**David Riley**

Second Edition

**Notes**

## Aunt Marj

When I was very young, I thought that Aunt Marj was as old as God. She certainly had the wrinkles to prove it. One time, when I was about seven, I asked Big Mom (Marj and my momma's momma) who was older, she or Marj. Big Mom laughed so hard she gasped for air. When everyone else found out why she was laughing, they, too, joined in the belly-shaking. Everyone but me, that is. I didn't understand what was so funny until I was ten. But that's another matter altogether. I always have been a tad slow on the uptake. This isn't about me, though. It's about Aunt Marj.

Aunt Marj was a lot like God in many ways, I reckon. I couldn't imagine anyone being wiser, or kinder, or more compassionate than she, especially towards little girls with a penchant for sticking their noses in places where they didn't belong. Not that she was a softy by any means. She had an iron will and a voice to match. Whenever I stepped beyond the boundaries of Marj's expectations I would be brought up short by a single word or "uhhu" as she cleared her throat. That was enough for me. As if I were a yearling learning to take the bridle, I would come to a dead stop and not move until she gave her permission. I wish I could train horses as well as she trained children: strong, yet gentle, flexible, but with unyielding limits. We learned when and how to behave, and when to run wild and free. We were civilized, but never broken.

Marj taught me many things. Through her gentle guidance I learned how to care for newborn kittens. I also learned the importance of respecting the earth and everything that lives upon it. Marj recycled long before it became fashionable. Her rule was, "Use what you have wisely. What little we have has to be enough for everyone." She meant everyone too, not just the members of our family. There was always enough soup in the pot for visitors or neighbors down on their luck.

Marj taught me too many things to mention. I'm most proud to say that she gave me her view of life. With that I've been able to face every battle (win or lose, I never tie) without fear. Not that I've never been scared; I have been, too many times to count. I've just never been afraid to try.

I learned from Marj that living was God's gift. Each and every moment of God's day was there for me to make the most of in whatever way I could. Every challenge was an opportunity for me to make a lasting mark on a receptive world. I would be judged, ultimately, not by how much I accomplished but by how much I tried to make a difference.

There were limits to what I could do. Cheating, lying, and stealing were all damaging to God's creation. Marj would say, "You came into this world honest and you will go out of this world honest if I have anything to do with it." I have always been afraid to test her on that one. Even today, when I am tempted to tell a fib, Marj's displeasure keeps me on the straight and narrow.

Honestly, though, it's not fear that motivates me. Marj had this great love for everything. She truly believed that each time a person sinned, creation was harmed. And each time a person was virtuous, creation was healed. If enough people lived caring lives, the world could be reborn. I'm convinced now that Marj was a true disciple of Jesus; nothing half-hearted about her.

Anyway, that's why I am the way I am. If my Aunt Marj continues to live through my actions, through my love and concern for the world and everything on it, then I am happy. That's the least I can do.

▲ *Who has been the "Aunt Marj" in your life? Do your students have an "Aunt Marj" in theirs? Find out who teaches them about the value of creation and what they are learning.*

## YOUR STORY

**1.** Who has been the "Aunt Marj" in your life? How has he or she shaped who your are and what you believe?

_____

_____

_____

**2.** What were you taught about creation when you were a child?

_____

_____

_____

**3.** What is your present attitude toward:

**(a)** your physical body and its needs?

_____

_____

_____

**(b)** the environment and wildlife?

_____

_____

_____

**(c)** natural resources?

_____

_____

_____

**4.** Why is the study of creation an important part of understanding theology?

_____

_____

_____

## All of Creation

A person's attitude toward creation is an interesting barometer. This attitude can:

- Measure the importance of the material world to that person.

- Say a lot about a person's attitude toward life and how he or she is living.

- Indicate where a person finds God—only in the spiritual activity of prayer and Sunday Mass or as a part of the everyday, material world.

From time to time, Christians have had an uneasy truce with the world, feeling confused about what their attitudes toward the material world should be. Some people think that creation is a temporary means for reaching what is truly important—life with God in another, spiritual world. Others view the world as a dangerous place, a mine field through which people must carefully and nervously find their way.

Gaining a proper understanding of creation can be difficult. Many of the major Christian writers from the past had some of these same attitudes. Yet, it is also true that Jesus spent his public life in the world and that his parables were situated in a physical setting. Although he rejected worldly, material standards, he appeared to be at ease wherever he went.

A proper understanding of creation is a foundation for hope in a world that sometimes seems hopeless. Such an understanding is among the central factors animating a Christian's way of life. It is a fundamental attitude and insight on which much of religious education is based.

### Scriptural Perspectives on Creation

The creation accounts found in the Book of Genesis were not intended to be history or science as we now understand those two disciplines. Rather, the creation stories (there are two) are theological reflections, mythological in nature, that express what the Israelites believed about God, the world, and humanity. Genesis 1 leaves no doubt as to what the Israelites believed. Presented in the form of a litany, God's actions are coupled with a response. As God completes each part of creation, the author says, God "saw that it was good." Just imagine a revivalist preacher working the congregation, "Can I get an 'Amen'?" to which the people shout, "Amen! Alleluia!"

The attitude found in Genesis 1 has not, however, always been the predominant one. Throughout history people have doubted the goodness of creation as well as the goodness of people. Various philosophers and religious writers have described reality in terms of a dualism—dividing the world into the material and the spiritual. They have considered the material world to be limited, flawed, imperfect, and, by implication, sinful. They have described the spiritual world as preferred, worthwhile, valued, honored, and beautiful. Such thinking has led to a devaluation of all life, the spoiling of the ecology, and an attitude of "It's mine; I can do what I want with it."

Because this dualism has been so rampant, Christians have not always had wholesome and positive attitudes toward the material world,

### Dualism

Dualism is a philosophical concept developed to explain how an all good God can allow evil to exist. Some people argued that the spiritual world was good while the physical world belonged to the forces of evil. Thus, humans were locked into a mortal battle, body against soul, to determine whether they would be good or evil. The Church has always rejected the teaching of dualism, believing, instead, in the goodness of creation because of the ultimate goodness of the Creator.

particularly the human body. For instance, to some, being Christian means "giving up the world" and "denying physical desires." In this mentality, one's body is regarded as shameful and sexuality an embarrassment. This attitude has drifted in and out of Catholic thought from the first century A.D. when such dualistic views of the body and spirit were so prevalent.

Somewhere between the extremes of the Victorian approach to sex and the permissive sexuality that is now prevalent in society lies the proper Christian perspective—one that views creation as the revelation of God's goodness shared as a gift with us. The following are some biblical perspectives on creation.

**Complex Reality.** It is true that we and our world are complex realities, often not easily understood. But, creation's complexity reveals the mystery of God and reflects God's love and beauty. Just as the spiritual aspect of humanity cannot be separated from our material selves, God's kingdom cannot be separated into spiritual and material creations. Our spiritual nature was created in unity with our material nature. Whatever dignity and glory we have (see *Psalm 8*) is contained in all the dimensions—physical, mental, spiritual—of who we are.

**Of One Body.** Another perspective on creation, found in Genesis 2:18–24, describes God's act of creation, taking Eve from the rib of Adam. The underlying message in this narrative is that man and woman are made from the same material. Although this may not seem very significant today, this message was most likely very disturbing when first shared approximately 3000 years ago when women were regarded as inferior to men. Ancient cultures often considered women as property to be owned and controlled. This creation story in Genesis communicates a completely different point of view. Women are not property; they are people—man's equal in dignity and value. One gender cannot own the other, use the other, or discriminate against the other.

**God Is Involved.** The writers of the Bible knew that God is involved in, and not removed from, creation. Where in other cultures the gods are often detached from the cares of the mortal world, living apart from and not involved in the daily lives of people, the God of Israel is intimately involved with each part of the world. Where the gods are described as thinking of creation as inferior and beneath their interest, the God of Israel is intimately involved with all of creation.

**In God's Image.** What is the position of human beings in the universe? Where do we rank with all of creation? Genesis describes the exalted position of the human race where Adam gives names to all the animals. God gives men and women dominion over all of creation. That dominion is one of stewardship: the responsibility to preserve, care for, and develop creation to its fullest (see *Genesis 1:28–30; 2:15*).

The Book of Genesis mentions this dominion a number of times. In Chapter 1, God instructs the first humans to "fill the earth and subdue it" (28). They are to "have dominion over the fish of the sea, the birds of the air, and all the living things that move on the earth" (29). Genesis 2:15 states that Adam (the human race) is given the task of cultivating and caring for the Garden of Eden (the earth). In Genesis 2:18–20, God gives Adam dominion over all the wild animals and the birds of the air.

Note this interpretation of the word *dominion*. Far too often, especially in western society, dominion has been interpreted to mean "domination."

*Memo*

Read the stories of creation to get a feel for God's action. In Genesis 1-2:4, the priestly writers' description of God's handiwork was actually the second story of creation. Genesis 2:5–25 is the earlier story. What attitudes do the different stories show about creation?

People intent on dominating nature have raped and pillaged the land, wantonly slaughtered animals, and fouled the earth. Dominion, better understood as stewardship, means that we are responsible to a higher authority for how we care for and nurture creation.

According to *Webster's Ninth New Collegiate Dictionary,* a "steward" is an overseer—someone who manages the concerns of a family or an institution or superintends another's affairs. A steward does not necessarily own what he or she manages.

None of the Genesis passages seem to imply human ownership of creation. Rather, men and women have been chosen as part of God's creation to be partners with God in the care for creation. We have a responsibility to care for and to improve the material world. Because each person is meant to share in this stewardship, the goods of creation should be available to everyone, not just a few. This point is repeatedly developed in the Papal Social Encyclicals published during the last hundred years.

Scripture teaches that all people are made in God's image and likeness. Therefore, one cannot have a prejudiced, negative view of any race or culture without implying the same about God. If we are like God, then we possess God's characteristics: we are able to relate to, care for, and love others, imperfectly as that may be. In Genesis, God creates man and woman and sees them as good. God's optimism should influence the Christian outlook about the goodness of humanity.

Even though humanity was made in God's image, we know that human goodness is not perfect. Genesis 3 points to the fall of the human race from goodness through sin. All of humanity's actions must be seen through that fall.

**Order and Purpose.** Genesis 1 speaks of God creating out of the void, out of chaos. Into this disorder God brings life that has an order and a purpose, proceeding toward a goal. This understanding of creation is far different from any other creation story found in antiquity.

Most other cultures did not share this understanding of revelation. For these cultures, life is often understood as a cycle that continually repeats itself. They think the material world is going nowhere, like a needle that is stuck on a record and plays the same thing over and over. By implication, these people could perceive themselves as being stuck in this cycle, with no purpose or goal, searching for but not finding any lasting meaning in life.

## The Notion of Ongoing Creation

The work of creation is not complete. St. Paul speaks of bringing the world to perfection. Writers today speak about how the development of this world is part of its continuing creation. By utilizing resources, developing technologies, and exercising the true dominion God gave us, we help move creation on to become more of what it is meant to be. We can appropriately describe ourselves as co-creators with God.

We somehow make the kingdom of God present in our midst, when the physical world is affected and developed as we act peacefully, joyfully, and lovingly. In this way, solidarity (being one with our brothers and sisters) and justice are also developed. An example of this is Mother Teresa of India, who, through her work with the poor and the dying, has brought much sensitivity and humanness to the world, adding to the hope of creation.

Frequently the ministry of Jesus is characterized by the words "priest," "prophet," and "king." Each baptized person participates in this three-fold ministry of Christ's. We share in the kingship of Jesus, responsible for the world as a guardian, a careful developer of its material resources, responsible for our actions, and a custodian for God's generous gifts.

We approach this notion of ongoing creation as people of hope. All creation—all of life—has a purpose in God's eternal plan. All of creation is sacred, filled by the Creator with its own unique dignity and sanctity. Extreme pessimism about the world is unacceptable. The doubt may be warranted if we rely solely on ourselves, but we don't. We are participants, along with God, in the continuing development of creation—a task that holds much promise.

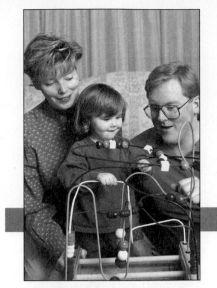

▲ *All creation has a purpose in God's eternal plan. As Christians, we have a responsibility to be guardians and caretakers of life.*

## REFLECTION

This section will give you an opportunity to personalize the ideas presented above.

1. What is your attitude toward creation?

_____

_____

2. What does creation's complexity reveal to you about God?

_____

_____

3. How does God dwell within creation? How might this affect your understanding of sacrament?

_____

_____

4. What is your favorite image of the earth: "machine," "living organism," "home," "mother," "work of art," or "resource"? What are the implications of each image?

_____

_____

5. Which of the following titles do you think best describes the place of the human race in creation: "fellow creature," "slum landlords," "managers," "stockholders," "strip miners"? What are the implications of each image?

_____

_____

## Pause a Moment . . .

• What does it means to say that we are made in God's image and likeness?

• Do you feel that creation has a purpose? What is it? Does your life have a purpose?

• In what ways do you co-create with God?

# Part III Discovery

▲ *How does Western society promote a consumer mentality? What are the dangers of affluence? How can affluence be used for the good of others?*

## Implications for Social Justice

We learn from Scripture that we are partners with God; we have dominion over the rest of creation. The author of Genesis believed that God intended this dominion to be in the form of stewardship.

We are challenged, as Christians to "live simply that others may simply live." We are to live in such a way so that we do not deprive others of what is rightfully theirs—adequate food, shelter, clothing, employment, and education. Affluence, it can be argued, does deprive others. Jesus' skepticism about accumulating more than one needs is evident in the parable of the "rich fool" (see *Luke 12:16–21*) and the story of the "rich young man" (see *Mark 10:17–25*). Too many possessions can restrict and even control a person.

Saint John, in his first epistle, also warns against accumulating too many possessions. "If someone who has worldly means sees a brother in need and refuses him compassion, how can the love of God remain in him?" *(1 John 3:17)*. In behaving selfishly, people are not exercising the proper stewardship over creation that God intended.

Saint John's question can also be asked of groups and nations. Can the United States, which comprises about five percent of the world's population, continue in conscience to consume 28 times the energy of a developing country? Can Americans continue to consume an inordinate share of the world's food resources while starvation remains a fact of life on this planet?

Issues involving creation can be very threatening to we who live in the United States and other Western countries. Every statement of a problem can seem like a slap in our faces and a condemnation of our lifestyles and values—no matter how ecologically aware we may live or generous we may be!

Developing a mindset of oneness with creation is not something that happens overnight. And it surely doesn't come from public humiliation. People must be given an opportunity to consider this information in a nonthreatening manner, and must be free to respond to its challenge at their own pace.

The National Catholic Rural Life Conference has developed a process to help Catholic adults gently come to an understanding of how their lifestyles affect the earth and then reach their own decisions about how to make a difference. This process, based upon the "Pastoral Circle," is used along with the pastoral letter "Renewing the Earth," published by the United States Conference of Catholic Bishops in 1992.

For more information about the "Pastoral Circle" see *Catechists in Formation, Book 2*, "Social Justice and the Catechist."

### A Moral Challenge

"Renewing the Earth" calls the environmental crisis "a moral challenge" which calls us to examine "how we use and share the goods of the earth, what we pass on to future generations, and how we live in harmony with God's creation." As an example of the crisis, the document points out the "effects of the environmental degradation" that surround us: smog, polluted water, eroded topsoil, loss of wetlands, toxic waste, and industrial pollution that threaten the health of all workers.

The bishops speak to us as pastors offering their thoughts to us on a global problem. Theirs are not final conclusions, but beginning reflections. Here are some of their observations:

- "The web of life is one. Our mistreatment of the natural world diminishes our own dignity and sacredness."
- "Our tradition calls us to protect the life and dignity of the human person, and it is increasingly clear that this task cannot be separated from the care and defense of all of creation."
- "It is the poor and the powerless who most directly bear the burden of current environmental carelessness. Their lands and neighborhoods are more likely to be polluted or to host toxic-waste dumps, their water to be undrinkable, their children to be harmed."
- "We invite Catholics and men and women of goodwill in every walk of life to consider with us the moral issues raised by the environmental crisis. We ask: How are we called to care for God's creation?"

After reviewing the scriptural basis (much as we have done in Part II), the bishops offer the following thoughts:

- There is an "urgent moral need for a new solidarity, especially in relations between the developing nations and those that are highly industrialized."
- The fruit of the earth is for the whole human family, excluding no one.
- "Created things belong not to the few, but to the entire human family."
- "The ecological problem is intimately connected to justice for the poor." They "suffer most directly from environmental decline and have the least access to relief from their suffering."
- "Solutions must be found that do not force us to choose between a decent environment and a decent life for workers."
- Everyone must be willing to sacrifice. "Where jobs are lost, society must help in the process of economic conversion so that not only the earth but also workers and their families are protected."
- Population is to be controlled by responsible parenthood.
- Reduced consumption is the first step to resolving the problem.

In the environmental crisis the bishops see an "exceptional call to conversion. As individuals, as institutions, as a people, we need a change of heart to save the planet for our children and generations yet unborn."

## Moving to Action

The National Catholic Rural Life Conference (NCRLC), using the "Pastoral Circle" approach to social analysis, attempts to accomplish this goal. Describing social analysis as "a means of widening our reflection on our experience to search our relationships between values, events, structures, systems, and ideologies," this process is built around the following four questions:

1. What do I see?
2. Why is this happening?

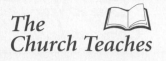

## The Church Teaches

Some would consider such hopes utopian. It may be that these persons are not realistic enough, and they have not perceived the dynamism of a world which desires to live more fraternally—a world which, in spite of its ignorance, its mistakes and even its sins, its relapses into barbarism and its wanderings far from the road of salvation, is, even unawares, taking slow but sure steps towards its Creator. This road towards a greater humanity requires effort and sacrifice; but suffering itself, accepted for the love of our brethren, favors the progress of the entire human family. Christians know that union with the sacrifice of our Savior contributes to the building up of the Body of Christ in its plenitude: the assembled people of God. (*Progressio Populorum, #79*)

# The New Commandment

*He said, "This is how it is with the kingdom of God; it is as if a man were to scatter seed on the land and would sleep and rise night and day and the seed would sprout and grow, he knows not how. Of its own accord the land yields fruit, first the blade, then the ear, then the full grain in the ear. And when the grain is ripe, he wields the sickle at once, for the harvest has come."*

(Mark 4:26–29)

3. What are my values?
4. What can I do?

By addressing these questions, Christians develop:

*a habit of thought which expands our approach to all of our experiences. Each time we move through the steps of the pastoral circle, we move to deeper levels of awareness and experience. As we continue, the process is one of development at new levels of understanding, rather than one of repetition.*

Let's look at these four steps in light of "Renewing the Earth" and see what we can discover.

**What Do I See?** Look around you. Pick up a newspaper or turn on the news and there is usually a story about some type of ecological problem. A nuclear waste dump in California threatens the water from the Colorado River. Plants in Pennsylvania produce air pollutants that threaten the northern forests. Floods in the Midwest wash tons of chemical toxins out of holding tanks into the Mississippi River, threatening fish and agricultural interests the length of the river. Locally, your headline may deal with the need for a new town dump, what you should do with your used motor oil, or whether you will have to pay more to have your trash picked up and garbage recycled.

Here are some questions to ask during this stage:

- When have you experienced God in nature? Describe the experience.
- How do you see God's creation in your local community?
- What are the businesses and industry in your area that might affect the environment?
- What is the major source of environmental concern in your life?

**Why Is This Happening?** After determining what is occurring, try to determine the causes of the problem. (This is not the time for solutions, only for understanding.) Does the chemical plant release gases in the atmosphere because the plant is old and because modern retrofitting would cost too much for the plant to be competitive? It may be a choice between releasing the gas or closing the plant.

Maybe it is chemical runoff from farm fields. Protective dikes have not been put in place to allow farm residue to settle out before the water goes into the stream. The farmer is aware of the problem but lacks the resources to solve it.

Follow this time of questioning with silent reflection and prayer. Come to your own conclusions as to the reasons for the local major problems.

**What Are My Values?** There are two kinds of values in the world: (1) spoken values and (2) lived values. Spoken values are the kind that sound good, especially when you say them to yourself. Spoken values are easy, because they are seldom, if ever, acted upon. Lived values are reflected in what a person does. Here are examples.

**Spoken Value:** I'm concerned about the effects of pesticide on the environment. When I go shopping however, I buy tomatoes from the commercial grower rather than the local pesticide-free producer because the tomatoes are cheaper.

**Lived Value:** I'm concerned about the effects of pesticide on the environment. When I go shopping I buy my tomatoes from the local organic gardener even though I have to pay more for pesticide-free produce.

Only you can determine what you value. A true value is something one acts upon and repeatedly practices. Be honest in your consideration. Although you may list both spoken and lived values, you ultimately want to end up with only lived values.

Consider the following questions:

- What are the values of my Christian tradition?
- How are my values shaped by them?
- How do my values affect my concern for the environment?
- How do my values improve the environment?
- How do my values harm the environment?
- What actions am I prepared to take to support my values?

**What Can I Do?** There are many types of actions that can follow from this consideration. The more realistic your decision is, however, the more likely you will be to follow through on it. Where a few people may be blessed with the courage and conviction to renounce everything that could be in the least harmful to the environment—use only renewable energy sources, bike to work on natural gum tires, burn candles for light, eat only vegetables—most people are not yet ready to live up to such a conviction. It's important that they not be forced into making that choice.

In the cartoon "Calvin and Hobbes," Calvin is ready to bash Susie with a slush ball when Hobbes challenges Calvin's values. Calvin, momentarily filled with remorse, drops his weapon and turns to a life of good works. However, he soon tires of the lack of pleasure his good deeds have brought, so he returns to his former ways, belts Susie, and takes great satisfaction in his action. Hobbes is left to remark that "Virtue needs more immediate rewards."

Living out the actions required to make an ecological difference are like Calvin's virtuous deeds. They often do not show immediate paybacks and so are often difficult to endure. That is the challenge we face. The pain of perfection may be more than we can bear, but we must do what we can to make a difference. This can happen only when a person freely chooses to make changes in his or her own life.

Begin by asking the questions:

- What new attitudes must I develop to make a difference in this problem? What will it take for me to develop this new attitude? What problems will I experience in gaining this new attitude?
- What action am I willing and able to take to promote a solution to this problem? What steps must I take to accomplish this action? What are the obstacles in my way that will prevent me from achieving my goal?

## Pause a Moment . . .

- Some people own things in order to use them. Other people own things simply to possess them. What is your reason for owning things?
- How important are possessions to you? Have your possessions freed you or made you more restricted? Explain.
- What can you do to promote justice in your community?
- How can you use the Pastoral Circle with the students you teach?

---

**Practice**

Practice the Pastoral Circle on an environmental theme of your choosing (e.g., local pollution, hunger, depletion of the rain forests).

1. What do I see?

_____

_____

2. Why is this happening?

_____

_____

3. What are my values?

_____

_____

4. What can I do?

_____

_____

# Part IV Response

## Applications to Teaching

▲ *How can you use what you've learned about creation with your students?*

Many issues are directly related to the topic of creation. As we have already seen, these issues include the following principles central to Catholic social thought:

1. All creation is good and holy, filled with the grace of God.
2. Men and women are equal.
3. God entrusted to humanity stewardship over creation.
4. All people are made in God's image.
5. Christians should develop positive attitudes toward sexuality.
6. We are co-creators with God.
7. Everyone has the right to be owners, but ownership is never absolute.
8. People must share the world's resources.

There are many ways to approach these issues in a religious education class. Possible teaching techniques include the use of objects, murals, stories, role playing, debate on a particular issue, research, reflection, essays or other written activities, liturgies, discussions, prayer, projects and creative activities, multiple choice value testing, and singing. The actual techniques used will vary according to the specific grade level of the students.

### Younger Children

**Kindergarten and first grade.** Lead these students to discover the wonders and beauty of creation. Bring in physical specimens—leaves, flowers, acorns, caterpillars, eggs, and feathers—or use colorful pictures. Also, teach these students to say short prayers of praise and thanksgiving for the wonderful gifts of God's creation.

These children have a natural eye for the beauty of God's creation. Help them explore part of it by asking them to bring to class some of their favorite natural foods—apples, oranges, peanuts—just as God made them. When the foods are all gathered, display them near the edges of the four sides of a large table. Have the students walk around the table, look at the food, and notice its various shapes and colors. Cut an apple open crossways to show the star shape made by the seeds. Do the same with a tomato to show its wheel pattern. Finally, cut the foods into small pieces so that everyone gets to taste several items. Then sit with the students in the prayer corner for a short litany of praise and thanks to God for these gifts of creation.

**Second and third grade.** These students can link their study of creation with the bread and wine used at Mass. Help them consider how wheat and grapes are grown and how they are eventually made into bread and wine. Help the children appreciate the role people play in the process of ongoing creation by transforming natural materials into food and textiles. (Some grade school religion textbooks stress that people are co-creators with God.) Help the students to consider their five senses as ways to experience and add to creation.

Begin a collection of colorful, striking pictures of the beauty of the world and its creatures. Mount these pictures on posterboard or cardboard. Perhaps attach to the backside particular comments or discussion questions for each picture. Invite your students to bring in such pictures from travel or nature magazines, or from the *National Geographic.* Let them help suggest the comments and discussion questions for each one. Rotate a small selection of such pictures for display during the year.

To reinforce the idea that each person is a unique creation of God, with worth and beauty like the other wonders of creation, have the students bring in a picture of themselves. Mount the photos on 5" x 7" pieces of posterboard. Let the students color and decorate the borders of their posterboards. Display the students' photos with the other pictures of God's wonderful creations.

## Middle Grades

When studying the Ten Commandments, you can show how each commandment guides people in relating to the rest of the created world. You can also point out how the symbols used in the sacraments are all materials from nature: water, wheat, grapes, wax, stone, oil, and fire. Many sixth-grade textbooks explore the Old Testament. Part of that study can be a thorough look at the creation stories in Genesis to really understand their origin, purpose, and meaning.

Try these activities.

- Provide your students with a sheet of white paper. Have them fold the papers into quarters or eighths and then cut out small notches or circles along the fold. When they unfold the paper they will have a snowflake. Point out that no two snowflakes are alike; each has its own special value and beauty.

- Have the students bring in photos of themselves. Make a bulletin board display with the snowflakes and student pictures with the caption, "Each One Is Unique, Each One Is Special." Snowflakes can be hung from various lengths of string from the ceiling to create a festive atmosphere.

- Make a series of creation collages. First read the story of creation from Genesis 1. Form six groups, assigning each group one of the days of creation. (If your class is small, form three groups, each to do two days.) Each groups is to use pictures from magazines and their own drawings to illustrate their day of creation on large pieces of posterboard, including a short title at the top. Use student displays to tell the story of creation.

- Discuss the meaning of "Sunday, the Lord's Day, the day of rest." How is it intended to be used? How should it be celebrated? Have the entire class look for pictures or make drawings to put on a poster for the seventh day. Display this poster with the others.

## Junior High and High School

Use the students' fascination with the subject of sexuality as a chance to stress how men and women are co-creators with God. Attitudes about the dignity of both sexes and a positive regard for our physical bodies relate to the basic creation theme. Foster interest in junior high students by dividing the class into two groups to debate both sides of a creation-related issue. Challenge high school students to consider the creation issues and analyze the values behind the options facing them. Try these activities:

*Notes*

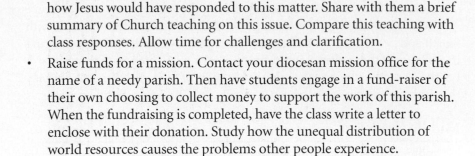

*Memo*

In light of what I have learned about creation, I want to keep the following considerations in mind for the next time I meet with my students:

- Use one or more of the eight themes presented in this chapter, or those of your own choosing. Reverse some of the statements to make students truly think. Have the students write a short statement "Why I agree (disagree) with this statement." Collect the statements (unsigned) and redistribute them around the room. Use student comments about their neighbor's statement to provoke a discussion. Have students discuss how Jesus would have responded to this matter. Share with them a brief summary of Church teaching on this issue. Compare this teaching with class responses. Allow time for challenges and clarification.

- Raise funds for a mission. Contact your diocesan mission office for the name of a needy parish. Then have students engage in a fund-raiser of their own choosing to collect money to support the work of this parish. When the fundraising is completed, have the class write a letter to enclose with their donation. Study how the unequal distribution of world resources causes the problems other people experience.

- Have students find stories in newsmagazines or the newspaper of pollution and ecological destruction. Have them report on the stories they find. Discuss their findings in light of the Genesis creation story. How are we being stewards over the earth?

- Working in groups of four, have the students develop brief public awareness commercials on a creation topic. The commercial is to be addressed to their peers and may take any form they wish.

- Discuss the issue of sexual harassment as it applies to student life. When have they been harassed in school? the neighborhood? among friends? How did they feel about this experience? How can they bring about the ideal of creation expressed in Genesis that men and women are made from the same "stuff" and consequently ought to be treated with equal dignity and respect?

- Carefully explain the many ways we can be co-creators with God. Have students write a paragraph about how they hope to be co-creators throughout their lives. You may wish to play instrumental music softly in the background as they write.

- Find a photograph of planet Earth taken from space. Have a prayer service, called "A Planetary Perspective," and meditate on this symbol of creation. Give thanks for God's goodness and generosity.

## Care for Students

Our attitudes toward ourselves, other people, and material things stem from our view of creation. Our Christian heritage offers us a unique and enriching perspective toward life—one that will help us to bring creation itself to its fulfillment.

Considering the biblical insights about creation, it is important that we, as catechists, avoid references that reinforce a negative approach toward the world. We need to remember that the material world and our physical bodies are not evil, although the misuse of them can result in sin. Finally, we need to realize that a dichotomy between the physical and the spiritual is a misconception. God created both in unity with each other.

1. Look over the various issues about creation raised in this chapter. Which three can you use most effectively with your grade level?

_____

_____

_____

2. Look over the teaching techniques offered above, as well as those listed in your teacher's manual. Which three do you feel are especially suited to the grade level you teach?

_____

_____

_____

3. Decide how you would explain to your students each issue you chose above. Then determine which technique or sequence of techniques you would use to teach the lesson.

(a) _____

(b) _____

(c) _____

## Pause a Moment . . .

- Reflect on the main ideas that you have studied in this chapter. What difference will they make to your teaching?
- Take a few moments to write your reflections, describing one implication of this topic in terms of justice.

## Prayer Response

Read the following Scripture passage. Reflect on a time when pessimism about the world threatened your Christian hope. Then consider the aspects of creation for which you are particularly grateful.

> Bless the Lord, O my soul!
>
> O Lord, my God, you are great indeed! . . .
>
> You have spread out the heavens like a tent-cloth;
>    you have constructed your palace upon the waters.
>
> You make the clouds your chariot;
>    you travel on the wings of the wind.
>
> You make the winds your messengers,
>    and flaming fire your ministers.

**Notes**

_____

*You fixed the earth upon its foundation,*
*not to be moved forever;*

*With the ocean, as a garment, you covered it;*
*above the mountains the waters stood.*

*You water the mountains from your palace;*
*the earth is replete with the fruit of your works.*

*You raise grass for the cattle,*
*and vegetation for our use;*

*Producing bread from the earth,*
*and wine to gladden our hearts.*

(Psalm 104:1a, 2–6, 13–15a)

▲ *What are your reflections on the glory of God's creation? Try your hand at writing a song of praise.*

## BIBLIOGRAPHY

*About Stewardship of the Environment.* Channing L. Bete Co., Inc.

Brieg, James. *Wave Good-bye to the Jones': Christian Used of Wealth.* Chicago: Fides/Claretian, 1981.

Donders, Joseph G. *Creation and Human Dynamism: A Spirituality for Life.* Mystic, CT: Twenty-Third Publications, 1985.

Flannery O.P., Austin. "Gaudium et Spes." *Vatican Council II: Conciliar and Post Conciliar Documents, New Revised Edition.* Grand Rapids, MI: Wm. B. Eerdmans Publishing Company, 1992.

Fritsch S.J., Albert J. and Angela Iadavaia-Cox. *Eco-Church: An Action Manual.* San Jose, CA: Resource Publications, Inc. 1992

Jenkins, Christie L. *Loving Our Neighbor, the Earth: Creation-Spirituality Activities for 9–11 Year-Olds.* San Jose, CA: Resource Publication, Inc. 1991.

*Jesus B.C.* Mahwah, NJ: Paulist Press. Video.

Jung, Shannon. *We Are Home: A Spirituality of the Environment.* Mahwah, NJ: Paulist Press, 1993.

McBrien, Richard P. *Catholicism.* Minneapolis, MN: Winston Press, 1981.

_____. "What Is the 'Kingdom of God,'" *Catholic Update.* Cincinnati: St. Anthony Messenger Press, 1980.

National Conference of Catholic Bishops. "Principal Elements of the Christian Message for Catechesis," *Sharing the Light of Faith.* Washington, D.C.: USCC Publications, 1979.

_____. *Catholic Social Teaching and the U.S. Economy.* Washington, DC: USCC Publications, 1986.

_____. *Renewing the Earth.* Washington, DC: USCC Publications, 1991. (See *Catholic Update,* March 1992 for a condensed version.)

National Catholic Rural Life Conference. *Renewing the Earth Study Guides.* Washington, DC: USCC Publications, 1992.

Soelle, Dorothy. *To Work and To Love: A Theology of Creation.* Augsberg, MN: Fortress Press, 1984.

Tobin, Thomas H. *The Creation of Man.* Washington, DC: Catholic Biblical Association of America, 1983.

Viviano, Pauline. *Genesis. Collegeville Bible Commentary, Vol. 2.* Collegeville, MN: Liturgical Press, 1986.

*Nihil Obstat*
The Reverend Gregory A. Banazak, S.T.D.

*Imprimatur*
The Most Reverend Kenneth J. Povish, D.D.
Bishop of Lansing
May 13, 1994

The *Nihil Obstat* and *Imprimatur* are official declarations that a book or pamphlet is free of doctrinal or moral error. No implication is contained therein that those who have granted the *Nihil Obstat* and *Imprimatur* agree with the contents, opinions, or statements expressed.

Send all inquiries to:

BENZIGER PUBLISHING COMPANY
15319 Chatsworth Street
P.O. Box 9609
Mission Hills, California 91346-9609

Second Edition

**ISBN 0-02-651222-X**

Printed in the United States of America.

1 2 3 4 5 6 7 8 9    BAW    98 97 96 95 94